<u>Do You Recognize</u> <u>These Emotional Types?</u>

★ **The John Wayne:** Super hero. Strong. Silent. Thinks he or she can do it all alone.

★ **The Greta Garbo:** Unassertive. Withdrawn. Unable to take action or make decisions.

★ **The James Dean:** Super-assertive. Fueled by anger. Control and power are the name of the game.

★ **The Marilyn Monroe:** Emotionally detached. Prone to depression. Can never see a silver lining.

★ **The Frances Farmer:** The eccentric. Views the world as chaotic. Goes her own way.

★ **The Charlie Brown:** The chameleon. A fragile sense of self. Changes colors to please the crowd.

EMOTIONAL HEALING

. . . sheds light on the coping personas you adopted to survive the pain of childhood and which you may still be assuming as an adult. Step by step, with compassion and insight, it also helps you overcome the need for control, an overdeveloped sense of responsibility, fear of authority figures, difficulty with intimacy, chronic lack of self-esteem, compulsive addictive behavior, and other problems.

▽

"A VERY IMPORTANT AND EXTREMELY HELPFUL BOOK. HIGHLY RECOMMENDED."

—Ken Wilbur
author of *No Boundary*

EMOTIONAL HEALING

A PROGRAM FOR EMOTIONAL SOBRIETY

KAREN PAINE-GERNÉE AND TERRY HUNT, ED.D.

WARNER BOOKS

A Warner Communications Company

The stories presented in this book are drawn from actual cases. All of the names of and certain other identifying characteristics concerning the individuals depicted in the stories have been changed to protect their identity and privacy.

Copyright © 1990 by Karen Paine-Gernée and Terry Hunt
All rights reserved.
Warner Books, Inc., 666 Fifth Avenue, New York, NY 10103

W A Warner Communications Company

Printed in the United States of America
First Printing: January 1990
10 9 8 7 6 5 4 3 2 1

Library of Congress Cataloging-in-Publication Data

Paine-Gernée, Karen.
    Emotional healing : a program for emotional sobriety /
Karen Paine-Gernée and Terry Hunt.
        p.   cm.
    Bibliography: p.
    ISBN 0-446-38770-3
    1. Adult children of alcoholics--United States--Psychology.
2. Problem families--United States--Psychological aspects.   3. Co-
dependence (Psychology)   4. Emotional maturity.   5. Self-actualization
(Psychology)   I. Hunt, Terry, 1951–   .   II. Title.
HV5132.P34   1990
362.29′23--dc19   89-14820
                                                                        CIP

Book design: H. Roberts
Cover design: Harry Nolan

We dedicate this book to our children
with the hope that the chain of denial
we were born into be broken with them.

KAREN PAINE-GERNÉE and TERRY HUNT, Ed.D., are well-known therapists who specialize in working with Adult Children of Alcoholics and other troubled families both in individual therapy and workshop groups. They are currently associated with Esalen Institute, the Omega Institute, the New York Open Center, Interface, and Hollyhock Farms in British Columbia.

Acknowledgments

We have always been amazed, when reading acknowledgments, how many people authors thank. But now that we've completed this project, we understand how many comforters, supporters, encouragers, and teachers it takes to write a book. To all of you who have added to our learning about these matters in so many subtle and important ways, we thank you.

Writing a book as personal as this one is a labor full of feeling—sometimes happy and sometimes not. To have the support and writing ability of Hester Kaplan and Larry Rothstein behind us made it possible to get through the hard times, have fun through the easy ones, and to grow in the experience. Our editor at Warner Books, Jamie Raab, offered us, as first-time authors, a measure of confidence that helped us get going and sustained us when we needed it.

There are several people who helped us by reading the manuscript and commenting on the content and organization. We would like to thank: Robert Jonas, George Whiteside, and Kiernan Stenson. For sharing their stories with us, thanks to: Annie, David, Jim, and all the adult children that we have worked with both in our workshops and in private therapy. For their love and support around this project from the beginning, thanks to: Richard, Evi, Gay, Sallie, Bud, Sara, Marion, John, Judy, Holton, Margo, John, the Sunshine Canyon Gang, and The Donuts, who showed us just how good we are.

A number of significant ideas in this book have been drawn from specific sources to whom we would like to offer special thanks. Leie Carmody, who over the years has served as Karen's teacher, therapist, mentor, supervisor, and now friend, was especially helpful in reading the manuscript and offering suggestions. Much of what Karen knows about therapy, she learned from Leie. Our friend Robert Gass read Chapter 9 and offered comments and suggestions that became the foundation of the present version. It was our experience as staff in the Opening the Heart workshops with Robert and wife, Judith, that taught us heart-centered therapy, the basis of our work today. Ginny Jordan made suggestions on Chapter 10, and she and her husband, Roger, shared their ideas on relationships with us. Out ideas about sexuality and aliveness were largely developed during Terry's study with the Massachusetts Society for Bioenergetic Analysis. The lessons learned from Philip Helfaer, Virginia Wink-Hilton, and Robert Hilton along with the writings of Alexander Lowen are very much woven into the fabric of this work. Several experiences with Ann Armstrong were crucial to Karen's understanding of her relationship with her mother.

The ideas in this book have also been influenced by those who have preceded us, the pioneers in the field of adult children of alcoholics. We are grateful to Janet Woititz, Sharon Wegscheider-Cruse, Claudia Black, Charles Whitfield, John Bradshaw, Tim Cermack, Cathleen Brooks, Terry Kellogg and especially Celia Dulfano, Julie Bowden, and Herb Gravitz, who were initially responsible for exposing us to this area.

Although this has been a collaborative effort, there are some acknowledgments that we choose to make separately.

Karen: This book could not have been written without my husband, Rick. Not only did he listen to my ideas, read my drafts, postpone his own vacations while Terry and I wrote; he also held me, loved me, and comforted me while I healed. Much of what I know about the damage my childhood did to me, and the steps needed to emerge from the pain, has been learned in his arms. His support and willingness to interrupt his own projects to listen to me as I struggled to clarify ideas got me through many difficult days.

I also thank my father, Bud Vervaet, whose love and support I always knew I could rely on and whose generosity in requesting no changes in the manuscript touches me deeply. I thank my children, Alex, Megan, and Max Dichter, three of the most generous young people I know. Being in a family with them has taught me that being close can be fun and that loving doesn't have to hurt. They did without me often over the past year when the book took precedence over family plans and they never complained. They are the best little cheering section we could have. Thanks to my sister, Gay, with whom I struggled to understand, and whose love and support have sustained me often over the years, and my brother, Alden, whose recovery inspires me. Thanks to Gale for her incisive editing skills, and her support to go for excellence.

Terry: The loving support and always available sanity of my wife, Gale, never ceases to cause my reverent gratitude for such good fortune in my life. To have the faith of another when the going gets tough makes all the difference. She is also a delightful friend and lover.

It has not been easy for my mother to witness this process of my recovery. There are few greater pains than to have to acknowledge that the home one helped to create was dysfunctional. However, she has always sought to encourage me in this and my other endeavors and had no need to censor my point of view. I will always be grateful for her openness and capacity for unconditional love.

I also wish to acknowledge the extraordinary input of

Evan, my two-year-old son, who with his still uninhibited aliveness is one of the great inspirations to work for recovery. Thanks also to my siblings—Marion, John, and Andrew—and to my stepbrother, George, with whom I spent many hours trying to sort out the family drama. Their thoughts, feelings, and unique perspectives on our family have been quite useful in our quest for understanding and recovery.

Acknowledgment also must go to David Lovler, Lisa Rung, and Elisabeth Malm, my administrative assistants, who were always there in the clutch through many rewrites.

And we thank each other. Writing this book and working together, we have learned that love has many ways of expressing itself, that it is possible to disagree creatively, that burdens can be shared, and that we are each safe to rely on and trust. We appreciate the "can do" attitude that each of us brought to our collaboration, and our ability to hear and learn from one another. Most of all we are grateful for the love and support we have shown each other and the fun we have had.

Contents

Introduction

Karen: The first time I met Terry was really more of a glimpse than a meeting. Terry, as I would come to know, was doing what he usually did: running around, trying to get three things done at once, unable to slow down for even a minute. But in the little time that we did spend together the day we met, I noticed his smile, his attractiveness, and his intense energy. I had no idea that day how important he would become to me.

It was the summer of 1976 at Spring Hill, a retreat and growth center in central Massachusetts. I had just moved there to be with my boyfriend (now husband) Rick. Terry was one of the founders of Spring Hill, and spent a lot of time there, and that summer I got to know him and his girlfriend Sallie. The four of us—me, Rick, Terry, and Sallie—became constant friends, and spent much of our time talking about the problems we all seemed to be having in our relationships. The bond between Terry and me grew stronger every day as we discovered many things we had in common, including the fact that his father and my mother were alcoholics.

Terry: Karen was dressed in white the first time I saw her. She was beautiful, shy, and clearly very much in love with Rick, my dear friend. That summer, we were both riding high on the excitement of new romances, and although there were problems in both relationships, we believed that if we talked about the problem enough, they would disappear. So, talk we did, and Karen and I became close friends because of it. That we each had an alcoholic parent was nothing to dwell on, we thought, and at that time, we didn't know that it had anything to do with our strong identification with each other. It was just a fact of life we both accepted, as we always had.

For both of us, things looked good that summer of 1976. Terry was a full-time graduate student, doing well and working on his doctoral thesis at Boston University in Humanistic and Behavior Studies. Karen had just finished advanced training in Gestalt therapy and an esoteric training in spiritual development called Arica. After a divorce two years earlier, she was now ready for a different direction in her life. Becoming involved with Rick marked her readiness to begin a serious relationship, and in moving to Spring Hill, she felt she was starting a new life for herself and her three children.

Over the next year, we both became strongly committed to learning about and teaching "heart-centered approach" therapy, a method that was emerging from within our community at Spring Hill and from our friends Robert and Judith Gass. The principles of this approach were founded in a faith in the resiliency of the human spirit, an idea we still cherish. All we needed to do to heal ourselves, we believed, was open our hearts to our deepest feelings, which would, with the support of friends and fellow seekers, allow us to find a more loving and fulfilling life.

Although we didn't see it at the time, this approach only

partially worked for us. Most of the people in our community had grown up in essentially healthy homes, and the pain and problems they carried into adulthood could be talked over and cried out. For us, though, there was something deeper and more scarring in our childhoods—alcoholism—that we needed acknowledged. To a limited extent, talking about how we felt was productive, but it just wasn't enough; there was too much denial in both of us. If our childhoods looked okay on the outside—good schools, comfortable homes, nice clothes— why were we so unhappy? We needed to know then that the unhappiness we had felt as kids, despite all the outward appearances of a healthy family life, was real, that it had affected us, and that it was called alcoholism. What we saw at Spring Hill was success for many people, and while we cried a lot, and had glimpses of our pain, it simply was not enough. We were still too caught up in the web of denial to acknowl- edge the depth of our childhood hurt.

Karen: I was the oldest of three children in my family. My grandmother, my mother's mother, lived with us for many years and all the children in my family loved her dearly. She was a binge drinker. This meant that she could go for months without a drink, and then she'd drink herself senseless. I remember seeing her passed out, getting drunk and falling down, and occasionally she was sent off to a "farm." My parents tried to treat this as though it was all perfectly normal, but I could feel their great sense of shame. They considered AA useless, and while they talked about how my grandmother couldn't control her drinking, there was still a lot of blame. Later, I found out that my grandfather's father had been an alcoholic, too, and that my grandfather had left my grandmother when she started drinking.

It took a long time for anyone to realize that my mother was an alcoholic, too, because she was such a different type of drinker. She drank daily but seldom passed out. She had dealt with her alcoholic mother for so long that she was convinced she was an expert on the problem, and wouldn't listen to anyone tell her about her behavior. My sister and I thought for years that there was no way our mother could be an alcoholic. It wasn't until I was eighteen, and my mother had been in the advanced stages of alcoholism for six or seven years, that I finally accepted the truth about her.

Terry: I am the oldest in a family of four children. My grandmother and her brother were alcoholics, although we never talked about that, and my father was what we called an "enthusiastic drinker." I was born in 1951, and my family settled into the vision of the prospering, happy family. My father had a good job that he loved, but his drinking made it progressively more difficult for him to succeed as he wanted. My parents' high expectations for me and my siblings hung over us like a cloud, so that normal failings became humiliating exposures of weakness and incompetence. As the years went on, my father's illusions of grandeur and the realities of his alcoholism made him into a very mean man who constantly put people down to build himself up. Clearly his children were his easiest target.

In spite of this, we adored my mother and looked up to my father's power. We could never understand what my parents were fighting about, and those years were filled with many broken promises. Time after time, we were told that things would get better, that they'd be different soon. But things didn't really change, and my mother turned more and more to her children for friendship and support. She desperately wanted to be thought of as a good mother, and became emotionally dependent on her children. We were confused by her dependence, and frustrated that so many promises were not kept.

* * *

Needless to say, the unresolved conflicts and injuries from our childhoods created seemingly insurmountable problems in our adult intimate relationships. During the summer of 1976 at Spring Hill, we all had each other to depend on, and the four of us became emotionally inseparable, alternately helping and commiserating with each other. We used our friendship as four-way couple therapy, and our personal lives became an extension of our professional lives. Both couples had plans to be married in the coming year, but the "honeymoon" seemed to be over, and we often discussed splitting up. For all four of us, the daily dilemma was "stay together or break up?" We listened intently to each other, but no one stopped to realize that we weren't having fun anymore, as absorbed as we were in the personal dynamics of the situation. Still, we were committed to the idea that if we worked hard enough, we could fix our lives and we could make it all work, because we were loyal and loved each other.

We were addicted to the process. In focusing on ourselves and our relationships, we were actually indulging in pain-avoidant behavior, because we looked everywhere but where it mattered. We were unable to look at the real, underlying problems. Terry was operating on his childhood belief that solving problems was up to him, and he could fix anything if he worked at it hard enough. Karen, after a relationship with a controlling and rigid man, was enjoying being with a man like Rick who didn't feel the need to control her, and loved her for who she was. Unaware at this point of the effects that her childhood had on her, Karen experienced a nagging dissatisfaction with Rick that imitated her own mother's criticalness toward her. She was unable to trust that Rick wouldn't abandon her the way her own father had for a time during the war, and then later when he did not protect her from her mother's alcoholic rages. Karen constantly questioned the permanence of her relationship with Rick, and when things went wrong, she blamed him. Neither of us knew at that time that our anxiety, our quickness to blame, and our fears were all products of having grown up in alcoholic and abusive homes.

We were confused. If we looked at our lives, they seemed

okay. It was easy to deny past effects if we looked at present reality. We know now that the denial in alcoholic and abusive families is so powerful that even as adults it allows us to look back and say, "Things weren't so bad." We needed help sorting out our feelings and making sense of the past. We needed to see what happened in the context of alcoholism, to see that our parents' bizarre behavior and chaotic life-style were caused by their drinking, not by us. That understanding, though, was years away for both of us. We needed to find Emotional Healing, and that is, in part, what this book will lead you toward. Both of us have tried to put our past behind us, without denying what went on, and by following the process we describe here, we have found a place where we can be peaceful while the seeming craziness of life continues around us.

As we have discovered over the years of working with adult children of alcoholics (ACOAs), everyone wants to fix his life right now and put the past behind him forever. We take a different approach toward recovery. We acknowledge that our past was our fate—we can't change or deny that—and that the hardships it created will always be there scaring us, making us anxious and angry. But when we finally find Emotional Healing, we accept our lives as they were and are. The pain has less impact on us as we enable ourselves to identify the behavior which draws us back into the hurt again and again. It is through Emotional Healing that we rediscover our self-esteem, a place where we can begin to live our lives as adults who embrace life rather than try to hide from it.

Unfortunately for us at the time we were at Spring Hill, we were not able to see this, and our lives really did not change much until 1982 when Karen discovered a course in California for adult children of alcoholics led by Herbert Gravitz and Julie Bowden.[1] This opened up new areas of understanding for us, and we began to read books on the subject and examine the issues of addiction that were involved.

We use the word *addiction* fairly broadly throughout this book to refer to a way of living that is essentially pain-avoidant rather than life-affirming. We see addictive behavior as a quick fix for a painful situation. Real healing, rather than a quick fix, involves difficult introspection, and requires maturity and a sense of self-worth that the addict does not have.

We use the term "addiction" to refer to both substance abuse and certain patterns of behavior. If a person's behavior pattern and/or use of a particular substance causes pain and suffering to himself and/or his loved ones, and he does not stop, he is addicted to the behavior or the substance. The people who form the social network of the addict are "co-dependent" on the substance or the behavior as well. Addiction is indeed a family problem with both a genetic and a behavioral predisposition, and co-dependents are forced into pain-avoidant and addictive behaviors simply to cope with the chaos caused by the addict.

There are other kinds of abuse as well, and they are often harder to define, since different cultures accept different parental behaviors as natural and helpful to the growth of the child. We consider any form of physical assault (either aggressive or sexualized) on a child to be risking that child's healthy development, and the effects of the abuse will show up in later life. Verbal attacks on a child injure the child's self-esteem and well-being. The experience of abuse is ultimately in the eyes and hearts of the abused. Since our aim here is not to blame, but to recover our emotional health, a useful principle to keep in mind is, *If you think you were abused, you probably were.*

Along with most experts in the field, we see addiction in the use of alcohol and drugs, in cigarette smoking and compulsive eating, in gambling, as well as in the abuse of emotional or physical power. We also see addictive behavior in so-called positive addictions, such as work, exercise, sexual activity, and meditation, where if practiced in excess the behavior enables one to avoid life rather than embrace it. In adult children of alcoholic or other unhealthy families, we see addiction in the mood disorder we call "addiction to excitement." In this kind of addiction, the addict is so caught up in the storm of his life that the pleasure of living a simple, peaceful, and loving life seems boring and unappealing.

Our view of addiction is also an optimistic one, because we like to think of the addict as a person on a spiritual quest for wholeness who has lost his way. The addictive behavior he employs makes him feel whole, if only for a short time, and stopping the addictive behavior causes so much pain and turmoil that he feels too weak to try any other way of living. This idea, put forward by Pat Perrin and Wim Coleman,[2] suggests that this quest to feel complete is a legitimate motivation for living, but that addictive behaviors simply do not work toward this end.

And if Janice Phelps and Alan Nourse, authors of *Hidden Addictions and How to Get Free*,[3] are right in their belief that addictive behavior is really a biochemical problem that may or may not be genetically encoded, then the addict can easily be encouraged to let go of any feelings of guilt or blame he has surrounding his inability to control his behavior. Problems of addiction are not problems of morality—the addict is not a bad or weak person because he is addicted—but they are problems of a physical craving too powerful to stop. And if you accept that the addict is looking for a way to make himself feel whole, then the next step for the addict has to be to find better ways to achieve this quest for wholeness.

Throughout this book, we will look at the range of problems connected with addiction, and through our own personal and professional experiences—both as victims of addiction and as therapists in the field—will lead you to a place where you can find a wholeness that is peaceful and fulfilling.

Until we both reached the point in our lives where we were able to honestly address how much we were hurt, how deeply injured we were, until we understood the devastating effect our parents' alcoholism had on us, we couldn't let go of the ever-present pain, no matter how hard we tried. Everyone around us made progress, but we stood still. While others moved smoothly toward growth, we created crisis after crisis, and we were burdened by a deep sense of grief and self-blame. However, when we learned about the dynamics of growing up in an alcoholic family, we also learned about certain predictable effects. We began to see that there were reasons why we were having trouble in our adult lives, and it wasn't all our fault.

As we learned more about the subject of adult children of alcoholics and children who grew up in abusive homes, we began to realize that there were many things missing in the kind of therapy we were conducting that made it inadequate for ACOAs, and that there were many things missing in the literature available on the subject.

We saw that in the therapy we were practicing, we had underestimated the power of denial that is so much a part of alcoholic and abusive families. We hadn't understood that the words "It wasn't so bad" were more powerful than any impulse to tell and accept what really happened. We believed that if we gave people enough support, they could release their pain and get on with life. We saw that they needed education, they needed to hear stories similar to their own, to disengage the mechanism of denial, and they needed to feel safe enough to make changes in their lives and move toward recovery. In this book, we'll lead you through those steps.

Obviously it isn't that easy. What we finally understood was that ACOAs and victims of abuse need to feel safe when they talk about their childhood pain. They need to be given permission by someone who has suffered as well, to stop blaming themselves and start feeling the pain. Both of us had felt the pain—we understood that "it *was* so bad," that the truth needed to be talked about and recognized.

The early literature on ACOAs and children of abusive families did just that—allowed victims to recognize themselves, and in a sense "come out of the closet." Authors such as Janet Woititz, Sharon Wegscheider-Cruse, and Claudia Black made great contributions and were a catalyst for public recognition of the problem. But what we saw lacking in the literature were practical guidelines on how to access the pain and accept ourselves as wounded people with injuries so that permanent healing *can* take place. They rarely discussed the issues of sexuality that are so central to many adult problems, and the concept of the "wounded child" (developed by Charles Whitfield) was still far away. We had training in, and utilized our knowledge of, various kinds of therapies, including bioenergetics and emotional discharge work. No one else, we saw, used the power of touching, music, and meditation in healing. For much the same reason we are writing this book, we felt that the combination of our experiences—professional and personal—along with our sense of what had been neglected and what we could provide, could make a difference to people who were suffering and looking for help.

It all came together in the first workshop we gave in the spring of 1983. In the beginning, the workshop was known through word of mouth only, and thirty-five people signed up for our first course. Their gratitude and enthusiasm spurred us to ask Interface Foundation, a Boston-based adult education center focused on spiritual and healing arts, to allow us to offer a course through their organization—a first for them. Until our workshop, issues around addiction were considered the province of AA and similar organizations. Our second workshop drew fifty people, and after that, they were filled to capacity. Soon we were giving workshops across the country at other similar centers, most notably at the New York Open Center, Omega Institute, and Esalen Institute. Eventually we opened the workshop up to people who had grown up with abusive parents as well as alcoholic ones, recognizing that growing up in a family whose dysfunction was similar to that caused by alcohol produced similar results. Everyone from an unhealthy home is an adult child who needs to find Emotional Healing.

Adult children of alcoholics have created a movement which now leads other people to heal as well. In the last seven years, our work has touched several thousand people directly, and has truly transformed our own lives. We feel lucky to be able to do the work we are doing, and our families are happier. We have developed deep friendships, and are better able to accept peace and fulfillment in our lives. Our energies are no longer so focused on the past, but focus instead on our present and the hopes we have for our futures.

Through our workshops, we developed a program we now call Emotional Sobriety, whose key aspects are discovering our capacity for contact with others and developing personal boundaries, learning moderation in our lives, and developing a sense of personal faith. Emotional Sobriety is a way of living that allows you to be the creator of your own life and your own feelings, a way of living that is peaceful and fulfilling. Together we have formed a partnership, and we teach what we have lived and continue to struggle with. Our lives have changed, as have the lives of so many people we have worked with. This book, then, is about a personal odyssey as well as a professional one.

We have learned that we don't have to live waiting for the next disaster, but rather we can live to embrace all that happens, the bitter and the sweet. We have learned that to live fully means facing the pain that, as children, we could not bear. When we can experience what is painful, we allow ourselves an entire range of emotions, and we can experience what is pleasurable as well. When we stop denying a part of us that is very real—the wounded child—we start developing a sense of self, one that is capable of pleasure and inner peace. The path we took to get to where we are today was a long and hard one, full of change and struggle, but the reward was inestimable—the gift of a full life.

Along the way, we have learned to have compassion for our parents, and realize that they were good people who tried to do the best they could while battling something—their addictions—stronger than themselves. Only recently has the public developed an awareness about alcoholism, abuse, and the effects on the family. It is unlikely that, even if our parents had borne the heavy social stigma of admitting they were alcoholics, they could have found knowledgeable and sympathetic professional help. We were both able to find some forgiveness for our parents before they died, and we find more as time goes on. Both of us experienced some sort of adult resolution about things that happened while they were still alive, but over the years since their deaths, the wounded child in each of us has had a lot of healing to do.

We no longer feel the need to blame, only to tell the truth, and the truth that we are about to tell is as best as we can remember it and feel it in our hearts. Others in our families probably remember things quite differently than we do. But we have faith in the truth that we tell, because we see that it has allowed us to embrace the pains and pleasures in our lives.

And finally a word about recovery. As it is used often when talking about addiction, recovery refers to a lifelong journey toward sobriety that follows an admission that an addictive behavior has taken control. We think that recovery is not a matter of creating something new, but rather a matter of reawakening something that was always there. It means rediscovering the energy and joy of the infant who was held, stroked, cared for, and loved unconditionally, even if only occasionally. It means no longer allowing pain-avoidant behaviors to run your life, and it means facing your pain, fear, and anger about the past. Recovery involves being able to withstand strong feelings of disappointment and elation, of accepting who you are and how you are. It means appreciating what is good and what is bad in you, what is good and bad in life, and finally it means forgiving yourself, and others, and trusting in your inner strength to love and guide you through life.

We will share with you in the following pages the personal stories of our own recovery and the stories of the many people we have worked with. At times we will speak from a distance, and at times we will speak as people who have lived it, suffered through it, and survived it. We will show you that through the painful struggle of accepting your past, you can begin to look at your future with a joyful attitude and an open heart. You can find Emotional Healing.

PART
I

THE
WORLD
OF
THE
ACOA

CHAPTER 1

How We Are, Who We Are

Recognizing the Injury

Our story begins in the fall of 1982 when Karen made the painful decision to separate from her husband, Rick. Although they loved each other very much, Karen felt there was something missing in her life and in their relationship, and she had a profound feeling of dissatisfaction and loneliness. Initially their relationship had been difficult, but they had worked hard, both in and out of therapy, to create a stable home. Professionally Karen was involved and creative, and life, at least on the outside, looked good.

Internally, though, she was not in good shape. Her self-esteem was so low she couldn't accept praise, and she derived little satisfaction from her work and her successes. She felt that at any minute she could be found out as a fake, and she could fall on her face. No matter how well things were really going, she felt a deep sadness and confusion, and an inability to accept love from her husband, her children, and her friends. To give herself a feeling of excitement and a sense of purpose, she continued to create crises in her life, even when things were going smoothly, by picking fights with her husband and threatening to leave.

Both Karen and Rick were unable to confront the problems in their relationship and were afraid of the pain that lay underneath the surface. Karen made some decisions she soon regretted—including promising her ex-husband that her children could live with him for a year when he returned from overseas. It was a promise that upset a balance that Karen, Rick, and the children had worked very hard to achieve, a decision Karen made because she thought she should, not because she believed it was the best thing for everybody. She was removed from her ability to hear her heart and believe in her right to have what she wanted, and as a result, many lives were disrupted and made unhappy. When the children were gone, Karen felt that there was no longer any reason to stay where she was or to stay with Rick, and she left her home.

Thinking that she had to go as far away as possible to achieve any real sense of separation, Karen left Boston for California. It was a choice that would affect the rest of her life. After a few weeks in California, she wrote a letter to Terry.

Dear Terry,

I think about all the things that have gone on in my life recently, and I'm realizing how lost and really lonely I feel. I miss you a lot. It isn't as if I haven't been busy and involved. In fact, I spent the last five days in a dance workshop which distracted me some and let me focus on my body, instead of my mind, for a change, but today I am awed by the depth of silence and sadness within me.

While I've been in Santa Barbara, I've been attending a series of lectures on adult children of alcoholics, and I've also gone to some Al-Anon meetings. For all my knowledge of alcoholism, I haven't really known much about the effects of it on nonalcoholics in the family. I am amazed by some of it and really touched by the relief and recognition that is happening for people in the class—and for me, too, although it's hard and it is making me look at my relationship with Rick and my leaving in a different light.

One of the most amazing things is to just talk about alcoholism. There is such a conspiracy of silence and denial in alcoholic families—the most incredible things can happen and no one ever talks about it—that just being with others and sharing our experiences breaks through a lot.

I feel reluctant to say this because my feelings change so fast these days, but this is something that has stayed with me, and that is why I am writing to you. I know that working with adult children of alcoholics is something I want to do as my next professional step, and I would like you to work with me. I would feel safer if we did it together. I have also thought for a while that you needed to look at the consequences of your having an alcoholic father. This is all very new to me and, I think, very important!

Rick is coming here for Thanksgiving. It was painful to talk to him on the phone last night, and at the end of our conversation, he finally expressed some doubts and fears about coming to visit. I don't mind hearing pain and doubt, but I do mind the absence of things between us. If there is any chance that we can get back together, I want to take it.

Children of alcoholics can't trust, have trouble with intimate relationships, need to control, deny their feelings, see everything as black or white, and don't know how to work things slowly. I see all these things in myself today. We want the changes to have happened yesterday. That's my contribution to the mess.

Kisses, Karen

Karen's letter, and what she described, hit Terry with a shock of familiarity. During the fall, Terry had gone through a series of incidents that had left him disturbed and unhappy, and Karen's letter reached him at a time when he felt most confused about the way his life was going. There was a recognition of the characteristics Karen described, yet up until that point, neither of us had ever labeled ourselves as adult children of alcoholics. In fact, until that time, we didn't even know that there was such a thing.

That fall, Terry had begun psychotherapy again after a four-year break, and his therapist was now asking him to look more deeply into himself than he had ever done before. He was beginning to examine his relationships and was allowing himself to feel what it was like to be a small child again, dependent on parents who awed and frightened him. For the first time, he was facing the fact that his childhood had instilled in him some destructive and self-defeating behaviors that he was having trouble shaking.

Terry reentered therapy for a number of reasons. Perhaps the most significant was that within a month and a half he had lost three part-time jobs. The first job he lost was one he had had for three years, working with inpatient alcoholics in a traditional mental hospital where he was responsible for running a psychodrama session once a week. The issue over which he would eventually lose his job involved self-disclosure. Week after week, Terry and his supervisor would disagree on just how much the patients needed to know about Terry's own experiences. Terry insisted that the psychodrama was enriched by his acting as role model, the two of them never saw eye to eye, and Terry was terminated. Terry was unable to see that this man was his supervisor, not his peer, and that there were some things he'd have to do, even if he didn't like them.

The second job involved teaching a psychology course in a master's program. Terry became entangled with the dean over the rigor Terry thought the program lacked, and once again, he was not "fitting in" with the structure of the organization, and was let go.

The third job loss illustrates even more clearly Terry's problems with authority. He had been working at a school for five years, giving a communications workshop for students. Terry never took the time to introduce himself to the new headmaster, adopting the attitude that if the headmaster wanted to meet him, he could initiate a meeting. The new headmaster never came forward, and instead, the budget for the workshop was dropped the next year, along with Terry's position.

The particulars in each incident were different, but the essential similarities pointed to Terry's inability to work with male authority and his failure to address the political realities of each situation. A common thread that ran through each job experience was his unwillingness to fit in and become one of the team. The realization on Terry's part that this was a problem that kept repeating itself, coinciding with the work he was doing in therapy, allowed him to be receptive to all that Karen was discovering and proposing. There was a relief in being able to name what was going on, to step back and look at the problem, to recognize a pattern in his behavior. For Terry, who finally admitted that his life was not working, it was the beginning of finding Emotional Healing.

When we look back at that time, we see that for both of us, there was great value in finally being able to label ourselves adult children of alcoholics. Never having felt like we quite belonged anywhere before, we could now sit in a room full of people who listened to our stories but did not judge, who accepted and believed, because they had been there, too. We should not underestimate how difficult it is to apply this label to yourself, and the realization and acceptance may be as slow for you as it was for us.

In our workshops we see people who listen to other people's stories, but isolate themselves by thinking, "It wasn't that bad in my case," or "That person really needs help. I'm not sure I do," or "My parents only did what they did because life was so hard."

We have all apologized for our parents' behavior time and time again. In our position as professionals who have worked with ACOAs for many years, but also as fellow ACOAs, we tell people with all sincerity, understanding, and empathy, "Yes, your parents did the best they could, but they didn't do a very good job."

Our parents taught us to live in a world that was centered around them and their problems. At an age when we needed support, attention, and focus, we got little but gave to them instead. As adults, by accepting the truth about what went on, we begin to give ourselves the quality of attention we never got as children. For many of us, the attention makes us uncomfortable, and there are painful things we must accept about our histories and our adult lives in order to begin our recovery. First, we must admit it really did happen.

We must also admit that despite all our efforts to exist entirely on our own, we sometimes need to ask for help, even though many of us have become quite expert in simulating control in all aspects of our lives. We have managed our lives remarkably well, employing all our repetitive, self-destructive behaviors that give us the illusion of control that we were deprived of as children. We have learned behaviors that hide our pain and distress from the world and keep it buried within us. The song that would best describe our lives is: "Whistle a happy tune/and every single time/the happiness in the tune/convinces me that I am not afraid." We begin to move toward recovery when we admit we can't fix it.

Understanding Pain Avoidance as a Way of Life

To admit that we can't "fix it" goes against everything we learned as children: that we have only ourselves to depend on, only ourselves to make sure we survive. By admitting that we can't do everything alone, we give up a basic principle of our lives and sacrifice an ideal image of ourselves as self-reliant, utterly self-sufficient people. We open ourselves up to real life, and by accepting the good and the bad that it has to give, we join the rest of the human race.

In our work with ACOAs, and also in our own struggles, we have seen that a key to recovery is understanding how our lives until now have been organized to avoid pain at all costs, and how all our energy has gone into that avoidance. In healthy families, children are sheltered from pain to a certain degree, but at the same time they are taught not to deny the reality of a situation, even if it hurts. Children from healthy families learn that pain and pleasure are parts of the spectrum of human experience, and that it's okay to act sad if you feel sad, and it's okay to act happy if you are happy. They learn that there are some things they can change, and some things they cannot. However, we were taught to deny, and denial has worked very well for us until now.

As children who grew up in alcoholic and unhealthy families, we were taught to manage our own lives, because support and advice were inconsistent, unpredictable, and often given without our best interests in mind. We learned to be in control of ourselves and other people at all times. That is why it is so hard to admit that our lives are out of control now. When we finally admit that life is for living, not controlling, struggling, and avoiding pain, we create a context for a transformation in our lives, and take a step toward recovery.

It is natural to avoid pain. As we grew up in alcoholic families, it wasn't just that we tried to avoid pain, but what is more debilitating in terms of our long-term development is that we learned to organize our lives around pain avoidance. We learned to crowd out and ignore the most precious thing we were born with: our capacity, and right, for pleasure.

If you are pain-avoidant, you treat life as a problem rather than a prospect. Pleasure may be a reward for something well done, something that occasionally relieves some pressure, but do you see it as essential to your being as food and sleep? Does it hold any real meaning for you?

Our pain-avoidant focus distorts our view of pleasure and we often see it as self-indulgent, hedonistic, and destructive. Our parents often equated pleasure with alcohol, and when they derived pleasure from alcohol, they hurt and neglected us. Nowhere has the concept of pleasure been more distorted than around sexuality, where the selfish acts of others have led us into situations of abuse and incest. What should be a naturally pleasurable experience becomes, for some of us, dangerous, devastating, and humiliating.

The pleasures we seek from the very moment we are born are none of these things. The pleasure we speak of is the pleasure an infant feels when he sees his parents, and it is the visible pleasure and vitality we see in children when they play. It is the pleasure of healthy adults in the satisfaction derived from good work, in fulfilling personal relationships, in the spiritual, in the beauty of all things.

Real pleasure is not forced, but it is the focus in a healthy adult, in the same way it is for children. If we have been hurt from the start by the ones we take most pleasure in loving, the ones we've depended on to return the pleasure of love, then the avoidance of pain becomes a greater priority than the seeking of pleasure. Who needs pleasure and love if it only ends up in hurt and disappointment? What we as adults can do, though, slowly and gently, is begin to shift the focus of our lives so that we can disengage from a preoccupation with problems without denying them and live a life that seeks pleasure, not one that avoids pain.

In order to make this switch, many ACOAs must look back at their histories, rediscovering and befriending a voice inside of them that we call the "wounded child." It is this child that has the real memories and the real feelings that our pain-avoidant nature has not allowed us to face up to until now. In rediscovering this wounded child inside us, we can also rediscover our original capacity for pleasure.

We begin by allowing the child within us to speak to us, and to others, about what really happened, and we allow this child to be believed. This means we must be specific as we speak—recalling real events, citing true examples—and we must see the world from the child's point of view, and believe the feelings even if they aren't familiar or easy to accept. In the following chapter, we will show you that the key to this opening up to the past is to continually remind yourself, "Yes, it really did happen." We have made it this far by denying, repressing, and rationalizing—all facets of our pain-avoidant behavior.

It is important to note that the effort to remember takes time and patience. You cannot force the memories and the feelings to emerge. It is also important to understand that you are not going to fix all the problems in your life. Recovery is related to telling the truth about things, not always fixing them. "Fixing it" is a pain-avoidant mechanism. We must learn to accept that pain is a part of life from time to time, and something we can deal with. When we begin to deepen our understanding and acceptance of the wounded child's point of view, we can begin to make the switch. The point is that by telling yourself the truth, you are no longer avoiding the pain; you are facing up to it. It immediately creates a new context for you to live in, and a new focus for your life.

And the new focus is on pleasure. As a child you were taught to deny pain and to seek pleasure, as you saw others do, from alcohol or other addictive behaviors, such as overeating or gambling. Eventually sex, like alcohol or food, was added to the list of things that brought you pleasure. We learned to treat sex like a commodity to make ourselves feel better rather than as a natural and precious expression of the most personal and loving aspect of ourselves.

Gratification sought for the relief of pain is not fun. In our workshops we teach that pleasure is an *expression* of healthy excitement—it is not *for* anything. We see healthy excitement as coming from the heart, undistorted by fantasy and fear, and in contact with reality and the true feelings of other people. Healthy excitement stirs up adrenaline, which is a pleasurable feeling in and of itself when it does not make one fearful and pressured.

Making the Switch from Pain Avoidance

If you spend your life avoiding pain, life is a struggle and there is little or no room for pleasure. We often hear from ACOAs that the difficulty is not in actually appreciating pleasure, but in keeping the focus on it, because they are always waiting for the next disaster to happen. Nothing good can last for long, we learned.

We can learn to focus on pleasure the same way we learn other things—with time and patience. An important part of learning to focus on pleasure is to also accept our errors and ask ourselves, "What can I learn from my pain?" We can stop being the victim, and be willing to embrace all of life instead.

Terry's switch began when he started having problems with his first wife. Perhaps if she had not taken the brave step of leaving, Terry would still be trying to make their relationship work, because he was loyal, persistent, and believed he could fix anything.

When the marriage finally ended, it was very difficult and painful for Terry. His pride was hurt, and he was forced to admit that while his emotional life may have been exciting and dynamic, it just wasn't working.

In typical pain-avoidant fashion, Terry made the decision not to get close to anyone for a while, and although he didn't know it then, this was probably the first step in changing the focus of his life; he would no longer be ruled by passion and excitement in a relationship, but he would look for what made him feel good instead, what ultimately brought him pleasure and peace.

During this time, Terry began to look at why he was continually drawn to women who were highly critical and distanced themselves from him. He began to examine his relationship with his mother and the depth of his misgivings about what had gone on between them, what we now call "covert incest."

Covert incest is not acted out, and often happens when one parent, in this case Terry's mother, stays with a spouse who abuses alcohol or physical power. The nonabusing parent draws the child in, as a confidant or as a protector, to make up for the faults and failings of the spouse. This level of intimacy can be dangerous and damaging to a child.

By feeling he was so important to his mother, Terry developed a false sense of his own potency and importance, only to cover up and deny the pain he felt over the relationship with his alcoholic father. By choosing to be involved with a critical woman, Terry was unconsciously struggling with his confused feelings about his mother and her needs. The more critical and distancing a woman was, the more exciting Terry found her. His overinvolvement with the woman's needs continued to help him ignore the fact that he had been deeply unhappy around women his entire life. Terry's behavior functioned in much the same way that not dealing with male authority distanced him from the pain of dealing with his father.

Clearly, though, neither of these pain-avoidant behaviors worked for Terry, and his life was a mess. But seeing the mess enabled him to make a switch. The switch was in admitting to himself the truth about his relationships and facing up to the fact that things could not always be worked out in his usual way. It was a hard lesson for him to learn.

Once Terry began making changes, things began to get easier in his relationships. His relationship with his new wife, Gale, developed slowly and securely, rather than through a flash of passion. She was a kind and attentive woman, and the fact that Terry was able to finally appreciate and value these traits was a sign that he was ready to shift toward pleasure-seeking and away from his addiction to passion, drama, and conflict. He wanted to spend time with Gale because she made him happy, not because she helped him avoid and forget the pain in his life.

In the context of his happy, married life, the loss of three jobs now offered the opportunity for more change. His psychotherapist gently helped him see that it was just an illusion that Terry was triumphing over his father by avoiding male authority. The switch came for Terry when he could look back and honestly say about his father, "You got me and I'm wounded." Once he admitted he was wounded, there was nothing left for him to fix, or to prove. He could begin to live his life without so much struggle, and he could say, "I am not a hero."

Terry continues to make changes in his life, and they are often slow and painful. A good example of how this operates in his everyday life is the discovery he made one day when writing this book. He found himself lying to Karen and his family about the process of writing for no apparent reason. The truth was he had missed deadlines and was anxious about it, but he was covering up the fact to everyone who asked, including himself. Anxiety grew inside him and he felt he had no one to confide in.

He couldn't let it go on forever, because the pain and anxiety he felt over the work were becoming intrusive. He was living out what he was attempting to write about. When he told the truth and admitted his anxiety, the pleasure of the work began to come back. The truth is that writing a book was the hardest thing he had ever done, and he needed help and support. The switch occurred for him when he accepted the pain he was in and asked for support, rather than covering the pain up and trying to fix it all alone. The switch allowed him to enjoy his work once again. The truth had freed him up.

For the most part, Karen had always seen herself as a bad person for being angry at her mother. She tried to ignore and deny the anger she felt, and by doing so, ignored a very real pain and something her whole being told her was true. When Ann Armstrong, a mentor she loved and respected, helped her see that her mother's involvement with alcohol made her unable to love Karen the way Karen wanted, things began to open up. Karen finally understood why she didn't like to be touched by her mother, or even to sit near her. Her touch felt poisonous.

Karen could finally accept that her anger came not from being a bad kid, but from the fact that her mother had been unable to truly love her. She switched from the avoidance of the pain to the acceptance of the painful truth—that she hadn't been loved the way she needed as a child. That was where she needed to start her recovery, from the child who was so scared and so hurt. The switch, like Terry's, was not immediate. She still felt quite a lot of guilt when she felt good or enjoyed herself. For so long, she had felt that she was to suffer as her mother had. When she could face her pain, her capacity for pleasure increased, bit by bit. She realized that because she had been so dedicated to avoiding pain, she left no room for pleasure. Her response before had always been to run away—as she did when she went to California—but now she felt she had the strength to deal with the ups and downs in life.

When both Karen and her husband, Rick, were able to face the pain in their marriage, they were able to move away from their old patterns of denial and blame. It was not until both admitted how unhappy they were with their relationship that they were able to begin to enjoy the pleasures that made it all worthwhile. Neither of them had been particularly good at being intimate, because neither of them could face the negativity they sometimes felt. The bad feelings accumulated and caused pressure and anxiety in both Karen and Rick. Until they were able to tell the truth about how they felt, they were not able to be close. Facing the pain in their marriage released their energy and allowed them to seek pleasure as a couple.

Paying the Price of Pain Avoidance

It is natural for us to move toward pleasure if we give ourselves a chance. The problem, then, is not that pleasure is elusive, but that the means that enable us to avoid pain also inhibit our ability to attend to, or even value, pleasure. The result is a deadening of the spirit.

To realize that we, as ACOAs, are pain-avoidant gives us the advantage of no longer feeling helpless with our injuries, of no longer feeling so isolated. This understanding gives us a positive direction for our personal growth, a point from which to change the focus of our lives to the pursuit of pleasure. As we've said before, this is not a quick or simple remedy, and it takes time, attention, and practice. As we begin to look at our lives, we begin to see how many of our characteristics were formed as pain-avoidant mechanisms.

Janet Woititz, in her groundbreaking book *Adult Children of Alcoholics*,[1] outlines thirteen general characteristics of ACOAs. Point by point, we've seen in our own work with ACOAs how these behaviors, originally adopted as survival mechanisms, also served as ways to avoid the pain of what was really going on in our lives.

1. *Adult children of alcoholics guess at what "normal" is.* We grew up in families that were bizarre, inconsistent, and often chaotic, so we may not know what normal family life looks like. Because we have never seen it, never learned normal behavior from our parents, we guess, often expertly, how we should behave and appear in a given situation. This functions as a pain-avoidant mechanism because living is organized around the idea that everything has to be right and appear perfect and "guessing" is a defense against feeling what is really there. We are too busy guessing at how fulfilling lives are run, to be in touch with our real emotions, desires, and self-expression.

2. *Adult children of alcoholics have difficulty in following a project through from beginning to end.* So often we have been disappointed by our parents, had promises made to us and then broken, that we don't know how to follow through, to maintain a necessary level of commitment to the end. We were told that when something hurts, do something else (watch television, have a drink), instead of sitting with the discomfort, waiting out the bad parts. We have learned to have so little faith that life actually has its rewards that we don't hang in there. When things get rough, we get going. We don't believe there is a light at the end of the tunnel, and if there is light, it's probably a train coming our way. When we complete something, it feels to us like a little death, and avoiding the grief of endings is pain-avoidant behavior.

3. *Adult children of alcoholics lie when it would be just as easy to tell the truth.* There is not a high premium paid for truth and integrity in many alcoholic families. If you grew up in a home where telling the truth usually got you in trouble and drew you further into the family drama, you may have learned that lying is the easier, less painful route to take. Lying is a small price to pay to avoid being hurt, and quite often we believe our stories and are not even aware of the fact that we aren't telling the truth anymore. In short, by lying we are

behaving in a pain-avoidant fashion, ignoring the pain of the truth and of the consequences the truth might bring about.

4. *Adult children of alcoholics judge themselves without mercy.* Many ACOAs are harsh critics of themselves and others. By harboring an ideal image of how life should be, we are furious with ourselves when we make a mistake. It is just one more sign to us that we are not in control, that we can't fix everything, that our lives are not perfect.

There is a phenomenon described by Erich Fromm that occurs in many victims of abuse called "the internalization of the aggressor," where the victim learns to reduce his own suffering by accepting the abuser's attitudes as if they were his own. In other words, I deserve the punishment, so I don't really feel the pain and suffering, and I have no right to feel bad about it. If we are our own worst critic, then we are immune to pain and criticism we may get from outside. By judging ourselves first, we avoid the pain of having others judge us.

5. *Adult children of alcoholics have difficulty having fun.* So often when we were growing up, we were ashamed and humiliated by our parents "having fun": getting drunk, being abusive, ridiculing, gambling, etc. Humor in many alcoholic families meant picking on or humiliating someone. It is no wonder, then, that we have trouble having fun. Pain-avoidant people don't have the time or the skills for fun. ACOAs often feel tremendous guilt for the pain in their families and do not feel deserving of a good time.

When we are pain-avoidant, we cannot see what will bring us pleasure, and having fun becomes a hard task for many of us. Having fun also requires an openness, and an ability to respond at the moment, impulsively and intuitively. This requires a belief that most ACOAs do not have, a belief that things will turn out okay in the end. We think that by focusing on the serious aspects of life we can avoid the pain of being surprised.

6. *Adult children of alcoholics take themselves very seriously.* Many ACOAs are obsessed with their problems and everyone else's, and feel that the drama in their lives is

never-ending. When your life is organized around pain avoidance, there is no time to let down, to hang out, and every moment must be meaningful. We are so afraid of rejection and disappointment that we find it hard to simply enjoy someone's company, or enjoy the pleasure of a sexual relationship, fearing the rejection and the pain that will inevitably follow.

7. *Adult children of alcoholics have difficulty in intimate relationships.* How can anyone who is so bent on avoiding pain get into a relationship in the first place? Because the power of love and sexuality is greater than even our greatest fear of pain. However, what you learned in childhood is that the potential for hurt is greatest when you care the most. The work of being close to someone becomes a struggle between the forces of love and the fear of pain and vulnerability that comes with caring. We are so committed to protecting ourselves against the pain of being hurt that it is impossible to truly open our hearts to another.

But there is a healthy reason for partnership—the simple pleasure of another person's company. Healthy relationships exist between equals, and pain-avoidant relationships usually involve dependency, because with dependency comes the false promise of control and stability. Making the switch toward pleasure in relationships involves opening up ourselves, and making ourselves vulnerable once again to being hurt by someone we love. It is for this reason that intimate relationships are the most valuable and hardest place to make the switch from pain avoidance to the active pursuit of pleasure.

8. *Adult children of alcoholics overreact to changes that they have no control over.* If your life has been filled with pain caused by those you loved and trusted, your parents, then you will inevitably overreact and become anxious when anything changes and you don't know what comes next. For most ACOAs, change has always meant a change for the worse. In our effort to avoid pain, we grew up desperately trying to maintain the status quo. Healthy people look forward to the unknown in their lives and look for support to help them

through hard times. They accept the fact that difficulty and change are a part of living.

9. *Adult children of alcoholics constantly seek approval and affirmation.* Throughout our childhoods, we were told that our parents' well-being depended on our behavior. If they drank, it was because we were bad. If they abused us, it was because we deserved it. Healthy childhoods, on the other hand, are primarily child-centered, and children grow up learning how to distinguish their own from other people's needs, and how to be sensitive and empathetic. But pain-avoidant people did not learn this. Instead, our hearts were constantly played with through either conditional approval or criticism, in crazy and unpredictable ways, and our wounded inner child continually seeks the nurturing and acceptance we didn't get as children. We are driven by the approval of others and by a need to please. We have no internal sense of our own worth. Pain-avoidant people are not self-regulating, but are organized around an internal sense of satisfaction derived from others.

10. *Adult children of alcoholics often feel different from other people.* It has been our experience that just about everyone, whether he or she grew up in an unhealthy home or not, sometimes feels that he or she is different. Equally painfully, most people have the experience at one time or another that no one understands him. These phenomena are actually the dark side of a very important part of one's humanness—that each of us is unique.

The pain-avoidant person, however, gets caught up in his sense of difference and in his fear that others will find out about it. He then isolates himself with the secrets that he believes make him different. Tragically, this denies him the many opportunities to find out that others think and feel in similar ways. The fear of pain of rejection and humiliation are just too great to risk exposing himself by reaching out and opening up to others.

11. *Adult children of alcoholics are either super-responsible or very irresponsible.* The key to healthy responsibility is in one's ability to be human, to find the place in our

hearts where we are touched by life's mishaps and pressures, able to respond, but not overwhelmed by them. ACOAs too often have had to take responsibility too early and become either grandiose about their abilities or shirk all responsibility. By being super-responsible we desperately hoped we could bring order to our lives.

The tendency toward irresponsibility is the flip side of the same coin. Rather than examine and deal with the problems presented us, we choose to bail out instead. We may believe that we have worked so hard, now it is time for someone to take care of us. Asking for help when we need it is the healthy thing to do, but sharing responsibility is not something the ACOA has learned. We believe that by taking all the responsibility, or none, we can avoid the pain we believe is inherent in sharing control.

12. *Adult children of alcoholics are extremely loyal even in the face of evidence that the loyalty is undeserved.* The key to understanding this loyalty can be found in something we often say in our workshop: "This is the only mommy and daddy we will ever have." This statement captures the context of the child desperately searching for a good family life, and while the child recognizes the awful things his parents do, he also recognizes that they are the only parents he has. Being loyal to our parents helps us avoid the pain of abandonment and failure. When we hang in there and act as though there is hope, we have something to believe in. Loyalty in this case is not the admirable kind. Rather, this is the loyalty of a child who clings to love that has betrayed and hurt him, because the prospect of being alone is even more frightening than the reality of abuse and neglect.

13. *Adult children of alcoholics tend to lock themselves into a course of action without giving serious consideration to alternative behaviors or possible consequences.* This behavior points to our acting on impulse that will inevitably re-create a painful but familiar experience. Impulsivity leads to confusion and regret, and time that could have been spent thinking about options and choices is spent cleaning up the mess. Pain avoidance is a natural reaction, but here it is carried to such an

extent that it re-creates familiar disappointment and further pain.

In our workshops, we say, "Don't just do something, sit there!" By sitting with our discomfort in a situation, instead of running to cover it up and avoid the pain, we are forced to look at the what and the how of a situation, and we give our inner self a chance to express itself. Many ACOAs have received so much positive reinforcement for what they can *do* that they have often lost their ability to value their "being," and they become mechanical and joyless. The "being" is what we call the eye of the storm. The eye does not negate the storm, it dwells within it. Making the switch from pain to pleasure means searching for that eye within the storm.

Reaching Maturity: a Goal of Recovery

Children who grow up in unhealthy homes are not free to explore the world of childhood that is filled with fantasy and play within the safe confines of home. Instead, they are pulled into the family drama of coping with alcohol, anger, or other addictions. They become old before their time, and they are cheated out of their childhoods. They become what we call "pseudo-mature," another characteristic of pain-avoidant behavior. For Karen, her pseudo-maturity was shared with her sister in the responsibility both girls felt toward their parents' happiness and well-being. Unfortunately, the energy they put into denying themselves and trying to make life work, not only for their parents but for their brother and friends as well, was supported by the praise they received from teachers and relatives for being so "good." The child in them, however, was lost, buried beneath their pseudo-mature attempt to take responsibility for others.

Healthy maturity involves an acceptance of life as it is, the ability to absorb the good and the bad as it comes. A mature person, through the assimilation of varied experience, is able to react to a new situation in a measured and thoughtful way. Mature people allow for spontaneity and do not always edit or censor themselves. Maturity, however, also involves a sense of timing and self-control, the ability to judge when to act and what to say, instead of acting out of impulse at the moment, and the mature person can recognize when no reaction is called for. A mature person has worked out a balance for himself between independence and the pleasure of another's company. Mature love allows self-expression.

Finally a mature person is able to take his knocks in life, stand by decisions he has made, and embrace all of life's experiences, even pain.

But the pseudo-mature person has never had the time or the freedom to develop the trust in life required for the longer view of things. ACOAs have had a lot of experience at an early age that leaves them shocked and wounded, and they are only able to cope by adopting adult behavior or pseudo-maturity. Pseudo-maturity is an act, designed to build up the wounded child's self-esteem and confidence, no matter how convoluted, as in Terry's case.

Terry was the oldest child in his family. As his father's alcoholism became worse and his drinking took priority over his wife and family, Terry was drawn closer and closer to his mother. Every child feels an attachment for his mother that he eventually grows out of, but in Terry's case, he did not grow out of it. Instead, Terry continued to adore his mother and learned to manipulate her in many ways. The look of love she gave him was not simply a mother's love, but something different and more intense, and Terry was drawn into an oedipal drama he was too excited about to resist, and too young to understand.

Aware of how important he was to his mother, Terry developed a clumsy pseudo-mature attitude that was too much for him to handle. While he excelled in school and in sports, he had trouble making friends. He was also abusive to his siblings, and his parents nicknamed him "Terry the Terror." He had no realistic sense of the importance of his place.

Recently we worked with Anita, a forty-one-year-old housewife, another example of someone who employs pseudo-mature behavior. She was the second oldest child in a large Irish family. Her father, whom she adored, drank himself to death by the time she was twelve, but it was Anita's mother who was the monster in her life. Sadistic and controlling, her mother would verbally and physically abuse her children, blaming them for everything from their father's drinking to the baby's dirty diapers.

As the oldest girl, Anita was responsible for the cooking, the cleaning, and the care of the youngest child. In her loyalty to her father, she took on the task of parenting this child and sacrificed her own adolescence while her mother continued to abuse her. Anita never gave away any secrets until she came to our workshop. She had raised her own family, suffered from cancer for many years, lost her husband, and finally admitted that she felt "all dried up." Her pseudo-maturity had been so strong that it supported her for all those years. Eventually, though, it just gave out.

She finally found people to listen and believe her stories. Previous attempts to tell the truth had gotten her in trouble, but now, at a time in her life when there was no one left to take care of, she broke down, and could finally begin to live her own life. Anita had had no choice, and had become a robot to live out her mother's ideal.

Unhealthy homes, like Anita's, have no room for children to be children. We adopted our pain-avoidant behaviors, as Anita did, as a way to cope with a bad situation. It was the best we could do. But being a parent isn't easy either, and the normal burdens of parenting are many times compounded by problems of addiction and abuse, creating unhealthy environments for children. In our workshops we explain the Golden Rule that operates unhealthy families: He who has the gold makes the rules. And in this case, the gold is alcohol, physical power, sexual abuse. Parents abuse their power by changing rules to suit themselves, and children learn to go along or risk punishment.

In unhealthy homes, children have no recourse. They are not allowed to express how they feel, and are often forced into nonverbal behavior to relieve the pain and anxiety. The parents then blame and criticize the children, and the children begin to believe that their misery is of their own doing. Unhealthy homes are filled with frustrated and self-centered people who place their needs above their children's.

Healthy Homes Do Exist

Many participants in our workshops do not believe there is such a thing as a healthy home, let alone any possibility that they could create one. They do not recognize what is healthy and unhealthy in a family system, and do not know what to shoot for. When we speak of healthy homes, we have certain, yet fluid, characteristics in mind.

• *Healthy homes have roles for each member that are clear, age-appropriate, and make sense to each member of the family.* Fathers are fathers, mothers are mothers, and children are children. In healthy homes, children are not asked to accept adult responsibility that has been abdicated by the parents. Roles are age-specific, and are designed to give a structure to the behavior and development of the child. A common example is of chores that a child can accomplish with his skills and abilities. Appropriate roles give a child a framework within which he can deal with frustration and distress. They give the child a sense of security and encourage development.

• *Healthy families set limits that are individualized, age-appropriate, and child-centered.* We often say in our workshops that "kids need limits." They don't know what the limits are and they shouldn't have to ask for them. It is the job of the parent to set the limits that are an appropriate balance between discipline and freedom, allowing the kids to push for pleasure and independence within the safety of their parents' support and best judgment. Parents in healthy homes are sensitive to their children's needs.

• *Healthy families are honest and do not deny problems.* Children do not need perfect parents, but they do want to hear the truth—it strengthens their conception of reality and gives them confidence in their judgment. Often parents lie to their children to protect them from pain, but children in healthy families can learn to cope with pain if they are allowed to express it and are supported through it.

• *In healthy families, there is focused attention.* This means the parents give their children undivided and nonjudgmental attention and, when appropriate, eye contact. The parents must be sensitive enough to know just how much, and how intense, the attention should be. In Terry's home, the attention he received from his alcoholic father was conditional. It focused either on achievement or on failure, but was rarely what Terry needed at that point.

• *In healthy families, feelings are expressed and attended to.* As a child, having one's feelings attended to helps one tolerate intense feelings without losing the fragile sense of self. The child's point of view is treated as legitimate and considered. When a child's point of view is honored, he learns to honor himself.

• *In healthy homes, there is unconditional love, empathy, and physical affection.* All these things are necessary for the child to thrive. In healthy families, unconditional love is nonmanipulative; it is not given only as a reward for good behavior. Empathy allows the parents to see the child's point of view, and physical affection in healthy homes is nonsexual.

• *Healthy families are good-humored and have child-centered play.* Play is not possible if the pain of the family threatens the child's sense of safety. In healthy homes, good humor and play release tension and help the children learn not to take everything so seriously. When a child is taught to appreciate the humor of family life, he becomes better equipped to see it in other areas as well.

• *Healthy families have consistent rituals and rules that are attended to.* Consistent behavior on the part of the parents gives the child a safe harbor in reality, from which they can venture into play and fantasy. Family rituals give the child a sense of the order of things, things he can rely on and expect.

Holidays offer the child a sense of continuity and a time to look forward to.

• *Healthy homes are flexible as well as consistent.* Flexibility allows the family to react to the particular needs of each member, and allows each member to feel that things are never set in stone, that they, too, can effect change.

As you read this book, you will no doubt recognize what is unhealthy in your home and the home you grew up in. The stories we tell throughout will resonate with memories and feelings. When you see how your pain-avoidant mechanisms have controlled and limited your life, you have won a major battle.

We begin to lift the secrecy and denial about our childhoods by looking quite specifically at what went on. We begin by talking about what happened, maybe to just a couple of people at first, and we bear the feelings that go along with this, though at times they may feel intolerable. Once you can understand and embrace your personal fate, you have created the opportunity to make a switch in your life from the avoidance of pain to the pursuit of pleasure.

CHAPTER 2

Learning to Face
the Pain

The essence of the alcoholic and abusive family is denial, secrecy, and the parental power to enforce it, and this is what keeps us from seeing just how bad our childhood was. Denial allowed our families to continue to function as though nothing was wrong, and it enabled us to bury the pain we experienced as children. The importance of keeping the family secret and maintaining the family status quo meant we didn't tell anyone who might have helped us about the things that were going on within our family. As ACOAs the fundamental principle of our lives has been to tell ourselves that things were not really so bad, to pretend we weren't hurt by what went on, and to keep our past a secret. To no longer deny the truth, and to finally face the pain, is to begin our recovery. When we face the pain, we are able to find Emotional Healing, and when we have learned to accept our feelings no matter how painful, we discover self-confidence, self-love, and our hope for the future. Recovery does not mean creating something new; it means uncovering and rediscovering what's been there all along, something that has been so deeply buried we don't even know it exists.

What is confusing for many ACOAs is that in retrospect our lives might look like they weren't so bad. But at the core of each of our families was a problem that twisted the family's emotional life and affected each member. It is difficult for us to recognize the problem because the inconsistent and unpredictable nature of life in the alcoholic family obscures and confuses the reality of what really went on. There were good times that at any minute could change into bad times.

Seeing That "It Was So Bad"

As children we had no way of comparing what went on in our family with what occurred in others. Karen and her sister used to ask each other, "Do you think we're having an unhappy childhood?" Who knew what happened in the privacy of other families? We certainly couldn't ask.

Terry continued to believe that he had a happy childhood even well into his second year of therapy. He guarded the warm memories of his childhood like a locked treasure chest, for fear that someone might get in and discover the truth. The family myth was that "Terry got the best of Dad," and in part, this was true. Although his father was attentive in many ways and proud of Terry's athletic achievements, his attention and pride were really based on his own needs to have someone (in this case, his son) make him look good. This left little room for Terry to act and grow as an individual. For many years, Terry worked hard at maintaining the family myth by trying to please his father at the expense of his own individuality.

For both of us, as we got older and problems began to surface, we were forced to look back, this time with an eye that neither distorted nor denied the truth. At first the past was a puzzle and the pieces didn't fit at all, but through years of therapeutic guidance and hard work, of painful self-examination and conscious change, of digging deeper and deeper, we were finally able to accept the truth and understand why we are as we are today.

For some ACOAs, the feelings associated with our childhood are completely buried, as if they don't exist. We were raised in families that avoided addressing the issues of alcoholism or abuse, that ignored problems, and spent much energy presenting a false face to the world. Our parents, like most, wanted to appear as though they were doing their very best for their children. So as children we suffered silently with our anger and grief. We were not allowed to talk about our pain, we were not allowed to let it show. When Karen cried, her mother would make fun of her saying, "Look at her, she looks like a turtle!" As a child Karen learned to cry alone, or not at all. Terry, on the other hand, did not know when he was scared. Early on, he had relabeled his anxiety, and had learned to talk himself out of whatever he was feeling. All his will and energy went into having everything look like it was okay.

No one told us that our parents were alcoholics and out of control, no one helped us name what was really going on. We needed to know that the unhappiness we felt, in spite of the fact that we might have had nice clothes, good schools, and frequent vacations, was real and painful. Our perceptions were questioned and denied, our reactions challenged, and we had no one to corroborate our stories. If, for example, Dad said something cruel to Mom and we questioned her, we were told that "he doesn't mean it. He had a hard day at the office." When Terry's father got up in the middle of dinner to vomit from too much alcohol, no one said a word, as if it was the most natural thing in the world.

We have worked with clients whose childhood stories are much worse than our own, people like Kathy who have survived incest, abuse, and illness, and who still do not really know that what went on in their childhood was destructive, who do not look at the past until their adult lives begin to fall apart and they search for reason and understanding. Kathy, one of eight children, came to us when she was in her early twenties because she was experiencing a nightly terror that left her trembling in her bed. She had trouble keeping jobs, had recently broken up with yet another boyfriend, and was lonely and depressed. She didn't know why.

Kathy: My father was okay when he was sober, but when he was drunk he became violently abusive and controlling. One night I tried to protect my younger sister from his violent rage and he was so angry that he disowned me right then and there. He threw me out of the house and told my sisters and brothers that from then on they were to think of me as dead. I was no longer any part of the family. I thought that when I left the house that night, I had left all the pain, but now I see that I didn't. Recently I've felt the fear every night, and am so scared I can't even get out of my bed.

Why didn't Kathy, as an adult, know that what had gone on in her childhood was destructive and realize how profoundly it had affected her? If alcoholism and child abuse are so obvious to outsiders, why didn't we understand how our families' problems had affected us? The key is in the point of view from which we choose to look at our childhood. Our adult minds tend to whitewash the memories, gloss over the abuse, and focus on the good times. But from the point of view of the child, vulnerable and devoted to his parents, the abuse and the bad times were profound. From the child's point of view, *"it was so bad."*

Seeing From the Child's Point of View

In our workshops, one of our tasks is to help the participants see their past from a child's point of view. This is not what they expect, because people in pain are often in a hurry to feel better, and they want to "fix" everything as quickly as possible. They search for techniques that will help them block out the past, but instead we teach the process of learning to live in a dangerous world, as they did as children, and to stop denying. As ACOAs we are trying to find that wounded child within ourselves, trying to help that wounded child move toward recovery. When we look back at the past from the point of view of the wounded child, we can share the pain.

As we've said before, life in the alcoholic family is based on denial and confusion, of avoidance of the truth and the pain, and to this day, we often don't even know something is wrong until our lives begin to fall apart. To better face the pain of childhood and understand *what* went on, it is important to look at the dynamics that operate in the alcoholic or abusive family, what we will call the unhealthy family.

• *In families where there is alcohol, physical, sexual, or emotional abuse, there is no consistency.* In short, the structure of family life is chaotic and arbitrary. Children seek consistency and predictability in their lives, but in unhealthy families, rules that are often inappropriate to the age of the child—the ten-year-old should make dinner, the seventeen-year-old should be in by 8:00—are set down one day and are ignored or changed the next. Children who have been given a curfew of 9:00 suddenly have to be home by 7:00, and no explanation is offered. The consequences of a child's behavior change arbitrarily and without warning, so that a minor misdeed becomes a major felony, depending on how the parent feels that day. The family learns to tiptoe around and avoid making anyone angry, even though it is nearly impossible to predict just what, or when something will cause a blowup.

Promises are made—to go to the zoo, to have a birthday party, to take a vacation—and are suddenly broken, often because the parent forgets the promise has been made at all, or because the need for a drink takes precedence over any commitment made to the child. There may be no consistency in meals: dinner may be served one night and forgotten the next. Plans change, promises are broken, and life is subject to the whims and impulses of the parent in charge. The endless cycle of hope and disappointment wears a child down and teaches him that life at home is not safe or dependable, and essentially deprives him of the security, joy, and curiosity of childhood.

• *Sexual boundaries are often crossed in unhealthy families, and children are subject to behavior that is sexually inappropriate.* Where there is sexual abuse (we define this as anything from inappropriate talk, to fondling, to overt sexual activity), the child becomes, in a sense, the property of the parent. The child is confused about the role she or he is to play in the family. Is the little girl the daughter or the wife? Is the little boy the son or the husband?

Alcohol has the ability to dissolve inhibitions, both physical and verbal, leading to actions that the same parent would never perform sober. Many alcoholic parents will not remember that they engaged in inappropriate sexual behavior with their children. What looks like simple affectionate play to the drunk parent draws the child in through seduction and fear, and leaves that child with confused emotional and physical feelings that he or she is unable to deal with. The child has no choice but to participate, and acts out of a combination of fear and hope that he will make his parents happy.

Often the spouse of the abusive parent may be so wrapped up in the destructive behavior of his or her partner that he or she is not paying enough attention to the child to see what is really going on. For some women, the sexual advances of their abusive husbands may be too much for them, and they are relieved to have a daughter take on their conjugal obligations. Often children are forced to listen to a parent complain about sexual problems or neglect, and the child is the holder of information he or she should not have. Sexually abused women often tell us that their fathers let them know that their wives didn't satisfy them sexually. This creates in the daughter a feeling of responsibility toward pleasing her father, while having to deal with feelings of disloyalty to her mother.

The area of sexuality has been introduced quite inappropriately to these children, and there is no one around to help them understand it. The only way they manage to cope with the confusion around sexuality is to separate their hearts from their excitement, their love from their sexual feelings. As adults they then find it hard to reconnect these components in a healthy way. We see victims of this who are sexually obsessed and incapable of love, or romantically obsessed and afraid of sexuality and sexual feelings. Often children can't say anything to protect themselves from the abuse; either no one will believe it, or they think it will cause too much trouble, and they are dedicated to keeping the family peace.

Sometimes the sexual abuse is not overt and thus difficult to identify, as it was in Tim's case. Even as an adult, Tim, a twenty-seven-year-old bookstore manager, was not sure that what his mother had done could actually be considered abuse.

> **Tim:** When I was a kid, my mother used to take me to bed with her lots of times when she was drunk. Most of the time she never touched me at all, but just said she didn't want to be alone and I should keep her company. I was really scared that my father would come home any minute and find us and he would kill me, but I felt obligated to my mother to give her what she wanted, and incredibly guilty if I even thought of saying no. This went on for a long time, and it became hard for me not to have some sexual feelings as I lay in bed with my mother against me. I knew this was wrong, but I couldn't help it, and one night I got an erection. I was devastated and embarrassed and I prayed she wouldn't notice, but she did, and she got furious. She threw me out of the bed and accused me of all sorts of things, and that was the end. She never even mentioned it again. I was sure I'd done something wrong and disgusting, but I had only meant to please my mother by keeping her company.

• *In the unhealthy family, unrealistic standards are set for the children.* The children are told that they should be better athletes, do better in school, have more friends, and be more obedient. We hear stories from people who tell us that as children they were never praised for the four As they received on their report card, but criticized for the one B. Both of Terry's parents relied on his good performance for their own self-esteem. When he did well, they did well. Terry's father had unrealistically high standards for his son, and since his own success was increasingly impaired by alcoholism, he counted on Terry to act for him.

The alcoholic or abusive parent who is full of self-loathing puts pressure on the child to make up for his failings, but there is no way for even the best child to be good enough to relieve the pain and anger in the family. Children grow up feeling as though they are never good enough, and whatever they do, they are subject to criticism. They suffer a lifetime for failing to meet impossible standards, even though by other standards, they do an impressive job.

• *In unhealthy homes, children are often blamed for everything that goes wrong, from Dad's drinking problems to a messy house.* Alcohol or parental outbursts are not the problem, they are told. At first, the family will deny that there is a member abusing alcohol or physical power, and then they will deny that he is dependent on it. Finally, when it is so obvious as not to be ignored, the family line is that alcohol or physical abuse is a symptom of a deeper problem such as trouble at work or financial worries, and not the real cause of distress. Something or someone else caused the alcoholic's problems, and he is not responsible. The family finds everything else to blame: Mother is having a hard time at work, John is misbehaving, Sue is failing in school. Because the family is unable to focus on the real issues of addiction, the children become confused and guilty about their role in the crisis. Children in this situation are often attacked and blamed for something they did not do, and they grow up learning not only to take responsibility for their own pain but to take on the responsibility for other people's problems as well.

Learning to Take Care of Ourselves

Children who grow up in unhealthy families experience deep emotional pain and have no way to relieve it, no outlet for expression. All children go through unhappy times and bad experiences, but in healthy families they are allowed and encouraged to talk about it, to work it through and allow the hurt to heal. Children from alcoholic families repress their pain until it surfaces in some other form—phobias, illness, or delinquent and promiscuous behavior—and their pain is treated as a nuisance, and seen as a result of their own inadequacies. The parents, confronted with their child's feelings and behavior that they can't control, react with anger, punishment, more abuse, and more drinking, instead of support and understanding. The child begins to blame himself for everything that goes wrong, and to keep his longings for comfort and security a secret. Isolated and frustrated, the child loses the thread of pleasure in his life and turns to anything that will keep him from hurting.

Simple pain that could have been eased with support and comfort eventually becomes monumental and consuming. In Sandra's case, her fear of being blamed for her problems kept her from telling her parents how a group of children beat her up on her way to and from school every day. How could she expect help from her parents, when they responded with anger every time she cried? She learned not to cry at all and to fight her own battles, and by the age of eight, she was street-wise and tough. It was only after facing her own problems of alcoholism in her early twenties that the memories of the wounded child inside her began to emerge. Even then, it was hard for her to cry.

Blaming Ourselves

Children in alcoholic families often try to solve the drinking problem themselves. They pour liquor down the drain and hide the car keys. They get in between their parents during fights, they beg for it to stop, but they are up against a force larger than they are, and their efforts are wasted. Even as a young adult, Terry agreed to "take care of Dad" after his parents divorced. He still believed he could fix things, he still thought he could make his father change by waking him up to the reality of his drinking problem. In the face of Terry's attempts, his father continued to drink. Children in this environment learn that they are powerless to solve problems and bring about change in their own lives, and when things go wrong, there is nothing they can do about it. They also quickly learn that anything that is going right will very soon go wrong. There is no safe place in this kind of family, no retreat from the pain and confusion, nothing to trust.

By nature, children are loyal to their parents and seek to love and be loved back. In the face of the confusion that exists within the unhealthy family, the child tries desperately to make order out of the chaos and put it in an understandable framework. In an attempt to order the chaos, the child accepts a basic premise: *My mother/father acts this way because I am rotten/unlovable/bad/to blame.* Accepting this premise allows the child to have a sense of understanding and reason— something so profoundly lacking in his life—and it feels like power. The power, although illusionary and fleeting, is preferable to confusion, and may help the child to survive, at least for the moment.

Sorting Through the Confusion

In the child's attempt to save himself from sinking into the chaos of the family system, from disappearing completely, he chooses a role that helps him cope with the situation. Often this role allows him to create a boundary between himself and his parents, and it is a role that can be hard to break out of. Take, for example, the way Elizabeth and her sister chose to work it out in their family:

Elizabeth: My sister and I coped with our mother's drinking in very different ways. I failed at school and withdrew from the family, seeking privacy in my failings. It seemed that every time I did succeed at something, my success belonged to my mother. To establish myself as a separate person, I needed to fail, and failure also allowed me to express my anger at her. My sister, on the other hand, decided to be responsible for all of us. She looked around, saw no love, and took it upon herself to supply it for all of us. In the end, she became the family doormat, never properly thanked for all she did, trapped in the resentment she felt at not getting back what she was giving. For a long time, neither of us knew how to step out of the roles we had gotten into. In the end, it seemed like my mother had won, because neither of us succeeded in making ourselves feel better and fix what was going on.

As adults, when we look back at our childhood, we may remember good times as well as bad, loving times as well as times of abuse and neglect. To admit life is rotten is too much pain for the child to bear. Only as adults can we begin to face the pain. Why are we so confused about what really went on back then? One of the more confusing aspects of alcoholism is that it can take many forms. There is not one set of behaviors common to all alcoholics, and all drinkers do not act alike. Moreover, any single alcoholic can act differently from day to day. The alcoholic, before full drunkenness sets in, can be a glorious person, full of fun and energy, and this is the person we may remember when we look back. When Karen's mother had just a few drinks, she was so bright and charming it was hard to resist joining her in her games.

> **Karen:** When I got home from school, my mother, who didn't start to drink until 4:00 P.M., would be vague and uninterested in me. After a couple of drinks, she was cheery, and would suddenly warm up and want to know everything that had happened in my day. After her third or fourth drink, though, her interest became intrusive and her endless lectures about how I should run my life became boring and difficult to listen to. By dinner, she was really tanked up, and spent most of the time criticizing me, often for the very things she'd approved of at 4:30. Most dinners, I left the table in tears, but the next morning, she'd chat on as if nothing had happened. Was I supposed to feel grateful for the interest she showed in me or angry for the abuse?

Similarly, Terry's father, when he wasn't drunk, was charming and dynamic, and would gather the family together for exciting outings. So who are these parents? Are they good or bad? As children we were so loyal to our parents, it was hard for us to admit that they were not perfect. Lacking the knowledge about the nature of alcoholism, we remained confused and unable to understand what was going on.

Equally confusing for us as we look back is that not all alcoholics are abusive. Some merely withdraw or pass out, but this is the abuse of neglect, as in Tim's case, described earlier. To deal with an extremely controlling and angry wife, Tim's father would get drunk every night and go into his study and fall asleep, leaving Tim to be the recipient of his mother's unhappiness. Although no one was actively abusing Tim, no one was supporting him either. As he struggled to understand what had gone wrong in his childhood that had left him so withdrawn and depressed, he could find nothing concrete to point to. In our workshop, Tim was finally able to see the lonely and neglected little boy that he still felt was a part of him.

Some alcoholics can stop drinking when it suits them. Terry's father prided himself on never missing work for any reason, not even because of his drinking. By passing out Sunday night, he would begin to sober up for work the next morning. Karen's mother stopped drinking for four days because she didn't want to be drunk at a family reunion. Karen and her sister were confused and heartbroken that their mother could stop drinking to please others, but never stopped to please them.

Another confusing aspect for us when we look back is that some of us come from families where the drinking stopped but the alcoholic or abusive behavior persisted. AA calls the untreated alcoholic a "dry drunk," someone who acts as though he is still drinking even though he has stopped. For children who saw alcohol as the problem, it was perplexing for them to see that things did not change when the alcohol was gone. When Karen's mother stopped drinking in her forties, she continued to control her family, this time through her illness, and the family dynamic continued as before. The family continued to revolve around her, protect her, avoid making her angry as though she was the queen bee, to focus their energy on her problems and her needs. One family that Terry was close to confronted the alcoholic father with his drinking, and he responded with the same iron will he had always been able to conjure up, and stopped drinking. He remained untreated, though, and the family continued to fear and avoid him, since he was the same raging tyrant he had always been.

In some families where no one drinks, there is still alcoholic behavior, because it is possible for alcoholic behavior to be learned from someone who doesn't drink. If a grandparent drinks, and his or her child, a nondrinker, has never been treated for problems associated with alcoholism, the child re-creates addictive behavior, because that is what he learned from his parents. Often alcoholism can skip a generation, so that a granddaughter of alcoholic grandparents may drink, although her own parents never did.

When the family operates with denial, the denied feelings must go somewhere; this is the nature of co-dependency. Everyone in the family must play the game, but no one deals directly with anyone else or with what is really going on. They react to what is going on by re-creating the addictive behavior, and find themselves drinking, hitting, and so forth, because addictive behavior is their only outlet for the frustration and fear found in this kind of family situation.

Another source of the confusion is that we don't know what to make of the fact that we remember good days as well as bad days. We then tell ourselves that it must not have been so bad. However, the fact is that a parent can be loving one minute and not give a damn a few drinks later. Karen remembers one Christmas when her brother was given a minibike.

> **Karen:** We were all in on the surprise, and when he got the bike we all cried because he was so happy. We had moments of love and sharing in our family, but at the same time, I was confused. I thought that things had to be either good or bad, and if they were bad, what was the closeness and family love I felt at that moment and moments like it? On the other hand, if things were good, why was I in pain so often? As an adolescent, in order to make my pain real, I had to see everything about my mother as bad, when, in fact, it wasn't like that. She wanted to be a good parent and never stopped trying. I wish I'd understood then what I do now, that she was in the control of something much stronger than she. I was unable to see that there was a basic goodness in my family that was in the destructive grip of addiction.

It is hard to evaluate just how bad things were, because alcoholism is progressive. Many of us had early childhoods where a parent's drinking was moderate, and there were days, maybe even months, without an episode. In the case of an abusive parent, the pressure grows greater and greater until it cannot be controlled, and eventually an abusive incident occurs, followed by remorse and promises that it won't happen again. But sooner or later, it will happen again, and what can the child think then?

Even without obvious incidents of abuse, parents can control their children in ways that are neither predictable nor even very visible. The Domestic Abuse Intervention Project in Duluth, Minnesota, has created a model to conceptualize the issue of male violence against women, which shows that the motive of establishing and maintaining power and control is central to an abuser's actions, and that often with just one violent incident, an abuser can maintain authority over his victim. Although this model was developed to describe the plight of battered women, if we adapt it to look at the relationship of children to abusive parents, we see how the aura of fear from the threat of an outburst can control children just as absolutely as daily hitting. Through the use of a wide variety of behaviors—intimidation, criticism, isolation, mind games, threats, sexual abuse, put-downs, using adult privilege, and restricting freedom—the parent can create an environment where the potential for violence is ever-present and the child becomes controlled by his or her fear that it will erupt. Because there may be no actual hitting or screaming, the child cannot identify him- or herself as abused, but the intimidation and lack of safety inherent in the power dynamic between parent and child are very real.

The messages growing up in an unhealthy family are confusing, and we don't know how our parents really feel about us. We were blamed and neglected and were the focus of much negativity, but sometimes we were coddled and supported. Life was full of mixed messages:

I love you/Don't bother me.
I'm proud of you/You're a failure.
You're my favorite/You make me maddest.
You're special/Don't show me up.
You're beautiful/You're cheap and seductive.
We love you for who you are/You have to work
   to be loved.
Think for yourself/Do as I say.

Recognizing Ourselves for What We Are and Being Specific About Our Own History

Identifying ourselves as adult children of alcoholic or abusive parents is an important and necessary step in reclaiming our past and identifying our pain, but we need to go further. By labeling ourselves, we have an explanation for what went wrong, and we can look at certain predictable problems we bring to our adult lives. The identification and the labeling allow us to feel less isolated and outcast, and when we meet other people like us, we recognize the things we have in common. Finally, we feel, there is somewhere we belong, and there are people who understand what it was like.

As we begin to identify ourselves as ACOAs, our recovery begins, but it is important to examine our individual situation and circumstances, and to correctly assess our own unique family dynamic. Part of our recovery is learning to focus on ourselves, and it is important not to get lost, as we so often have. As a way to assess just how badly and in what ways you were wounded, psychotherapist Stanley Keleman, in his book *Emotional Anatomy*,[1] suggests four ways of looking at our individual situation, based on the timing, the number, the source, and the duration of insults and abuse you received as a child. We have adapted his approach somewhat to relate to insults and abuse that occur in situations where there is alcoholism and/or abuse.

Timing of insults: Some of us had parents who were in the

advanced stages of alcoholism while we were still quite young, while some of us had fairly stable early childhoods in which alcohol was not yet a problem. The earlier you were exposed to the use and abuse of alcohol, the greater and more destructive the effect it has had on you. If the character of the child is fairly well formed by the age of six or seven, as some theories suggest, and alcoholism was present in the family at this point, the child will grow up pain-avoidant with a limited capacity for pleasure. If you had a few years of relative calm and stability, support and love from your parents, you might have these years as a foundation to build a future on. If that was not the case and you were brought into the family chaos the minute you were born, the damage done to you was profound.

Pauline, a thirty-four-year-old book editor, is an interesting example of someone whose entire life was affected by early trauma in the family. When she was five, her father contracted polio, and while her older and younger sisters managed to escape severe trauma from this, Pauline was asked to take responsibility for his health at this crucial time in her own development. She was asked to always be quiet and understanding of her mother and father, and she was told in many ways that her father's life depended on her and her behavior. With this great burden hanging over her, she learned to hide her own needs and fear, and began to substitute food for loving contact she should have been receiving from her parents. Soon she was obese, isolated, and sending out the message that she didn't need anyone in her life.

Hank, twenty-seven, was as profoundly affected as Pauline by what went on in his family when he was young. When he was three, his parents began to fight all the time, and his mother expressed her feelings of resentment toward her husband and children. Hank's father drank, and his mother's rage reflected the situation. When Hank entered therapy in his twenties, he was depressed. Overtly the source of depression was his father's alcoholism, his mother's rage, and his own career problems. More careful examination revealed that underneath Hank's depression there was intense anger at his mother. When he was three, he had been torn between the natural feelings of wanting to be close to her and nurtured by her, and the feelings of wanting to escape her anger and abuse. The struggle had created a conflict within Hank that he was still wrestling with as an adult.

The occasions on which the episodes occurred are an important factor to consider as well. For many children growing up in an alcoholic or abusive family, Christmas was often a time of trauma and upset. A time that was supposed to be happy was full of anger and violence: the Christmas tree was pushed over, Father stormed out of the house in a rage, Mother cried all day. What about your birthday or vacation? Were these times that were consistently ruined by drinking? Did the episodes occur during obvious times of stress or during times that should have been happy? For Karen and Terry, despite the chaos that occurred during the rest of the year, they remember Christmas as being a truly happy event. For Kathy, however, Christmas was a horror. Her father would get drunk and then spend a lot of money on only one or two of the children, leaving the others miserable and the favored kids guilty and confused.

Frequency of insults: Clearly, daily abuse has a greater impact than occasional abuse. If traumatic events occur once in a while, there are also some relatively peaceful times when the child can leave family problems behind for a moment and focus on other things. But if fear and abuse are ever-present, there is no time for anything else, and the child becomes hyper-vigilant, waiting for the next explosive episode.

Source of insults: Was it your mother or father who was abusive? For young children who are with their alcoholic or abusive mother all day, it is worse for the child because there is no escape and no "downtime." Obviously, the worst circumstance is one in which both parents are abusive, for the child then has no safe place to turn. Additionally there are different implications according to the sex of the child and that of the parent who is abusive. If it is the same-sex parent, the child grows up without a positive role model. If the opposite-sex parent is abusive, the child may learn to be suspicious of love from anyone of the opposite sex, and sexual boundaries are more likely to have been violated. Karen, for example, had always turned to men for help because her experiences in childhood had taught her that women would always hurt her. Most of Terry's good friends were women because of a deep distrust he felt toward men, and his fear that they would criticize and shame him.

Duration of insults: Most children can live through periodic episodes of trauma, but they cannot when the episodes are relentless. How soon were you able to get out of the home? As teenagers both Terry and Karen were sent to boarding schools, which allowed them to have a place where they could be safe, be themselves, and live with consistency and rules. How soon were you able to develop other important affiliations outside of your home? Are you still involved with your parents, and are they still present in your everyday life? Are their criticisms and their demands still clamoring in your head?

These are some things to consider as you discover the exact nature of the pain you have to face. For some of us the pain has been vivid and constant, and we do not doubt for a moment that the abuse, the trauma, and the violence have hurt us badly. For others, though, the abuse has been less obvious, less easy to recall. In every workshop we give, there are always some participants who doubt they should be there at all, because they're not sure that what went wrong was really so bad. They have nothing dramatic to point to, no incidents that really stand out, yet the tension was always there. Some of us feel crazy because we know that something was wrong but we can't name it. As we have said, prolonged and early trauma is the most difficult to recover from, but living with an alcoholic or abusive family, no matter the degree of intensity, affects who we become as adults.

Learning Patience and Focused Attention

So how do we finally face our pain?

We focus attention on ourselves. In our workshops, we give nonjudgmental attention to the person who is trying to recover the feeling and memories of his childhood. This is something we didn't have when we were children, someone to listen without criticizing us. As children, when we attempted to express ourselves, we were squelched or told we were wrong, and made to feel bad for our feelings. When we receive focused attention, we gently and patiently attend to what it is we feel inside, forcing nothing. Some of us will recall incidents, but will be unable to reconnect with the feeling. Sitting with the emptiness is a way to start. As we've said, some people will have no memories of their childhood, but this is not important. What is important is to have those *feelings* associated with childhood, *from the child's point of view*. The memories will not set us free, but our capacity to feel the pain instead of avoiding it will.

Some of us have to develop the emotional muscle to cry convulsively, and we may have no idea what tears are about. Others of us will have to learn to have our feelings without letting them control us and without losing ourselves in them. What is important is to accept ourselves where we are now, and start from there. We are who we are because of our work to survive and we have done a great job. In each moment, we have only done the best we could. Recovery takes patience, attention, and an acceptance of who each of us is.

It is helpful, as you work on your recovery, to work with others who have done and experienced the same. This will provide you with inspiration and safety. We've clearly seen this in our own personal experiences. Until Karen talked with other ACOAs, she had never articulated—not even to herself—what had happened when her mother got drunk. The pain of her mother's alcoholism was so deeply repressed that it was not until Karen heard others talk about their experiences that she realized how deeply she had been hurt. We've seen it work for our clients; Kathy particularly needed the support of other women. When she had shared her experiences in groups previously, all she saw were reactions of disbelief that caused her to doubt herself and her own sense of what had happened. Before joining our workshop, Tim had never told anyone about the experiences with his mother, because he was ashamed and thought people would think he was exaggerating or lying. It was not until he heard other men talk about their relationships with seductive mothers that he was able to open up and talk about his own feelings of anxiety and fear connected with women. People who have forgotten much of what went on often remember when they listen to others' stories.

As children we did not receive the focused attention we now ask you to give yourselves. As children we were not able to bear the pain, and as adults we have carried over behaviors that allow us to continue to deny it exists. In the following chapters, we'll talk about how we survived as children, how we learned to cope, and how we have learned to deny the pain until now.

CHAPTER 3

Learning to Face
Our Addictions

Lessons in pain avoidance come particularly early for ACOAs. These lessons serve to create a way of dealing with life in the child that is so bound up with denial that there is little attention left for the experience of pleasure.

Terry: My earliest memory of making the decision to turn my back on pleasure and organize my life around the avoidance of pain happened when I was eight. On a Thursday night my grandfather died in his sleep from lung cancer, which I hadn't even known about. Not knowing how to deal with me and the whole situation, my parents sent me away to spend the weekend with my cousins, as had been planned before my grandfather's death. When I returned on Sunday, I found my family acting as though nothing had happened, and I was confused. My grandfather had died and I felt very sad about it, and when I expressed it, I only got blank looks back. I was angry at having been sent away, and also felt guilty because I'd had a good time over the weekend, and I didn't know what I was supposed to feel or how to act. I got angry at my sister for laughing, and asked her how she could be having fun when our grandfather had just died. I now see that I coped with everything I was feeling— sadness, confusion, anger—by being in control. I saw that everyone was supposed to act a certain way, despite how they really felt inside.

When you grow up in an environment organized around the denial and avoidance of pain, you are unlikely to pursue pleasure in a natural and healthy way. As much as we may now resent and distrust our parents, they were once god and goddess to us. As we were growing up, we idolized them. They were our most powerful, if not also at times our most destructive, role models, who themselves were dedicated to avoiding pain. As adults many ACOAs have promised themselves that they, unlike their parents, will never become substance abusers or addicts of any kind. Some of us achieve this, but most of us don't, and we find ourselves locked into patterns of compulsive, addictive behavior. We are not necessarily addicted to drugs or alcohol, but we are addicts of excitement and crisis. An addiction to excitement can take many forms, but it serves one purpose: to hide our pain and make ourselves feel vital.

When we observed our parents, we saw in their reactions to the stresses of daily life that if a person feels out of control, an addiction, whether it is drinking, taking drugs, overeating, or abusive behavior, has the power to make him feel whole and strong. We thus learned from our parents' behavior the importance of avoiding the painful realities of life, and when there was tragedy or sadness, what we saw was denial and control, not grief and distress.

Terry: By the time my second grandfather died, I played the part of the perfect little soldier. I copied my father, and never let on that I was sad, and never cried in front of anyone. I was sure that this was the manly thing to do.

Learning to Feel

Terry never grieved for his grandfather because he was unconsciously afraid of the feelings of sadness and vulnerability, and had learned that his own father's sense of self was not associated with a capacity to feel (be alive), but with his ability to control his feelings. Terry learned early on that a man's strength is dependent on suppressing life, rather than feeling and fully experiencing it.

As with Terry's father, what is lacking in the addicted individual is as basic as a lack of connection with the natural forces of life—the human drives for gratification and pleasure. It is a connection that was broken very early on in most of us, a connection that would have led us to pursue pleasure in a natural, healthy way.

Every child comes into the world with a sense of wonder and spontaneous excitement characterized by natural movement—touching, reaching, seeing, talking—and we see this in the constant movement of a baby's mouth, arms, and legs. Initially this movement is toward some kind of pleasure and gratification, and as the child matures, he learns from experience that not all movement is pleasurable, and he begins to be more powerful with his energy and avoid certain situations. Healthy parental attention is the primary acknowledgment of the child's sense of self as the parent responds to the child's movements with rocking, singing, caressing, playing. All too often in unhealthy homes, however, there is a short supply of attention, and family members are forced to fight for what little is there, while the addicted person gets attention for himself by being abusive, controlling, and demanding. A child in this environment not only feels neglected but is called upon to give attention to others before his own needs have been met. In this way he is not given a chance to develop a strong sense of self.

Unhealthy families place a priority on appearance and

control over natural childlike movement, and there is enormous pressure put on each family member to look happy, healthy, and successful, despite what's really going on. The tragedy occurs when the parents' stress and pain divert the child from natural, healthy excitement and the pursuit of pleasure, and the connection with the natural forces of life is broken. The focus instead becomes the avoidance of a direct reexperiencing of pain. In the unhealthy home, the child's developing sense of self is replaced by parental preferences and needs. The child aims to please his parents, no matter how irrational or inappropriate their demands are. Instead of learning to "go with the flow" of our painful feelings, we learned to do something to make the pain go away, because that is what our parents taught us to do.

Some parents turned to alcohol, drugs, abuse, or other addictive behaviors to avoid and suppress deep pain and daily pressures, and their addictions became a way of life for them. They couldn't deal with their pain or ours, so they looked for the "fix." Their addictions are fruitless attempts at escaping reality. As role models, these parents set an example to their children of placing priority on pain avoidance, and in this way they are clearly teaching their children addictive behavior.

As adults we find that we are also involved in the storm of addiction and abuse our parents created. In following their example, we find ourselves falling back on the same addictive behaviors we promised ourselves we would avoid. We may successfully avoid addiction to drugs or alcohol, yet become trapped in a destructive cycle of pain avoidance and denial. Many of us are addicts of a different sort: we are addicted to adrenaline, an internally generated substance, and to the excitement it produces.

Defining Excitement

It is important to understand what we mean when we talk about excitement. Many people believe that excitement is always a positive thing, but we want to broaden its meaning here and explore it in all its forms. No excitement is good or bad in and of itself; excitement is what we make of it. Some of us search for excitement in everything we do: our jobs, relationships, even in the food we eat and the clothes we wear. Others find the quest for excitement trivial and immature. Most of us feel somewhere in the middle, and we look for excitement when we think it is appropriate.

When we talk about excitement here, we refer to any situation or thing that activates the nervous system to respond and release adrenaline into the system, a mechanism familiarly known as the fight-flight response. We became addicted to adrenaline when, as children, we were denied the right to live our own lives, and were instead drawn into the all-consuming drama of our parents' addictions and their alcoholic, sexual, physical, and emotional abuses. We were intoxicated by the adrenaline our participation in their drama produced within us, and we became addicted to the excitement inherent in it. This addiction involves a constant production of adrenaline to make us feel alive, through creating situations of crisis or drama. At the same time we present a challenge to ourselves to be in control of our excitement at all times. Eventually we become exhausted doing this, but it is the only way we know. Since the adrenaline is addictive, we feel that life is boring when it isn't flowing.

Excitement should be a movement toward pleasure, but when it is an addiction, it gets perverted and becomes unsafe and unfulfilling. Sometimes healthy excitement also involves pain, but in the healthy family, the child is helped to tolerate this. In the unhealthy family, the parents treat the child's pain as unacceptable and as an annoyance to them, thereby preventing it from being a learning opportunity for the child.

Those who grew up in unhealthy families know the excitement involved in trying to block the path of the addict to his drug. We know the drama that occurred when we poured liquor down the drain or took away the car keys or saw violence and attempts at reconciliation. We didn't need to go to the movies to see excitement; it was happening at home, every day. It happened when we thought things would finally change—and they never did.

As a result, for many of us now, peaceful, uncomplicated lives appear boring and unstimulating, and we search for situations that will get our adrenaline flowing again, that will re-create the excitement that we grew up with. When we feel excited, we feel alive, and the excitement, no matter what it is about, feels reassuringly familiar. As adults many of us are still addicted to the excitement this roller-coaster kind of life provides, and many of us are not sure we want to, or can, get off it.

Understanding Addiction

To see how this hunger for excitement can develop into a full-blown addiction, we need to examine the nature of addiction itself. In our generalized definition, we believe that if a person employs a pattern of behavior (through substance abuse and/or attitude) that causes repeated difficulty in his personal, professional, or spiritual life, then those behaviors, to varying degrees, constitute an addiction. When we look at the nature of addiction, we can say that the addict is simply looking for a way to make himself feel whole, no matter how self-destructive his methods of achieving that wholeness may be. The addict incorporates his addictive behaviors in a unique way of life that works just for him, and it is almost impossible for anyone else to understand, let alone accept. Drinking makes the alcoholic feel less uptight, eating gives the overeater a feeling of fullness, and managing anxiety with nonstop activity makes the person who is addicted to excitement feel involved, alive, and in control. We may experience our addiction to excitement physically as adrenaline, psychologically as anxiety or depression, and socially as overreactive and controlling behavior.

When we explore the nature of addiction, we see that it

has three components: compulsion, tolerance, and dependency. *Compulsion* is simply that we have to do something, whether that means having a drink, getting into a fight, or taking drugs. The something is "a way of life" for the addict. Those who are not addicted cannot understand that the addiction is not caused by a lack of willpower (don't have that cigarette, don't eat so much), but is the fabric of the addict's life. Terry remembers his father complaining after his first year of sobriety, "Why did God have to take away all the fun in my life?" His compulsion to drink was his pleasure in life. Similarly the roller-coaster, anxiety- and crisis-filled life many of us have chosen may not look pleasurable to other people, but for us it is all we know, and we have an addictive compulsion to create the drama in our lives.

Tolerance in addiction is when we seem to be able to have more and more of the addictive behavior (or the drug, the drink, the abuse) with less and less of a disruption in our lives. For example, a parent who hits his child at first feels shock at what he has done, then regret. The regret leads to guilt, which eventually becomes too much to bear, and the abusive parent begins to rationalize and justify his behavior, thereby distancing himself from the event. He can say, "The kid wouldn't shut up and I couldn't stand it anymore." The distancing of oneself from one's actions through rationalization and denial leads to a tolerance of that behavior. Eventually the parent will even go so far as to excuse his behavior by saying, "It builds character," or "The child has to learn sometime." The abusive parent will soon hit again.

With food addictions the pattern is similar. The person who gorges himself feels initially sated, but soon feels full of self-loathing and regret, which prompts him to then eat again to allay his discomfort. It is an endless cycle of despair fueled by rationalization, which leads to greater tolerance, both physically and emotionally. In an addiction to excitement, the tolerance is of problems and crises, and if there are none at hand, we seek them out or we create them. If we can't find the excitement externally, we create it internally with guilt, anxiety, and self-absorption.

Dependency, the third component of addiction, is insidious. Dependency implies that the addict must continue the addictive behavior in order to feel normal, and withdrawal from that behavior or substance will produce anxiety and discomfort. People who find that they have a headache because they haven't had their morning coffee are dependent on the caffeine to make themselves feel right. Those who must have a cigarette and drink in hand in order to interact socially feel they have no choice in the matter. These behaviors, they are convinced, are necessary parts of their lives. People who are addicted to excitement create problems with their friends and crises at work, because they are dependent on the familiar and secure feelings of their adrenaline rush. If there is no issue to work on, no problem to solve, no crisis to be involved in, things just aren't right, and they feel bored and lost. They need the excitement.

What does it mean to be addicted to excitement? Let's look at some symptoms. A person who is addicted to excitement will tell you that there is always something better (meaning "more exciting") to do than sit still and think about a problem. Moreover, when we stop the flow of adrenaline caused by excitement, we begin to feel uncomfortable. In the same way that an alcoholic is addicted to his drink, the workaholic to his job, the chocoholic to his candy bar, we are addicted to excitement. People who are addicted to excitement are suffering from a mismanagement of their emotional lives, and this affects the level of energy they have for living. By avoiding healthy excitement because we are afraid of it, feel it is foreign and not in our control, we throw our emotional lives off balance.

Healthy people need pleasure as part of their daily routine, and they can get it from such simple acts as eating, loving, and working. When you don't get your share of pleasure, you automatically shift to filling up your life with other emotions. Every healthy child has an instinct for experiencing feeling. When the full range of feeling is not allowed us, we aggrandize the feeling that is allowed, namely the excitement of the chaotic drama.

This drama may take many forms. For example, the woman who continually seeks out men that treat her badly is addicted to the excitement of the breakups and make-ups, of the dramatic scenes and outbursts, and she cannot appreciate the healthy pleasure that can be found in a good relationship. To her, a man that treats her well is "nice but boring." As an addict she is simply looking for a way to make herself feel whole and alive, no matter how self-destructive her methods are. Because she is unable to pursue healthy pleasure, she is satisfied, at least for the moment, with the pseudo-pleasure she derives from her addiction to excitement.

Understanding Pseudo-pleasure

We make a distinction between pseudo-pleasure and real pleasure by suggesting that real pleasure is not *for* anything, and it is a "being" state rather than a "doing" state. Real pleasure can also give one a physical feeling of well-being and satisfaction. Many people have lost the capacity to experience pleasure naturally, and instead equate pleasure only with the results achieved through an addictive behavior. There is pseudo-pleasure to be found in getting drunk, because it makes all problems fade away and makes one feel powerful and alive. There is pseudo-pleasure to be found in fighting and making up, because it is dramatic and satisfying. It is a pseudo-pleasure because once the positive feelings fade away, one is left with the down side of the addictive behavior: the guilt, the hangover, the resentment, the embarrassment.

In the same way, compulsive eating can provide pseudo-pleasure, but eventually victimizes the people who overeat. The compulsive eater has found a forum for pleasure that is real at a certain level, but it is a pseudo-pleasure in that the behavior is fueled by a compulsion to cover up the pain and anxiety that underlie the problem. This was the case with Susan, a thirty-two-year-old writer.

Susan: I guess I just love to eat more than anything else in my life. I've ridden the scales up and down for years, but I'm hooked on food. I love anything to do with it: talking about it, cooking it, serving it, and certainly, eating it. In fact, I feel good when I eat and never think about getting fat or destroying my body. That, unfortunately, comes later, and by then I feel disgusted at having gorged myself. I'm feeling so lonely and depressed that the only thing I can do to make myself feel better is eat again.

Susan's eating provided her with pseudo-pleasure that allowed her, at least in part, to feel that she was in control of her life. As in Susan's case, most of us are just trying to make our lives a little better. When we feel despair and anxiety, we look for that thing that will ease our pain right now, and that is often an addictive behavior that will ease the situation, if only temporarily.

Playing God With Our Lives Through Our Addictions

Addictions help us manage conflict in our lives by easing tension, suppressing anxiety, and alleviating depression. But the reality is that when we use an addiction to get by in the world, part of us ceases to function. The natural feeling system that enables us to successfully interact with our environment has been replaced by the mood-altering effects of our addictions.

The feeling system of a healthy person works quite spontaneously. If you cut yourself, pain draws your attention to the wound; otherwise you might bleed to death. Emotional pain works the same way by drawing attention to the injury. Unfortunately, as life becomes increasingly complex, it is harder to see one's pain directly. This is especially true if we are adept at denying or suppressing it through addictive behavior.

Addictive tendencies are compounded by the fact that our society reinforces the patterns of addiction. There are many addictions—working long hours, running many miles, making many sexual conquests—that our society appears to approve of. We see on television, in magazines, in advertising, a glib, easy, and fast way of dealing with problems and pain. There is no suggestion that we should sit back and examine what pains us, and attempt to break some of our repetitive patterns of behavior that continue to get us in trouble. The message we hear is that smart, successful people "don't have time for the pain." In our society, there is a tendency and temptation to choose the quick fix rather than take the longer view. Why wait when you can have it now?

Pain is often treated as a problem that needs a quick fix, and never a symptom of something deeper and more serious. Pain can be a real friend if you are prepared to embrace it as part of life, because like the wound that hurts, it tells you that something is wrong. It is a message from the engine room to the captain: "Hey, something isn't right down here." All too often, we squelch that message and try to cover up the internal noise, most tragically through addictive, pain-avoidant behaviors. When your stomach aches, do you quickly pop an antacid, or do you slow down to think about your diet or what might be making you anxious? Telling yourself that you need a drink to relax after a day at work helps you avoid the reality that you hate your job. When you ignore your pain, you might be ignoring an opportunity to change your life.

Our addictions are our attempts to gain control, and through our addictions, we attempt to "play God" by altering the reality of our lives: by choosing what we will acknowledge and by denying our pain. Playing God with your life means taking control of things that are not meant to be controlled, specifically the way you feel. When an alcoholic reaches for the booze to take away his pain, he is playing God with his life by trying to cover up what he feels. In trying to "fix" his life, he is acting on the assumption that he has the power to control how he feels. The truth is that the emotional body has its own reality. By becoming drunk, using drugs, or creating crises in

order to distract ourselves from true inner experience, we are
trying to go around the problem instead of moving through it.
It is too painful to focus on the problem, so we play God by
pretending it doesn't exist. When all is said and done, the
problem still remains.

Learning to Listen to Your Real Feelings

If you are addicted to excitement, you can change this
pattern only by opening up to what you feel, and realizing that
not all of life is controllable. In homes where there was too
much pain to bear, we grew up resisting the natural course of
life. We bring that resistance into our adult lives. As a result of
our work with ACOAs, we have come to believe that finding
the way to Emotional Healing entails working backward from
the addictive behavior through the defenses that protect the
underlying pain and anxiety.

Learning to surrender to the inner voice of our feelings is
like learning to breathe. Everyone knows how to do it, but
most of us don't do it efficiently or effectively. Our greatest
tools in learning this are our desire and our willingness to
practice and work at it.

Discovering the Body's Wisdom

In our workshops, we use a bodily experience based on
bioenergetic therapy to give our participants a clear sense of
what "letting go" feels like. We do this by placing them in
physically stressful positions—standing on one leg, holding
arms straight out—and asking them to verbally express their
discomfort. When they have had enough, we tell them to relax
completely and drop over like rag dolls. Then we suggest they
do the same exercise lying on the floor, this time exacerbating
their discomfort by recalling a painful memory. Then we allow

the group to have a "temper tantrum"—a commonly used exercise in various expressive psychotherapies—to fight against their discomfort. The participants beat their fists and feet against the floor, scream and cry "no." There is an intense feeling of relaxation that follows this exercise, and while the tension will return at a later time, the participants have learned to assert themselves through their tantrums and accept their pain at the same time. By saying "no," they have learned to say essentially, "I exist," and fight against the injustice done to them.

Jane, a forty-two-year-old housewife and mother of three, suffered from a weight problem and repeatedly tried to avoid her deep pain. She said she felt an intense pressure in her chest all the time, but whenever we asked her to talk about her feelings, she told us how difficult her father's life had been and how his abuse had affected her brother so badly. She preferred to tell stories about other people rather than have to deal with what she was feeling.

Toward the end of the workshop, the pressure around her chest grew so intense that she cried out for help. We asked her to lie on her back and breathe in a relaxed fashion, bringing her attention to her body. We asked her to locate her emotional pain within her body, and she found herself going back to the time when she was a little girl, terrified that her father would kill her brother and then come after her. She was so afraid at that moment that she began to choke for air. She kept trying to leave the feelings, to explain how she felt rather than experience it, but we encouraged her to stay with her feelings even though she was terrified. As she felt her fear again, her body began to shake, and she sobbed. She was that little girl again, afraid for her life.

For the first time, Jane was seeing that she could feel the terror and survive. When her breathing eased and her crying stopped, she told us that she felt the band around her chest loosen, and instead of tightness, there was now light. She began to feel calm as light suffused her body, and we saw her terror being replaced by a radiant glow, a profound experience of inner peace. The tightness in her chest had protected her from her terror, but had also prevented her from feeling her true feelings. For the first time she could remember, she could breathe freely and experience this brief glimpse of something divine.

In order to address our addictive tendencies, the first step is to recognize our behavior as addictive, and fully own up to the way we defend ourselves against pain. In our society of instant gratification and the quick fix, we seem to believe that to be hurting is bad. Unfortunately, when we block out the painful side of our existence, we block out the pleasurable side as well, and deny the spiritual aspects of our nature. We must begin to face our pain, to be with it rather than try to suppress it. There are no shortcuts to this. We must jump into the depths of our pain before we can emerge on the other side.

Identifying Your Own Addictions

The first step in addressing your own particular problems of addiction is to look at the aspects of your life that involve addictive behavior. This can be approached in two ways. The first and most obvious way is to examine your use of mood-altering substances and behavior, such as drinking too much, acting out sexually, or constantly creating crises. The second approach involves digging a little deeper, to examine what it is in your life that hurts you inside, and what it is that hurt you as a child. As the feelings and memories emerge, ask yourself what you do to make yourself feel better. Are your actions self-destructive, repetitive, hurtful to others?

When you look at your dependency on substance abuse, on self-destructive behavior, and on excitement, don't rule anything out, even the seemingly small things. When things are going well, do you create a crisis? Look at the amount of coffee you drink. Do you need more than a few cups to keep you going? Do you overeat, or eat when you're unhappy? Do you, as Karen did, create your own self-destructive excitement through repetitive behavior?

> **Karen:** I was often so out of control around sugar that I couldn't go past a candy store without going inside and buying something. Even when I swore to myself that I would stay away, I couldn't, and I'd end up eating so much candy I'd feel sick afterward. There was a definite pattern to this. I could be feeling anything really—sad, depressed, nervous, scared—it didn't matter, because any feeling was really enough of an excuse for me to eat. After I'd eaten the candy, whatever it was that I'd originally felt would be gone, and instead I'd feel this rapid vibration in my chest. I felt energized and happy, but instead of just sitting with that, I'd eat more until the vibration increased to the point where it was unbearable. Then I would start on the downhill slide from the sugar high, and I'd feel so blasted inside from the amount of sugar I'd eaten that I could barely stand up straight.

Karen realized that this behavior was alcoholic in a sense, the only difference being that she ate her drug instead of drinking it. (Alcohol, in fact, is derived from sugar.) She also realized that the downhill spiral of the candy experience was as important as the high. When she felt terrible after eating so much candy, the feeling was so intense it blocked out all other feelings. In addition, she preferred to hate herself for eating too much than to face deeper concerns that were making her more miserable than the overeating. Eventually Karen stopped eating candy, but then turned to diet soda, and then to beer, always involved in the same patterns of highs and lows. What remained constant was Karen's dependency on food and drink to make herself feel something other than what was really going on, to provide herself with the excitement and adrenaline of the ups and downs.

The truth is that Karen has an addictive personality, and her story shows that when one is addicted to something, he or she can also be addicted to many other things. Karen avoided pain throughout her life—dentists, doctors, having a splinter removed. She made life decisions based on her avoidance of pain, including not to get a hepatitis shot before going to Morocco. The irony in this particular case is that in being pain-avoidant, she caused herself more pain in the long run, for she got hepatitis. The pain of a series of shots would have been nothing compared to the pain involved as the hepatitis ran its course. Denied pain and sadness never really go away, and in Karen's case, her addictions compromised her health and natural ability to feel energetic and alive.

Albert, a man in his midthirties, is another example of a highly addictive personality, and during the time we knew him, he was addicted to marijuana, food, exercise, women, and eventually cocaine. Albert had joined our workshop at the insistence of friends, but he resisted exploring and talking about his alcoholic and abusive father. Instead, he preferred to handle things his way, and play God with his life. He tried to create an order to his life, as well as constant excitement, through compulsive behavior—overexercising, overeating, overdieting.

When we met Albert, he was in the middle of a court case and was subsequently sent to prison for possession of marijuana. His arrest and time in jail satisfied his hunger for excitement for a while and gave him a chance to explore some of his problems, in particular, his dependency on drugs.

While in prison, he decided to earn an undergraduate degree, making him the first person in his family to do so. Once out of prison, he worked toward his degree and pushed himself hard to succeed in his job, and for a while, this satisfied his need for excitement. He constantly reminded himself that he was just a poor boy trying to make good and that he could fail at any minute.

Albert made it, at least for a while. He earned his degree, got a good job, began a relationship with a woman, and bought a house. But Albert could only stand an absence of excitement and crisis for so long, because having things go smoothly opened him up to the anxiety and self-doubt he tried to bury. The little boy in Albert still believed he deserved nothing but failure and bad treatment, and the growing intimacy with his girlfriend awakened intolerable feelings of vulnerability within him. He began to have affairs, saying his girlfriend wanted to be closer than he did. His work suffered, and his friends were annoyed with him.

Slowly he became dependent on cocaine, until he lost his job, his house—everything. Cocaine was the substance of his abuse, but his need to abuse himself, to generate excitement, was the underlying addiction. Albert could not tolerate quiet, healthy pleasure, because it made him feel vulnerable to his repressed feelings. Whatever addiction Albert was currently involved in—drugs, women, exercise—the motivation to avoid pain was always the same. Because he was so busy dealing with self-perpetuating crises, he didn't have time to face his pain. He'd been beaten up as a child, and he was still beating himself up.

The only way Albert could break this pattern was to stop trying to fix his life and allow himself to feel his pain. In running from it, he guaranteed that it would be re-created again and again. He was so committed to an image of himself as a loser that he continually put himself in situations that would reinforce that image.

Where can we find our own addictions if they do not show up in substance abuse?

• *We are addicted to crisis in our personal and professional lives.* In part, this is because we are unable to view our lives in any long-term sense. As children of dysfunctional families, we knew only how to live from one minute to the next, never being able to predict or count on what would happen next. Now, instead of letting little issues remain simple and pass by, we overreact and blow them way out of proportion. If a problem was a mere annoyance when we first noticed it, it will soon become a crisis. We continue to involve ourselves in crisis partially because we receive praise and gratitude for being adept at handling the situation. Moreover, many of us feel that life is dull if there is no crisis at hand, and we ride this crisis roller-coaster for our excitement.

• *We are addicted to pain*. Our addiction to pain is our overinvolvement with it and our obsession with avoiding it at all costs. It is no surprise that so many ACOAs go into helping professions, because it puts them in the position of the "good listener" or the desperately needed friend. People who are addicted to pain are overly interested in what causes pain in other people's lives. They want to hear about it all the time, and they want to be involved in working it out. This addiction to pain is shown in the discomfort we feel when things appear serene and happy.

• *We are addicted to working on our problems*. ACOAs are generally very introspective and enjoy talking about their problems or working on their "issues." Once the problem is solved, they simply look for a new one. There is excitement in trying to solve not only your problems but those of the people around you as well.

Tanya is a good example of a person who was overinvolved with working on herself and others. She was an active member of AA, Overeaters Anonymous, and Debtors Anonymous, and attended at least one meeting a day. Obsessed with recovery, it became a way of life instead of a means to an end, and she rarely had much fun. She associated pleasure with the time spent assessing herself and her problems, and, therefore, she avoided the true pleasure of opening up to herself and interacting with friends.

• *We are addicted to work*. Although most workaholics will claim that they really do enjoy their work, when we look closer, we generally find that idleness makes them anxious and uncomfortable. Working all the time can be seen as a reaction against the reality of the emptiness of their lives, because it uses up the energy and fills the time with pursuits such as making money and getting ahead.

• *We are addicted to our sense of responsibility or our sense that we have no responsibility at all*. The attitude is either "It's all up to me" or "I can't deal with any of this." If "It's all up to me," then every situation demands complete attention and involvement, and a commitment to be in control. On the other hand, a lack of responsibility or control creates a drama through continual crisis. Either attitude keeps the adrenaline flowing.

• *We are addicted to sex.* Eddie is an example of someone who denied his childhood pain yet re-created the drama of it over and over. His behavior of regularly flirting with women he did not know seemed innocent enough. It was this behavior, though, that successfully buried his underlying painful needs that were not met as a child, the needs to be loved and comforted. His parents had been cold and formal, and Eddie remembers little warmth as he was growing up.

Eddie entered therapy in his early thirties at the urging of his fiancée, who was also in therapy at the time. Handsome and charming, Eddie was a successful entrepreneur who had recently sold his business for a small fortune. It was clear early on that Eddie derived little pleasure from his success, and was made anxious by all the free time after the sale of his company.

> **Eddie:** I had a problem, or actually, my fiancée did. I had what I called "secret sex" all the time. I seemed to be able to meet and attract women wherever I went, and sometimes it seemed as though they flocked to me. I'd had some great sexual experiences, but I was trying to be faithful to my fiancée. Still, I met women all the time, and even when I didn't sleep with them they'd write me letters and call me, and generally expect a lot. They seemed to depend on me and want me, even though I was pretty sure I'd made it clear I was not available.

It wasn't hard to see the pain Eddie caused these women who poured out their hearts to him. When Eddie began to realize this, the term "sexual slavery" came to his mind. Understanding that his seductive behavior toward these women was a promise he never intended to fulfill was initially a relief to him, and he accepted the fact that he was a sexual addict. His life seemed simpler then, and his devotion to his fiancée more intense.

This was really just a quick fix for Eddie, because when

he broke through his addictive behavior, he was left with an enormous capacity for excitement and no way to fill it. Soon Eddie found that he and his fiancée were talking about their problems all the time, and they were constantly "processing" their relationship. Their sexual interest in each other diminished as they focused on their problems and began to fight about little things they had never bothered with before. It became obvious to them that Eddie's "cure" was worse than his "illness."

The fact was that Eddie was exploring the dark side of his soul and was finding the anxiety and loneliness so devastating that he was substituting one addiction with another to cope with the changes in his life. Rather than deal with the childhood pain he had denied for so long, he began to create problems where none had been. He became an emotional drunk. Eddie didn't know it at the time, but he had come to us to learn to make the switch from pain avoidance to the pursuit of pleasure. The switch for Eddie meant less talk and more feeling, staying with the anxiety long enough to feel the pain and anger that fueled it. The result was that the child in Eddie began to mature and feel less needy and more able to stand alone, less dependent on an addiction to hide behind.

• *We are addicted to control.* This addict's life-style is organized around a search for problems to solve that will make him feel needed and vital. Andrea, a social worker, is someone addicted to control:

Andrea: I have only sad memories of my childhood. My father died from drinking when I was five, and his family blamed my mother for it and pushed us out of the family. My mother couldn't handle it and started up with a lot of men. Sometimes I would get up in the morning to go to school, and I'd find my mother and a man I'd never seen before, naked and passed out in the living room, surrounded by empty bottles. But I hid it all very well. I was an A student, a leader, and popular. The boys liked me a lot, but I stayed a virgin for a long time, because it was the only way I knew how to be really different from my mother. I was the kind of "nice" girl who got more than her share of marriage proposals.

While Andrea's mother was busy acting out her pain, Andrea was giving the impression that she had no pain at all. She gave the impression that she was everyone's best friend, but inside she was unsure, insecure, and withdrawn. She made others feel good by being attentive to them, and the anxiety that fueled her came out right—dressing nicely, doing well in school, being popular. One could say that Andrea's heart belonged to her father, who had died at such a critical stage in her life. Trying to get Andrea to stop and sit still was like trying to stop a freight train. The internal noise was too much; there were things to do, people to help, dates to keep.

Her career choice was obvious, and she became a social worker. In her early thirties, she married a physician who was an alcoholic. Instead of seeing this as a problem, Andrea saw it as a challenge and was able to convince him to stop drinking. Although he was sober, his emotional recovery was limited. His problem stayed within the family as another secret to protect.

Throughout this period in her life, no one guessed that Andrea's internal life was anything but perfect. Emotionally, however, she was dead. She had sacrificed her life in order to suppress her anxiety and pain. She chose an appearance of control and competence instead.

• *We are addicted to acting out*. This kind of addict acts out to draw attention to himself in order to create a personally meaningful life. This was the case with Sandy, a thirty-year-old receptionist. On the outside, her family had always looked healthy. Although her parents drank, both of them worked, and homelife appeared to be stable. But what was lacking in the family was a genuine interest in Sandy's autonomous identity. She was her parents' daughter, and she and her brother were expected to be part of the picture of normalcy shown to the outside world. Who Sandy was—what her needs were and how she was different—was a source of tension for the family. Acting out became Sandy's only alternative, the only way she could say, "I exist and my life has meaning." Only by uncovering her childhood hurt could she begin to make sense of her need to draw attention to herself by being self-destructive.

> **Sandy:** I began acting out pretty young, first with shoplifting, then with drugs and booze, and then with sex. Eventually I ended up with a heavy addiction to Valium. But when I did all these things—stealing, getting in trouble, being bad with men—I felt like I was a person, that I was being noticed for being me. Being bad was the only way I ever got acknowledged.

Tragically, as Sandy acted out, she buried her damaged sense of self in a flurry of excitement. Eventually she got tired and admitted that "turning thirty is a sobering thing, even for me." Settling down for Sandy was not easy, and it meant breaking an addiction to drugs and a bad relationship. When she came to therapy after two years of being drug free, she was depressed and felt that her life was meaningless. Therapy soon became extremely stressful as her self-examination made her increasingly anxious. The lack of focus on her real self in childhood was dramatically reversed by the attention and questions of her therapist. Slowly and painstakingly she was able to learn to bear the feelings associated with being the focus of positive attention.

This came only as she was able to feel the pain of the fact that her parents had little interest in her as a separate person, that she had often been abused by her father at the request of her mother, and that when her parents drank, they were harsh and critical. Finally she was able to admit that her childhood had been "that bad" and it might not be that she was the "bad" person.

• *We are addicted to our involvement in other people's affairs and the problems of the world.* By being overinvolved in a relationship or a job, one can avoid an examination of oneself and the associated pain that is buried with the true self.

An addict of this sort is often acutely sensitive to other people and may pick up cues that most will miss. This person, however, does not develop a strong sense of personal boundaries, rights, and responsibilities, because he is not connected to or interested in experiencing his inner life. It's just too risky an enterprise.

Brenda, a lawyer in her midtwenties, grew up in a well-to-do family, the elder of two children. The family was determined to present a perfect face to the world, but problems arose as her father's drinking increased and he became abusive. At first the family grew inward and tried to protect itself, but eventually Brenda's mother left, leaving the two children with their father. Brenda was disgusted by her mother's lack of loyalty, while her brother just wanted to live where Brenda did.

As the years wore on, Brenda's brother's emotional problems increased, and her father's alcoholism and abuse revolved around his son's failures and breakdowns. Brenda's father called her daily requesting her attention to his problems. Since she felt so obligated to help with her brother, she had little sense of her own rights.

> **Brenda:** I had moved away from my father and brother and had really tried to live a life of my own. I'd paid my own way through college and graduate school, and I was trying to make it as a professional. I had a constant, nagging guilt about being on my own, though, about how things were so bad for my brother, and how I ignored and avoided my father's demands. I smoked a lot of pot because it mellowed me, especially when I had to talk to my family. It was a defense for me, because not much bothered me when I was high.

Therapy for Brenda involved recognizing some basic goals. The first was to tell the truth: her father was an alcoholic and had been seductive toward her. Her breakthrough was in realizing that his pleas and demands for her attention were inappropriate.

Why couldn't Brenda simply manage to stay away from the family that caused her so much pain? The answer only appeared after a year of careful self-examination, a year during which, at her request, her father and brother didn't contact her. She found herself feeling increasingly anxious and often wanting to be back in the family drama. She also found that she was creating crises with her boyfriend at this time. There had to be a problem Brenda could involve herself in so she didn't have to face her own feelings, especially her feelings of grief over the fact that her family was not what she had always hoped for.

Steps Toward Recovery: Confronting the Reality of Our Lives

When we look to change the direction our lives are taking, we must confront what our lives are actually about. Each of us has a different "way of life," and each of us tries to cover up a childhood pain that is uniquely our own. We must accept this and bring it out into the open. From our own personal experiences as we have moved toward recovery, and from our work with people who are doing the same, we have recognized five important steps. Each step involves a redirection of energy toward life-affirming choices, rather than a continuing use of energy to cover up and suppress.

Step 1. *Realize that it is an addictive behavior to try to control everything.* In Andrea's case, she knew how unrealistic and manipulative her attempts to control were, but she couldn't stop herself. As a substance abuser, Sandy had no trouble labeling herself as an addict, but she had such a habit of rationalizing her behavior that she could not see that her acting out was also an addiction to control. Brenda needed to see that her involvement with her family was an addiction to control and an addiction to an emotional roller coaster. Because her habit of responding to every demand and crisis was so deeply rationalized as the right thing to do, she had no sense of what she needed for herself. She only knew that it was up to her to respond and fix every situation.

Step 2. *Understand that self-destructive behaviors are an expression of a damaged identity.* When we understand this, we understand why the movement to help and work with ACOAs has captured so much attention. It has given us all a context in which we can ask for help for our problems without feeling weak or self-indulgent, and it has allowed us to see our self-destructive behavior as a cry for attention.

Andrea would have never taken the time to address the problems in her life and enter therapy had it not been for an article about ACOAs in the newspaper. Until that time, her life moved forward, and she never looked back. The older she got, the less sad her childhood seemed, but when she found herself angry at her children for no reason, she began to question what she was doing and look at her life.

Sandy knew she needed help, and she had been in many programs to help her stay sober, yet nothing had calmed the chaos of her life. It was not until she understood that she had truly been hurt in childhood that things started to change. She could stop looking for a quick fix and start working on the deeper issues.

Brenda joined the ACOA movement with the same overinvolvment she brought to her dealings with her family, and she quickly adopted the role of advocate and good listener. It was a while before she was secure enough to admit that she was involved in the same self-destructive process of denial.

Step 3. *Be specific about what you learned about pain and pain avoidance from your parents, and how they served as role models.* Often we meet people in workshops who pass this off by forgetting that the behaviors they learned from their parents, they learned and reacted to as children. Children imitate behavior and believe that if their parents are doing something, that something must be okay. As adults we may be able to look back and say, "It was wrong that my father got drunk every night," but we must remember that as children we were unable to make that judgment.

For Andrea, this was particularly difficult, because the

memories of childhood were so terrifying that she was afraid her whole life would crumble if she opened herself up to those feelings. Sandy wasn't afraid of feelings, but she was unable to stay with one feeling long enough to really feel the pain. Brenda was so cynical about the competency of her parents that initially she was not even able to accept the fact that she had once loved and admired them, and that she had learned from and been affected by them.

Step 4. *Focus energy on pleasure by learning to bear the pain of being wounded.* When you allow yourself the time and room to be a wounded person, you give yourself a great gift. In order to give yourself the time and room, you must change your life in many ways. Above all, you must embrace pain and anxiety, not as enemies, but as parts of real life. It is the child inside us that constantly says that pain is bad. As adults we must reeducate that child and teach him that he will never be able to feel truly good if he is too busy trying not to feel bad.

For Andrea, this meant accepting the truth about her childhood and finally speaking openly about it. Until she sought help, Andrea was so busy trying to control every situation, and take care of everyone else, that she had never allowed herself to feel the pain and ask for comfort. Sandy had to break her habit of self-destructive behavior and realize that negative attention is not the only kind. The only time Brenda felt alive and needed was when she was involved with her family's affairs and problems. By learning to distance herself from her family, Brenda would learn that aliveness does not always entail selfless overinvolvement in other people's problems.

Step 5. *Finally, be fair with yourself and admit that you can't always be perfect.* The part of recovery that involves breaking addictions is perhaps the hardest, because it means changing your way of life and changing the way you see things. It is shifting your energy from avoiding pain to pursuing pleasure and happiness in your life. Be compassionate with yourself. Substance abuse and an addiction to excitement are the inevitable results of having grown up in an unhealthy home.

For Andrea, Sandy, and Brenda, as with most people on the road to recovery, this step is perhaps the hardest. For each of these women, it meant an acknowledgment and acceptance on their part that the way they had been living their lives was not necessarily the best way for them. When they could admit this, and ask for help, they learned that everything is not always up to them and, most important, that they were not failures because of it.

Getting off the roller coaster of our addictions may initially seem callous and selfish to the people we care about, because in some cases what we have to withdraw from is our over-preoccupation with their lives. When we get off the roller coaster, we also feel that we have failed because we haven't solved every problem, and we've let people down. It is a humbling experience to look at yourself and admit that the life you are leading is not your own, but belongs to the substance you abuse, or to all those people who need you so much, or both. When we admit this, we can begin to change.

Connecting with our true selves and exposing our addictions to the light of honest assessment is a slow process. The rewards are a clear sense of identity and an ability to view life today as separate from the past. When your life becomes yours, the reward is being the author of your own excitement and discovering your capacity for love and satisfaction.

In the end the only reasonable choice is one in which we move toward our own life and living independently because the feeling of real aliveness is worth working for. We want to move beyond the child within us that is still struggling to be loved, and see that we are lovable simply for who we are. Healthy excitement lives inside each of us and is always available. We need only choose feeling over control and aliveness over fear. As we shall see in the next two chapters, there are specific obstacles and opportunities to making this healthy choice. Recognizing our own obstacles and opportunities can make the difference in our ability to switch from pain avoidance to pleasure-seeking.

PART II

GROWING UP

IN

AN

UNHEALTHY

ENVIRONMENT

CHAPTER 4

Learning to Survive

As we've discussed previously, when we grow up in an unhealthy home, we learn from our parents to avoid pain at all costs. In response to this, we adopt certain behaviors that enable the family to function, that hide the truth from the outside world and allow us to act as though nothing is wrong and nothing bothers us. The coping child is adept at simulating control over life, no matter what the obstacles are.

In the unhealthy family, as Sharon Wegscheider, psychotherapist and author of *Another Chance*, suggests,[1] family members are organized around the sickest and most needy individual. The goals of the family are to maintain the status quo by not causing upset that would result from addressing problems directly, and to avoid a scene by not challenging the alcoholic. Family members are forced to dedicate themselves to making sure everything runs smoothly and ensuring that the addict has easy access to his drug. Each member thus learns to compensate for the alcoholic in many ways—by standing in for him, taking care of his duties, making excuses to friends and bosses, tending to his needs. Children who grow up in unhealthy homes believe that in order to survive, they must deny reality and bend the truth. Eventually they exhibit some of the psychological symptoms of addiction themselves, including a concerted effort to avoid and deny the existence of anything painful.

Over and over, we see people in our workshops who believe that they were responsible, in an adult sense, for what went on in their childhood. But children are not, and should not be held, responsible for themselves, their feelings, and their actions—that is the role of the parents. Alcoholic and abusive parents fail to perform as responsible caretakers for their children and, instead, train their children to believe that they should be responsible for dealing with their own pain. Wounded children then adopt this as their mission in life. It's as though the pilot of an airplane blamed the passengers for the turbulence, saying that if the passengers were more understanding, more attentive to the pilot's needs, there wouldn't be any problem. Like the frightened and dependent passengers, children believe their parents and dedicate their lives to calming the storm, in the process cheating themselves out of childhood.

Playing by the Family Rules

To admit that Mother and Father are crazy and out of control is just too painful, so as children from unhealthy homes we construct our lives in a way that never forces us to face the truth. It was intolerable for us to sit with the confusion and unpredictability of life in an alcoholic or abusive family. In *It Will Never Happen to Me*,[2] psychotherapist Claudia Black discusses three fundamental, unspoken rules that operate in an alcoholic or abusive family, rules that enable the child to cope with life while avoiding any real feelings connected with it. These rules are "Don't talk," "Don't trust," and "Don't feel."

Don't talk. In our families, we never spoke of the things that were really going on—abuse, drunkenness—and chances are we didn't speak of the issues to our siblings either. We may have talked in our family, but we never told the truth. Most likely we didn't speak it to people outside our home, people who might have been able to intervene and help, because our family loyalty was so strong and we didn't want the family secret to get out. The message from our parents, as Claudia Black tells us, is "There is nothing wrong going on here, and don't you tell anyone!"

Often there were angry scenes at night, scenes that caused someone to leave the room in tears, or violence—dishes broken, food thrown, someone slapped—but the next morning everyone acted as though nothing had happened at all. When you grow up in that kind of environment, you quickly learn not to talk about the reality of family life.

In Karen's family, it was unheard-of to admit that the reason she was sad was her mother's drinking. When Karen did confront her mother, her mother denied that she drank too much, and then accused Karen of being hostile and ruining a nice family dinner once again. So when Karen was asked why she looked sad, she made up stories—she'd had a fight with a friend, she was nervous about a test at school. But even her stories opened her up to criticism about how she handled her friends badly, about how she never studied enough. For her own protection, Karen discussed things that were neither true nor important to her instead of the very critical and painful issues she felt deeply.

The key message was: Don't talk about real issues. In both Karen's and Terry's families, there was talk, but little attention was paid to what was really going on. Children were taught to act as though they were immune to the storm that raged around them. Leila, a physical therapist in her midthirties, says that in her family, abusive incidents were treated as though they never even occurred, teaching her to doubt her ability to perceive and understand the reality of what was happening.

Leila: My father sometimes got very drunk and beat up my mother while we all watched. Sometimes I just couldn't stand it anymore and I'd try to pull him off her. Of course he was so much stronger than I was, and I couldn't really help my mother, but he would get so angry at me that he'd turn around and start beating me up. In the morning, I'd come down for breakfast, and there was Mom at the stove, with a black eye or a cut on her lip, acting as though nothing had happened. Dad drank his coffee as though it was just another morning. Since Mom didn't mention the night before or complain about her bruises, neither did I. As the bruises on my body faded, so did my memory of what had happened, until I wasn't really sure what I had seen in the first place. If my mother didn't think there was anything wrong, why should I? I even told myself that nothing had happened, and that I'd made it all up.

We learned as children to never say what we really felt, to never disclose our inner feelings, because we would inevitably get in trouble for it. If anyone asked, we bottled it all up and revealed nothing. As adults some of us now can't control ourselves when it comes to self-disclosure. We have so much to say that we have no sense of what or to whom or when it is appropriate to talk about our feelings. The words just tumble out of our mouths, and we don't even notice whether the person who is listening is receptive or being alienated from us.

Don't trust. In alcoholic and abusive families, we quickly learned not to trust. We couldn't trust our parents to stay sober or not abuse us. We couldn't trust them to pick us up after school or remember our birthday or not betray a confidence. We couldn't trust that they would be nice to us or behave well in front of our friends. They could be loving one minute, but we couldn't trust that they would be loving the next. We trusted their explanations for things, only to find out later they had lied. We learned that our greatest hurt, and our greatest disappointment, came from those we loved, and we learned to be distrustful of those we wanted to depend on most. It is important to remember that as children we did want to trust our parents, and we tried again and again. Even though they continued to let us down, they were the only parents we had. It is painful to mistrust your parents, but it is worse to mistrust even yourself. Our families demanded that we deny what our senses told us—that physical abuse is bad, that passing out drunk every night is a problem—and ignore our own healthy perceptions about what goes on. We take our cues from our parents; if they treat abuse as normal, so eventually do we. To challenge them is to risk being punished or ostracized from the family. Our survival depended on our compliance. Now, as adults, we often find that we can't rely on "gut feeling," as many people do, to guide us in certain situations. That was the case for Jill, a forty-one-year-old art teacher.

> **Jill:** My mother was an alcoholic, and by the time dinner rolled around she would be fully drunk. While the rest of the family ate, she would sit at the head of the table, with almost nothing on her plate, and a full glass by her side. As dinner wore on she would get drunker and drunker, and if she had to get up for some reason, she'd weave and stumble and barely make it out of the room. Still, no one said anything. If a guest or a relative was over for dinner, sometimes she'd straighten out a little, but often she didn't at all. Even people outside of our family never commented on her behavior. I wondered if I was the only person in the world who thought there was something wrong going on. These nightly scenes taught me to dismiss my own perceptions. I consciously remember deciding I must be crazy to be disturbed by her behavior. If something was wrong, wouldn't someone have told me?

Sometimes in our adult lives we find that we trust the wrong people, and we trust those who are bound to hurt us. Or we may act too soon, without evidence that the person is trustworthy. We may not trust at all and close ourselves off from intimacy, and not allow people to really know us. We never lift up the veil that hides our true feelings.

John, a medical technician in his twenties, tells a story that reveals the depth of internal confusion that can result from this crisis of trust.

> **John:** When I was ten, I was confronted by my male Sunday school teacher who said I had cheated on a test of names in the Bible. I was terrified of being publicly humiliated, so I was eager to return in the afternoon to do penance for my misdeed. To my shock, my Sunday school teacher sexually assaulted me, and then gave me an A to keep my mouth shut about what had happened. He told me he had some big plans for the future and if I talked, I would jeopardize them. I was also afraid to tell my parents what had happened. I know it sounds stupid, but I didn't trust them not to punish me, and I told myself, "This is what you get for cheating in Sunday school." I decided not to trust my parents or my teacher.

Don't feel. As children what we often felt was so painful and so horrendous that without comfort or reassurance, we learned to turn feelings off. Children of alcoholic and abusive families don't remember being held when they were scared, or comforted when they were sad. More likely they were teased about being scared and babyish, punished for being angry or sad. There was no parent to hold the child and assure him that things would be better, that it's okay to feel bad sometimes. They learn that there are some feelings that are intolerable and too painful, and should be shut off. Why else would their parents pretend the feelings didn't exist, or substitute them with other feelings? Why would Daddy always get drunk when his boss yelled at him? In this kind of family system, the truth is too much to bear, and children in this kind of family are gifted at learning the ways of survival.

Unfortunately, when the true self is covered up, the richness of each person cannot shine through. Only as an adult did Karen realize that as a child she had separated the part of her that felt from the part of her that experienced life.

Karen: When something bad went on in the family—my mother caused an incident and screamed at me—I just went numb. When I heard my parents fight, I heard things that should have scared me—hate, divorce—but I felt nothing. Even when my mother slapped me across the face I didn't care. There was a joke in my family about how "cool" I was. They said that if I went away for a very long time, and didn't see my family for years, when I returned I'd just stroll on in with a casual "hi" as though I'd never been away, never missed them at all.

By trying to hide her feelings of vulnerability that were ridiculed by her parents, Karen ended up hiding all her feelings. Recovery for Karen involved reducing the amount of time between an event and her awareness of how she feels about it. It was a painstakingly slow process, and at first it was years before she felt anything. Gradually it became months, and now, after much hard work, it is minutes. It was through reassurance and support from those she loved and trusted that she learned it was okay to feel.

There is a great price to pay when you turn off your feelings. What you cannot express emotionally often ends up being expressed physically in illness and pain. Sometimes, as in Karen's case, so much feeling was clogged up that when it came out it did so in explosions, in hysterics, and she would have no idea what the feelings were connected to. When she had expressed enough to take the pressure off, she felt relieved, but nothing had really been dealt with. Often she was consumed by guilt for having screamed at her child, or horrified that she was acting just like her drunken mother. Guilt and shame covered up what was really going on and pushed the real feelings further and further away.

Trisha, one of our clients, learned that as a child she could simply leave her body when she was feeling too much. She had trained herself to "disappear."

Trisha: Often at dinner with my family, I had no awareness that I was even eating. I taught myself to "lift off" when I felt things getting tense. People used to complain then, and they still do now, that I'm not really "present" much of the time.

Leila, on the other hand, as an adult, gravitated toward people who were violent and impulsive. She continued to seek out what she most feared. Her fears were so buried, though, she didn't know what they were, and had the attitude that she could handle anything that came up. She involved herself with people who, like her father, were abusive. Sigmund Freud said that if you have a situation in your life that remains painful and incomplete, you will feel compelled to re-create it again and again in an attempt to finally complete it. He called this "repetition compulsion." Leila needed an awareness of her feelings about her father in order to break this self-destructive cycle of behavior.

Choosing Roles as a Way of Ordering the Chaos

Just as we were forced to give up our right to talk, to trust, and to feel as children, we were forced into assuming particular roles in the family (first discussed by Sharon Wegscheider in *Another Chance*). These roles were just one more component in the smooth running of the system, dedicated to protecting the family from facing itself. The roles provided a structure for predictable behavior and gave us a context within which we could act, and a sense of control over what happened. They created a pseudo-identity for us because our real identity was not being supported. The roles were an attempt to save the family and ourselves from more pain, but they did not grow out of the needs of any individual except the alcoholic or abusive parent. They were merely attempts to save the status quo by perpetuating the denial and allowing the abuse to continue. As we explore our behavior within our roles, we must now remember that we were innocent bystanders pulled in by something much stronger than ourselves. We didn't create the drama; we were forced to act within it.

The roles we discuss here are related to birth order, but are not limited or confined to it. As you read about the various roles, you'll identify yourself primarily in one, but you'll recognize aspects in others that can also apply to you. Children within the family often play more than one role and often trade off, but even a combination of roles does not allow a full and free range of expression, and stifles the child's development. You may play different roles in different situations, and if you are an only child, you might have played them all at various times.

The Hero

This child, since he is most often the eldest, is doted on and taught to distract his parents, at least for a while, from problems and pain in their lives. "Look at what a lovely child we have," the Hero's parents say. "Things can't be that wrong!" The Hero learns to dedicate himself to succeeding so that his parents can feel good about him and themselves. He learns to do well in school, in sports, to be a leader admired by classmates and teachers. This child doesn't draw negative attention to himself, and by all appearances, he is a success. The problem is that despite all the Hero's successes, he continues to fail at the one thing he has devoted his life to—making the family pain go away. Inside, he feels like a failure, full of guilt for not being able to make his parents truly happy.

In our workshops, we occasionally meet the pure Hero type, and he or she is a great person. They look good, are attractive and well dressed, and they are succeeding at whatever they have applied themselves to. Often these people are greatly admired and envied. Many ACOAs, while they may be heroes to their own family, are not such stars in the larger world. His family might rave about how brilliant and special he is, while the Hero compares himself to his peers and doesn't think all that much of himself. In fact, most Heroes learn to be good, but not too good, because that might threaten the fragile ego of the alcoholic or abusive parent. This creates an anxiety and confusion within the Hero, and one more unbearable feeling that must be buried.

Believing that you are special, as the Hero often does, can be a terrible burden, because it means never being satisfied with just being ordinary. It means that doing a job well isn't good enough. Thus, the Hero is sometimes unable to focus on anything, and he becomes a person with unattained promise, rather than someone who accomplishes things. And despite how successful he actually is, the Hero still carries around a feeling of isolation and loneliness that, if not buried, would be extreme. Like every child in the unhealthy home, the Hero is under a lot of stress and feels that he has to win a race that he is running not only for himself but for the entire family as well. He is driven by an inner voice that says the family happiness depends entirely on him.

Diana is an example of a pure Hero type. At forty-two, she held a good management job in a business, wrote poetry, maintained a well-kept house, and cooked and entertained lavishly. She was sweet, friendly, politically active, and volunteered her time to various causes. She was liked and admired, but her private life was a mess. Her husband acted like an adolescent and would continually involve himself in one crazy scheme after another. Not only did he not bring in money, but he spent whatever Diana earned. The people who knew of Diana's problems thought she was a special woman saddled with a difficult husband. All sympathy was for her.

As she began to tell us her story, though, we saw that it was not just her husband that was a problem. Her children were furious at her, and in fact when she left her husband, they wouldn't live with her and often even refused to visit. Diana was so busy being the heroine that appearances were more important than truth. Even though her relationship with her children was severely disturbed, when she did see them, she created fights by fussing at them and correcting their behavior. She was so afraid of losing the patina of success that she sacrificed rebuilding trust with her children in order to teach them manners.

It was hard for anyone to be intimate with Diana, and even her children believed that they had been sacrificed to her need to appear successful. Her husband had been a trophy on her shelf, and when he refused to go along with her program, their relationship fell apart. Diana was filled with resentment about how hard she had to work to keep the family afloat.

> **Diana:** I was the eldest of five children. Both of my parents were alcoholics who, quite simply, assigned me the parental role for my siblings. No one in school would have ever guessed at the chaos that went on at home, because I took pride in keeping my secrets. I learned to cope with my parent's drunkenness by rising above it, and I didn't let it bother me. I did what was necessary and believed that their drinking wouldn't affect me if I didn't let it. I didn't even let the fact that my father sexually and physically abused me get to me very much.

The problem for Diana is that in order to have survived her childhood, she became such a superhero that she lost touch with her feelings and humanity. The anger and resentment she felt for having to be the Hero, as well as the abuse she suffered, were unacknowledged by her, since she had learned to deny her feelings.

David is an example of a tarnished Hero. He came to our workshop when he was twenty years old and a part-time college student because he noticed that he was always screwing up. He would get right to the edge of success, and then he'd not hand in a paper, or not show up for an interview, or not fill out an application. He constantly put himself back in the role of boy-with-promise-who-can't-quite-make-it.

Good-looking, articulate, and bright, it wasn't hard to see that David was a person with promise. Instead of delighting in his promise, he felt it was a heavy burden. His father had been much the same way and never quite made it, but he had wanted his son to succeed. Even when David was a baby, people had stopped his father on the street to comment on how lovely and intelligent his baby was. In therapy, David discovered that his father didn't really want him to succeed. So David had been trained to hold back from being a success so as not to threaten his father. If he shut his eyes, he could still see the terrifying look of resentment on his father's face.

When David entered high school, he was no longer the brightest student. Being the star was no longer assured, and he assumed other ways to get the attention he was so used to having—dressing in three-piece suits, riding a motorcycle. His parents and teachers were disappointed in his grades, and he found himself unable to study and be disciplined about his work. The burden he felt for his parents' happiness was showing, and he was sinking under the pressure. He had devoted his life to the impossible task of making his parents' problems disappear, and was unable to live up to their stories of how brilliant he was. He was a smart boy, but he wasn't a genius, and the family's praise, their need for him to save them, and his father's demand that he not be too good were too much to live with. David was sure the failure was all his, and he didn't understand that he had been put in a no-win situation. Even if he had been perfect in everything and had fulfilled all expectations, his parents still would have been dissatisfied with their lives.

The Scapegoat

The next child in line learns a different way to cope with his life and the painful reality of his parents' failings. Since the role of the good child has already been taken, this child dedicates himself to being bad. He learns to act out the family's pain so that his parents can point to him as the cause of all the trouble instead of facing their own shortcomings.

The Scapegoat covers his fear and vulnerability with

anger, so instead of saying, "I'm hurt," he says, "I'm pissed off." The tough-guy act not only fools his parents but fools himself as well. He becomes the mouthpiece for the family, and he allows all the others to deny their anger because he is so busy expressing his and drawing negative attention to himself. It's not a nice position to be in, but if no one takes the heat, the family will eventually explode.

Donna, now a clerk in a department store, was a problem from the time she was born. Even as a baby she was cranky and fussy, and most often did not sleep through the night. Her endless crying put more stress on an already strained family, and she became the focus of the family problems. As Donna got older, she began to express her discontent verbally, but her family discounted what she said, thinking she was just "complaining as usual." No one ever asked her what was really going on.

When Donna was able to escape into the world of her peers, she did so, but she was perpetually disgruntled, and so used to things not going her way that she was not fun to be around. The group she fit in with was comprised of unhappy kids like her. As a group they didn't do well in school and stuck together by ridiculing everything around them. By the time Donna was a teenager, the school authorities agreed with Donna's parents that she was a problem. She failed most of her courses and was suspected of smoking marijuana in school, but no one in the school felt they had the right to confront Donna's parents about any difficulties at home. By this time, Donna had learned to cope with the family pain by estranging herself from it as much as possible, and looked for love, although often not successfully, from her peers. Anything was better than the constant criticism and blame she got from her family.

At sixteen, Donna became pregnant, proving to herself that at least someone loved her. Her family was forced to pay attention to her to work out the crisis, and by having a baby, Donna found a purpose and structure to her life, and she was able to punish her parents. As far as disappointing her parents, she had done the ultimate. Often Scapegoats like Donna are noticed by others who sense something wrong. Ironically, by acting out the family problems, the Scapegoat is often the one to bring the family into therapy.

The Lost Child

By the time this child comes into the family, one sibling is already doing only good, another only bad, and both are involved with an ongoing drama with the parents. There is no room for the third, and lost, child. To cope, the Lost Child withdraws and keeps to himself. He may spend a lot of time alone, or in his room, or out of the house, and doesn't interact much with the family, especially when things heat up. The irony of the Lost Child's role is that the family can say, "Well, at least there's one child in this family we don't have to worry about." This, unfortunately, is not true. The Lost Child has learned that there is no one to count on, no one to care for him, and he is really truly alone and without guidance. Just because he's quiet doesn't mean he doesn't need attention. The Lost Child is forced into withdrawal by a family that is already stressed by other problems. There just is no other place for him to go. The message that the Lost Child hears is that he is not worth chasing after, not worth too much attention. The role he has found himself in teaches him that he is of no value.

Joy was the second child in her family, and while her brother flipped between the Hero and Scapegoat roles in the family, Joy withdrew, terrorized by the nightly fireworks at home. She spent most of her childhood avoiding trouble of any kind. When she avoided the storms that raged around her, she also cut off any real contact that she needed for her development. Her parents' attention always seemed so terrifying that being ignored was preferable.

Joy didn't learn about give-and-take in a relationship because she had been so shut off, and it was no surprise that at twenty-two she married an angry, erratic man who had no room for her. Her childhood had taught her that there was no other way than withdrawal to survive, so inevitably she chose a man that would allow her to repeat old patterns of behavior.

The Mascot

The Mascot is usually the last child, the baby of the family, and everyone takes some pride in protecting him from the horrors of family life. They teach him to get along by teaching him nothing at all. They don't tell him about the pain and the resentment, or what's going on, and he learns that confusion is normal. By the time this child arrives, the family is in need of a break in the emotional action, and the Mascot provides this by playing the fool for their diversion and delight.

The primary trauma for this child is that he doesn't have much real, calm contact with the world around him. The Mascot learned early on that the only way to get attention was to make a fool of himself, obviously a mixed blessing. People don't really listen to Mascots or take them seriously, because they're always joking around. Often they don't take themselves seriously either, and they have come to believe that they don't need to listen to other people. The Mascot receives a kind of attention he doesn't need—humiliation and embarrassment—and his parents treat him with the attitude that they know so much better, and so much more, than he does. The Mascot is then forced into a dependent and humiliating position that is hard to break out of and may exact a very high price. Often he is treated as a "special" child because of learning disabilities or an attention deficit.

Marie, a twenty-nine-year-old designer of children's books, says her family probably wouldn't characterize themselves as cruel, but that is how they were to her, despite their good intentions. Marie was the youngest of four children in a family that appeared to have a happy home. It was not a healthy home, however. The problem was that there was so much emphasis in the family on achievement that errors and failures were treated with condescension and derision instead of compassion and support.

> **Marie:** I couldn't read very well as a kid, and I'd get words mixed up. My family's laughter at the things I'd say by accident, at the things I'd get mixed up on, began to wear thin. At this point in my life, I hope to never have to see my family again. I can deal with them one-on-one, but whenever it's more than that, I see them looking at each other, being careful not to upset me. You'd think I was a mental case by now. They make me feel like I'm five again, and I do seem to get mad when I'm around them, fulfilling their expectations of me. I'm so tired of being thought of as "cute" and not treated like an adult. I think my anger is what saved my life. I simply had enough of the "happy home" routine. Sometimes I feel as though I've let my family down by going my own way.

The roles we have discussed are designed to satisfy the needs of the parents and the family system. The child sacrifices his own true identity and does the work required of him to keep things intact. Each family member becomes dedicated to serving, and being responsible for, everyone but himself. When this happens, the child's needs become confused with the parents' needs. As in Terry's case, no child knows that the expectations set out for him are unrealistic.

> **Terry:** I was completely lost in my role as Hero of the family. I was my mother's "little man" even though I was just a kid, and I felt it was my responsibility to make her happy and support her because my father didn't. I was very uncomfortable and guilty about taking over my father's role, but I was driven by some sense of duty to my mother. Instead of being a kid, I had to be a man.

Creating the Stories

The fundamental premise that underlies each role is that the family chaos is the child's fault, and the child learns to accept the responsibility of ordering that chaos. That is the way a child's mind works; he sees the world solely from his own point of view and internalizes parental expectations. Parents reinforce this perspective by expecting more from a child than is age-appropriate. The child would rather shoulder the entire burden than admit that his parents are so crazy nothing he can do will ever change them. When parents support their children taking the blame, they tell them that they wouldn't drink if they didn't have rotten kids, they wouldn't hit if their children would just be obedient. Since children believe they are the *cause* of the problems, they believe they can *solve* them, too. In truth, there is nothing the child can do to relieve the pain of the parent if the parent is unwilling to do his own Emotional Healing.

However, the child persists in believing that he can make the difference, saying, "If I were only prettier, smarter . . . then things would be better." No matter how much the child sacrifices his individuality, energy, and self-esteem, things remain essentially the same. Eventually, as the child grows older, he begins to feel less hopeful and more helpless about ever effecting a change, but never stops his attempts entirely.

In order to perpetuate the denial of reality, lies are told and stories are concocted, both by the parents and by the children. Problems are never addressed and real issues are not discussed. When life is so confusing and unpredictable that it becomes intolerable, stories are made to provide a little rhyme and reason to an incomprehensible situation.

> **Karen:** Around the time my sister and I were seven and eight, we went to my father one day and tried to tell him that our mother wasn't treating us very well.

He responded by telling us a long story about how my mother really wanted approval from her own father, to have him say she was a good mother, but he withheld his praise, and that was why my mother was so upset all the time. He never mentioned her drinking as a problem, and ignored the fact that we were expressing pain and asking for help. We believed his story, though, and spent much energy then, and for many years later, in trying to make our mother feel happy and appreciated. We focused ourselves on her needs, and from that time on, our own needs were buried and forgotten. My father's response told me that I didn't have a reality separate from my mother and that, in fact, I was responsible for her.

Like Karen and her sister, children in this kind of environment persevere in their attempts to solve the family problems. They continue to make excuses to one parent about the other, they continue to be quiet about what they see, and they try to do too much, asking nothing for themselves. Or they act out so the family can point to them as the trouble causers, they joke to distract the family from pain, they dedicate their lives to it, losing their own selves in the process. Children love their parents and will use all their tricks rather than admit the parents are crazy. We see sometimes that the bond between parent and child can be so strong that children beg to be returned to parents who have abused them. Children count on their parents to know what they are doing and handle the demands of life, and it is from them that reality gets defined.

Dr. Alexander Lowen, a psychiatrist who practices Bioenergetic Analysis in New Canaan, Connecticut, and who is the author of numerous books on bioenergetics and teaches internationally, talks about defenses being a matter of life and death. As children, we often felt that to face up to a feeling would kill us, so we defended ourselves against those feelings. In our childlike minds, we believed that our survival was dependent on denial. We also saw our parents do this expertly.

When we try to discover how this worked for us as individuals, we need to look at the lies we accepted as truths. Primarily we were forced to lie about ourselves and about the fact that our parents were failing us. As small children we made decisions about how to live life, and the kind of decision we made was based on the role we played within our family.

The Hero, for example, may decide: I'll be so good that my mother and father are happy. I'll ignore my "bad" side, and never attempt things I know I can't succeed in. I'll take care of everyone in my family and be helpful at all times. I'll be the perfect child. But what the Hero may end up with is: I'll never learn to deal with failure. I can't help myself from being drawn into relationships that aren't good for me, because I think I'm helping. I'll put everyone else first, and as I wear myself out, I'll completely ignore my own needs and development, and lose myself in the process.

The Scapegoat may decide, mostly unconsciously: I'm going to be a real problem for my family so they can focus on me instead of admitting how bad things really are. The only time I ever get any attention is when I'm bad, so to get the attention, I'll constantly act out the family pain and hostility. What the Scapegoat may end up with is: By being a problem for the family, I end up being a problem for myself. In always being bad, I don't learn how to ever be good. When I act out the family's pain and hostility, I lose myself in the process, and only get pain and hostility thrown back at me. I miss out on love and affection.

The Lost Child may conclude: I'll stay out of the way and not cause any problems, because I'm not important in the family and my thoughts and feelings don't really matter much. I can take care of myself better than anyone else can. What the Lost Child may end up with is: I learned never to be included and noticed. When I act so self-effacing, I end up thinking I'm not important either, and I don't pay attention to my needs. When I close myself up, I also never learn to open up to someone else's love.

The Mascot may decide: I'm going to be funny and disruptive so the family will be distracted from fighting. I can't bear the pain so I'll make everything into a big joke. I have to be cute and funny to get any attention anyway. The Mascot may end up with: When I distract my family from what's going on, I also distract myself from what's happening inside me, and I get caught in this pattern of behavior. Since I can't face what's really going on, I develop a lifetime habit of making jokes. The fact is that if I wasn't funny and the clown, no one would love me anyway.

These conclusions are life-influencing decisions. They are so basic to the way the child views himself and his world that everything else he does is based on them. Thus, it can be very hard to change ourselves, because we may be trying to alter life decisions that we're not even aware we made. Even as adults it is often hard to change, to get out of these roles, because we don't realize how essential they were to our survival and how they determined our responses to what went on around us.

Marybeth, for example, made a decision when she was a small child that would affect her adult life. At thirty-one, Marybeth loved her husband very much and considered their relationship to be good, but she was concerned about her lack of sexual interest in him. Most of the time she felt unenthusiastic about the prospect of making love with her husband, and often felt burdened by his desires and attempts. She did everything she could to change this, and bought sex manuals, sexy lingerie, talked to her husband and others about the problem, but nothing seemed to change the way she felt, until she remembered back to something that had happened many, many years before.

> **Marybeth:** When I was a very little girl, my mother, father, and I had a ritual every night before I went to bed. My mother played the part of minister, my father the groom, and me, in my nightgown and veil, the role of bride. Each night I "married" my father and he would carry me upstairs and lay me in bed. Once I was alone, I would wait for my father to come and be my "husband." I was terrified that he would come, and I guess I sensed that it was wrong and would be hurtful

to my mother. Still, the idea excited me, and I was hurt when he never showed up. I felt torn between all the feelings of wanting him but being afraid of it, and I decided, then and there, that the best thing to do would be not to have any sexual feelings ever again. This way I wouldn't hurt my mother and I wouldn't have to be afraid of my father. I wouldn't have to experience the confusion I felt. I was four years old.

Once Marybeth could remember the decision she had made so long ago, she was able to reconsider the choice she'd made at four, a decision to turn off her sexuality because it caused in her a dangerous combination of desire and fear. She began to understand that she had not been at risk of being seduced by her father—it had only been a game to him—and that she had been afraid of something that was not going to happen. Her mixed feelings had created an unbearable conflict within her that she re-created in her marriage—acting sexually sophisticated while feeling nothing—and she was able to slowly and painstakingly rediscover her buried sexuality. In other cases, the danger that children in alcoholic or abusive families are trying to protect themselves from is very real. Many girls from this kind of family are in fact seduced or sexually assaulted by their fathers, and like Marybeth, tragically bury their sexuality.

The Gifted Learner Adopts a Coping Persona

The life decisions we make as children, based on lies we were forced to tell ourselves, are the foundation of our behavior. As we grow older, we adopt what we have come to call a "coping persona," a habitual way of life that incorporates both an attitude and a stance with which we characteristically approach life. When we no longer live within the confines of our family, our roles become more fluid, but no less important for our survival. Most people see their coping persona as "the way I am," but they often do not go the extra step to see that the way they approach difficult situations may not be the best, may be pain-avoidant and not life-affirming, may be an automatic, programmed response instead of a heartfelt reaction. As we began to separate from our families, these coping personas worked for us in terms of our survival. Now they are part of an addictive way of life.

The coping persona begins when the mood of the child must be altered. Whether the child's tendency is toward anxiety or depression, the coping persona absorbs these feelings and integrates them into an identity he can live with, given the surrounding family circumstances. Eventually the coping persona becomes woven into the fabric of daily life until we no longer even notice that it is there. Creativity, spontaneity, and individuality become buried under the coping persona, so that when you attempt to understand how yours functions, you are taking a crucial step in freeing yourself from the trap.

When we discuss coping personas, we describe six different types. No one person fits exactly into one of these archetypes, but try to notice how each description touches you, and whether it rings true to your behavior. The roles we played in our family also do not correspond to one particular coping persona. To make their characteristics more easily identifiable, we have given each of the coping personas the name of a well-known person, and have drawn upon the public impression of these people to illustrate their visible qualities.

Pride: the John Wayne

This person has mastered the art of control early on and appears masterful and self-sufficient. Having received much praise and admiration for his competency, the John Wayne believes that if something is going to be done right, he has to do it, and the John Wayne thinks that he always knows best. He never needs to depend on anyone—he can take care of himself—and as a result, never really gets close to people.

Terry fits this description to a certain degree. Encouraged by his mother and father to be highly competitive in athletics and academics, Terry became the pride of the family and nurtured the illusion that he was, or could be, the best one around. He was adored by his mother, who praised him lavishly for everything he did, and he held the prize seat of firstborn son. His coping persona of pride allowed him to view the failures in many areas of his life as minor setbacks rather than as a message that something was wrong in the way he was operating. His pain-avoidant and prideful approach to life allowed him to ignore the truth of what was really going on by reminding him that he was getting better and better all the time. Pride is hard to let down, and in Terry's case, it took the breakup of a marriage and the loss of three jobs for him to start examining his approach to life.

The task of the John Wayne in recovery is to accept his own human frailty and need for affection. This type does not view life and loving as mutually enhancing experiences, but tries to cope with and conquer life all on his own. Of course, the rewards for this attitude can be high. But the John Wayne is too busy trying to make life work rather than letting life be.

Withdrawal: the Greta Garbo

The famous actress succeeded in a way that many others have failed: she was able to have a highly successful career yet maintain a very private personal life. She rarely granted interviews or was seen in public, and protected her private life fiercely. The withdrawn person does the same, believing that if he remains essentially hidden, yet admired publicly, he will not open himself up to being hurt.

Growing up in a strict, authoritarian, or repressive home often encourages a child to withdraw into himself. This child can also be the Lost Child, the one who is rewarded for being good and receding into the background, for seeming to have no pain or visible needs.

Rick, Karen's husband, fits the description of this type, although you wouldn't guess it. As a workshop leader, a therapist, and a friend, he could hardly be called an introvert or unenthusiastic about participating. In stressful situations, though, he automatically retreated. When pressed for an explanation of why he did something, he had no answer, as though his feelings were locked away deep inside himself, in a place even he couldn't get to. Rick still tends to defer to others when it's time to make a decision, or he makes decisions on his own and doesn't let people know.

The Greta Garbos must learn to tolerate stress without disappearing into themselves for safety, learn to tolerate disappointment and rejection. Often they lose the opportunity to act on something because the stress of making a decision causes them to retreat. The Greta Garbo ends up justifying what happened by saying, "It wasn't worth it anyway," or "I didn't really care to begin with." That is how the Greta Garbo learned to cope as a child: to never be assertive, to never have a preference that might cause conflict.

Anger: the James Dean

This coping persona constantly proclaims to the world, "I am." The assertion of rights and opinions becomes a pattern early on, as the child matures in an environment of disappointment and aggression.

James Dean achieved a certain notoriety because of his anger and violent outbursts. He was the "angry young man" in several films, and died at an early age. A highly aggressive approach to life often earns the respect, if not attention and fear, of others. There is a sense that the James Dean is always trying to prove something, and can never just "be."

For people who were raised in alcoholic and abusive homes, there is much to be angry about, but why does it show in some people and not in others? The answer lies in the role the child took on and the behavior he chose to model himself after. If the parents wanted a tough child, they probably got one. If the parents themselves were explosive and angry, the child may have followed their example and become like them.

Anger is what fuels the James Dean type. Whether this is exhibited in political heroics or self-destructive and addictive behavior, the underlying message of control and power is always the same.

Karen, for example, has an angry core. As the oldest child, she was the one to speak out, the one that pointed to problems everyone else ignored. It is her anger that impels her through rough periods in her life. It is no accident that she leads workshops: she wants to speak out against what makes her angry.

The task for the James Dean coping persona is to stop long enough to realize how grief-stricken he is about the way things have turned out. Tragically this realization often comes too late—in prison, in trouble—or never at all. The James Dean type is often so angry and defensive that he will do anything but let the world know that he is in trouble and affected by all his pain.

Hopelessness and Depression: the Marilyn Monroe

The sentiment of this coping persona is often, "Life is so terrible, and there is no way out. I would rather be dead." This seems hardly a good solution, but one that many adopt. If anger and frustration were not allowed as a child, but punished instead, depression and hopelessness become a way of living. If the child's needs are not met, then the thing to do is deaden all feelings so there are no needs at all.

The Marilyn Monroe may actually accept reality in a way that the others do not. It was depressing to grow up in unhealthy families, and hopelessness was a real feeling. This may not be the reality of their adult lives, but the Marilyn Monroe still says, "I will focus on how bad things are so I can never be disappointed again." She never gives herself the chance to find the good.

There is also some of this persona in Karen. As a child she was told that her family, and her father, who was mayor of the town, were much respected and admired in the community.

The secret about her mother being an abusive alcoholic never got out. Karen's coping persona of hopelessness and depression kept the lid on the truth, because she was told by her family that telling the true story never solved anything. In her heart, Karen felt a responsibility to speak the truth, but also to remain quiet so she wouldn't cause problems. When she suppressed her anger and her feelings of protest, she became depressed and emotionally dead.

In recovery, the Marilyn Monroe coping persona must talk about how her life really was, feeling the anger beneath the depression, and by doing this, come emotionally alive again. She needs to take pleasure that can be found in relationships with friends and lovers.

Confusion: the Frances Farmer

Frances Farmer, a Hollywood actress of the 1930s known for her unorthodox style, was eventually hospitalized for what her parents believed was mental illness. Hers can hardly be thought of as a coping persona with many positive character-istics, but the sum total creates a person who is able to live in a chaotic family situation. The child who eventually adopts this coping persona responds to the inconsistency of life and lack of boundaries with a belief that nothing at all makes sense. Why, then, should this child make sense himself? When the chaos and unpredictability become so intolerable that the child must disengage, this coping persona functions efficiently by giving him a personal consistency in an inconsistent environment.

Terry's persona is part John Wayne and part Frances Farmer. It is no surprise that he became a psychologist. Sorting out the confusion in his family and his own life was, and still is, a great fascination to him. As a child Terry was often hyperactive, but at the time, he was seen as just being a very active boy. Clearly he was out of control and overexcited, but this was merely a response to the chaos he saw around him.

The Frances Farmer needs to put herself in a situation

with people she trusts, so that she can open up to the pain and isolation of her confusion. She has been keeping one step ahead of herself all the time, and now she needs to slow down and let things catch up with her.

The Chameleon: the Charlie Brown

The chief skill of the Charlie Brown coping persona is adaptability. The Charlie Brown type will do whatever it takes to get along and keep the peace, and bow to any authority that is present. At the core of this type is the sense that "I am so afraid of being abandoned that I will be whatever you want me to be." The Charlie Brown remains a child emotionally, since he is always dependent on the moods and whims of the people around him to tell him what and how to be. Like a chameleon, the Charlie Brown can change his colors to blend into the environment.

The Charlie Brown makes compromises and changes to avoid conflict and rejection. He is usually a people-pleaser and a peacemaker, because he is scared of antagonizing people. Since he has such a fragile sense of self, there is a strong need to be around people. He is often a person who wins the affection of others, and prides himself on his ability to cope with, and fit into, any situation he finds himself in.

The task for Charlie Brown's recovery is straightforward: to find himself through his fear and assert that self with confidence and respect. This often entails a lot of false starts. There are difficult conflicts to overcome, because many people would prefer a people-pleaser to a person who constantly asserts his rights.

By now you have probably recognized parts of yourself in several of the descriptions of these coping personas. When you do become aware of how you act and respond in this fashion, you allow yourself the opportunity to step back and question your actions. Beware of being too hard on yourself when you do this. Don't fall back on your tendency to be overly critical and judgmental about yourself. You adopted these behaviors early on in childhood because they helped you survive in the chaos, and because they were based on decisions and needs that seemed clear and necessary at the time. The coping personas we adopted were based on the lies we told ourselves as children to deal with our feelings and to explain our parents' behavior.

The coping personas have served their function, and the coping skills you adopted have been your line of defense against pain. As an adult the goal in your recovery must be to identify your coping pattern so that you can make a choice about how you will act from now on, from the point of view of an adult, and not as a gifted but still immature child. We can learn to respond with our hearts and feelings, something our coping personas do not allow as they block the flow of feeling.

As we'll see in the next chapter, the coping personas play a significant part in the growth of the adolescent, helping him maneuver his way through a stressful period of life. This makes the task of shedding our coping personas today even more difficult.

CHAPTER 5

Adolescence: Discovering the World of Sexuality

For ACOAs to achieve the goals of healing and recovery, it is extremely important for them to examine and understand their adolescence. During this period, adolescent hormones imbue almost every encounter between the sexes with romantic overtones. Relationships take on monumental passion and drama, opening up for perhaps the first time the possibility of adult sexual intimacy. Unfortunately the fragile resources ACOAs bring to relationships are often overwhelmed, triggering the first of the emotional "defeats" of adulthood that ACOAs encounter, and reinforcing the pain-avoidant mechanisms that ACOAs developed to deal with the shattering experiences of childhood.

The non-ACOA adolescent, of course, also faces romantic defeat, but it is a normal part of growing up where trial and error ultimately lead to maturity and adult responsibility. In a healthy family, parents explain the child's loss, and place it in the proper context of the passage into adulthood. The parents usually add a generous ladle of love and compassion that reinforces the child's self-image and identity, thus enabling the adolescent to get back into the saddle after being thrown.

In alcoholic and abusive families, there is little of this support. The ACOA adolescent draws inappropriate conclusions about himself that pull him away from pleasure-seeking and direct him toward pain avoidance. This is what happened to Terry when he experienced sexual excitement for the first time.

> **Terry:** My first erotic experience ended disastrously. I had invited a girlfriend to a holiday weekend at school and during the course of our time together we kissed heavily and I felt her breast. I fell immediately in love. The next time I called her for another date, she wouldn't give me the time of day. I couldn't understand it and felt shattered. Unfortunately I couldn't talk about my feeling to my parents and I was too ashamed to discuss what happened with my friends. I trusted no one with my pain, not even myself. No wonder I continued to deny it.

When life is full of successes in the healthy home, emotional losses like the one Terry suffered can be taken in stride, because sexual awakening is in itself such a positive and compelling experience that it propels us forward even in the face of defeat. As we will see in this chapter, however, the energy awakened in the ACOA adolescent is almost never channeled into a healthy sexual life. (In Chapter 10, we will show how one's sexuality can be the fountain of hope and excitement which culminates in ACOAs achieving what we call Emotional Sobriety.)

The feelings of loss that Terry had may be denied, as they are in unhealthy families, but they do not disappear. They can be ignored for a while by whistling a happy tune but they will eventually reappear, and for many adolescents, they will cause depression, anxiety, and self-destructive rebellion. In the most extreme cases, the inability to come to terms with such feelings can lead to teenage suicide and drug abuse. A fear of intimacy and a sense of inadequacy are more common symptoms of the same phenomenon of denied reality.

While the quest for identity is at the root of adolescent

development, in an unhealthy home the parental needs and demands are often at odds with this, causing a deeply felt conflict within the adolescent. Alcoholic or abusive parents either suggest or openly demand that their children be people they can be proud of, people they can continue to control, and people that will take care of their needs. Sometimes their demand is that the children respond to them sexually or join them in their alcoholism or other abuses. Such parents are neither adequately mature nor stable enough to see and accept their children as individuals who are separate entities, with desires and wills of their own. It is the very nature of this conflict that makes adolescence so difficult for those who grew up in unhealthy homes.

In most cases, no matter how unhealthy and angry the family is, the adolescent has some degree of admiration and respect for his parents and tries to live up to their expectations and be a tribute to the family. A problem develops for the adolescent over how much he will try to fulfill family demands at the expense of his own individuality. People fall back on their coping persona when life becomes painful.

As we have shown in our discussion of roles in unhealthy homes, there may not be enough support or opportunity within the family system for the adolescent to attempt being a success and fulfilling expectations. While most parents will say that they want the best for their children, the reality is that success for a particular child may impose a tax on the family that is too high. If the family "requires" a member to be an object of humiliation or abuse—a human dumping ground for anxiety and anger—the parents will, in the end, inadvertently sacrifice the child's individuality, self-esteem, and desires, rather than face their own pain. A depressed parent may not be able to rob his child of success in dating, but he can certainly color and diminish it by being critical or uninterested.

Rebellion in this kind of environment is a reaction to abuse suffered at the hand of authority. Those in the family who make the rules do so to suit themselves, with little or no regard to what other family members really need. The teenager's rebellion often has less to do with an attempt to find his own ground to stand on than it does with an unconscious desire to treat his parents with the same lack of respect he is dealt with, and to challenge his parents' power in the same way his power is challenged and squashed.

Losing the Opportunity for
Adolescent Independence

Adolescence is a time of life that provides the individual with an opportunity to reconnect with spontaneous, natural pleasure through the budding of sexual awareness and everything that sexuality implies—autonomy, maturity, responsibility. But those adolescents who grow up in unhealthy environments lose touch with the thread that is crucial to a satisfying life, that is, the pursuit of pleasure. They continue throughout their adolescence to make pain avoidance the focus of their attention and energy. They have never been shown how to give pleasurable feelings priority, nor have they been taught that pleasure is valuable. All along, they have just been doing what they needed to do to survive and get along in the world. Many teenagers carry on fantasy relationships because they simply never get the nerve to pick up the phone and ask for a date. The fear of being rejected—not the possibility of acceptance—becomes the controlling force.

When the avoidance of pain is the focus of your life, you cannot pursue pleasure because it and its implications are too frightening. Tragically life becomes a self-fulfilling prophecy. If you always look for problems, you will find them, but if you allow yourself to search for pleasure, you will eventually find it as well.

As you read this chapter, we hope you will keep memories of your own adolescence in mind, and ask yourself what really went on. Adolescence can be viewed as a time of great opportunity and change. What opportunities were there for your personal development? Who encouraged you? How did you feel about the changes in your body and the changes you saw taking place in your friends' bodies? Did excitement make you anxious or depressed? Did the inevitable blunders that everyone makes in adolescence cause you to withdraw or become overly controlled? Who helped you through? For many of us, there was no one.

The Value of Pleasure

Sexuality plays a key role in the forming of healthy self-esteem, particularly with adolescents, because it is sexuality that determines one's capacity for independence. A healthy person's moral system is centered around his attitudes toward pleasure and love, both familial and erotic. The pleasure we speak of here is spontaneous and natural, felt as an emotional and physical/visceral experience that is neither hedonistic nor forced. It leaves one feeling peaceful and with a sense that one's feet are firmly grounded.

The experience of pleasure is based on the principle of harmlessness; that is, that the pleasure one derives is not at the expense of anyone else's comfort or happiness. For instance, a healthy person doesn't feel good after a one-night stand when seduction and deception were involved, because the feeling of having used another person is distasteful. Most of us learn this through experience.

Erotic love plays a special part in the life of the adolescent, because it deepens the individual's sense of self and limitations, particularly with respect to pleasure. It is on this foundation that adult self-esteem is launched. Without a strong sense of positive personal identity, we are constantly faced with experiences and trials that erode our confidence that life is fulfilling and pleasurable. With self-confidence, we can take setbacks and failures as part of life, not measures of our self-worth.

Forming Gender Identity in Adolescence

To embrace life, we must embrace our own personal sexuality and gender identity, rather than a generic identity that is prescribed for us. When we embrace what is uniquely ours, especially our male and female identification, we can begin to explore what brings us pleasure and what makes us afraid.

A solid sense of gender identity allows men and women to take pleasure in those of the same sex without automatically feeling competitive and jealous. It allows them to take pleasure in those of the opposite sex without dependency and seduction. Sexual preference—homosexuality, bisexuality, or heterosexuality—is not a factor in determining one's capacity for pleasure and self-esteem. The important factor is an individual's ability to embrace life fully within his or her own body, while recognizing this unique body's preferences, strengths, and limitations.

The tragedy that many of us suffered in adolescence was that we didn't have the parental support, beginning in childhood, to allow us to take advantage of the potential potency of our emerging sexuality. There were opportunities provided by adolescence that we could not see, blinded by our fears and insecurities. Just what did we miss out on?

In adolescence, our emerging sexuality provides us with a new sense of personal pleasure that is ours alone, one that can be uniquely expressed in relationships and in caring for others, in creativity and self-expression, and in the pursuit of a sexual identity and fulfillment. It is in adolescence that the notion of self-responsibility begins to make sense, while it is sexual excitement and energy that provides the motivation to step out and explore the world. But the fear of pain and rejection, if too strong, provides all the negative motivation a teenager needs to withdraw from the sexual arena entirely. The misdirected energy is then put into the same pain-avoidant behaviors that the child's parents employ: overeating, drug abuse, alcoholism.

It is important here to add that it is not sexual activity that creates a sense of identity, but the ability to accept and tolerate the feelings that arise out of sexual excitement. Quite often sexual acting out leads many teenagers away from the very opportunities puberty offers. To be able to contain one's sexual excitement takes practice. Terry, for example, vividly remembers being flooded with emotion when he was invited to kiss the girl next door. His emotions were so intense that to kiss was simply too much to bear, and after accepting a kiss on the cheek, he fled. It was, however, a very positive experience for him and built up his self-esteem. There was enough acting out to get his excitement flowing, but not so much that he lost himself in endless rehearsals and fantasy, a compulsive and pain-avoidant habit that can follow many people into their adult relationships.

With puberty also comes a certain level of autonomy and awareness of self that gives the teenager a sense of his individual rights. In particular, this right is established by his being able to say "no." In very young children it is much the same, when "no" becomes the first expression of the individual who is no longer willing to be completely controlled and dependent. Although appropriate for a child, dependency is no longer appropriate for an adult. Adults may find some satisfaction in dependent relationships but it comes with a price of lowered self-esteem. We all have an inherent capacity to be creative and find fulfillment, but in order for this to unfold, one must gain some measure of autonomy. Until that time, we look outside ourselves for pleasure and reward. Teenagers often exhibit their struggle for independence by rebelling and refusing to cooperate with parental or societal norms. This can lead to some very self-destructive behavior, but we can all relate to the underlying impulse: to be independent and autonomous, no matter what the cost.

One man in our workshop, Jack, twenty-seven, spoke of this period in his life as characterized by his attempts to assert his autonomy, even though he still had a poorly developed sense of himself. Jack began working when he was twelve years old, and only later saw it as his attempt to be out of the house as much, and as early, as possible. "When I was home I was sleeping," he said, "and when I woke up, I left as quickly as I could." At seventeen, he entered military service, unaware that it was yet another attempt to escape from his family and gain a sense of control over his own life. It was all so natural to him at that point.

> **Jack:** There is a story in my family I never liked to hear. It was the story my mother would tell about how she had given birth to me. "I waited for your father to come home before I gave birth to you," she said. It used to make me angry when I heard the story, because my father was off getting drunk instead of being home for my birth. But then I had a revelation. I felt angry at my mother for the first time: how could she control me so much that she could decide when I would be born? I had always thought my feelings about the family had to do with my alcoholic father, but now I see that it was more than that. Of course Mom couldn't control when I'd be born, but if she could have, she would have. She tried to control my entire life and justified it by saying, "Mother knows best." I felt I had no choice but to resist my mother and be on my own.

Jack paid an early and very high price for his premature autonomy—he was on his own but he was also alone—driven by a desire for the control that had been taken from him so early on.

The Development of Autonomy

Another opportunity presented by adolescence is the ability to be introspective. With puberty comes the chance to see oneself as truly separate while still existing within the safe confines of the family. Healthy families support an introspective search for identity, whereas unhealthy families are threatened by it, and the child is often accused of being moody or difficult. Healthy parents help children to think for themselves and find their own point of view.

In a family where there is a fear of losing control, children who think for themselves are a threat. When Karen was sent to boarding school at fifteen, she picked up some ideas that were more liberal and radical than anything her parents entertained. When she came home advocating sex before marriage, for example, her parents responded by being angry at her. Karen was given the message that her thoughts and ideas were bad, and she was bad for having them. It was clear then that she better cut out any thinking that did not conform to her parents' values, or suffer the consequences.

Terry took little advantage of the opportunity to be introspective, because it made him too anxious. Instead of looking inward and maturing emotionally, he learned from his parents to look outside himself for the answers and the means to make himself feel good. He was impulsive and was always quick to change his behavior to correct any error he'd made instead of simply accepting the truth that he was fallible. Young people from healthy homes are more easily able to learn from their limitations and from their experiences, both good and bad. The rest of us are so afraid to be hurt that we hardly venture out into the world at all or, as in Terry's case, deny our mistakes and never learn from them.

The Joy of Self-expression

In adolescence there is also the opportunity to reconnect with a childhood experience of pleasure in physical movement. Parents often try to control their young child's movement, and children are corrected for their errant behavior. Some parents, believing that all movement must have a purpose, cannot see the joy their child derives from movement itself. The adolescent rediscovers the pleasure of movement that occurs with the awakening sexual energy and the changes of the physical body.

Healthy pleasure arises from movement as small as breathing or as large as running a marathon. Few adolescents understand this, and finding the balance between spontaneity and control is always difficult. In the best situation, a teenager is aware enough of his feelings to discover that harming others is distasteful before he's broken too many hearts. To learn to steer oneself away from these heartbreakers is no easy task either. Adolescence is a time when there is pressure to partake and join in, and to be able to pick and choose, to act responsibly and appropriately, and to learn to demonstrate healthy control of movement.

In adolescence the teenager can experiment and learn to handle energy well, to neither overcontrol and kill it nor be controlled and impulsively impelled by it. It is a thin line to walk, especially in an atmosphere in which one's peers are all struggling with the same difficulties. Handling the energy of sexual feelings can be the hardest of all.

Just about everyone has had a crush at some point, and Terry had several. When Terry told people about his crushes, he was ashamed and humiliated, but he had no sense of when and when not to say how he was feeling. Things would have been easier for him if he had just learned to keep his mouth shut about such things when it wasn't safe. Most teenagers learn to be "cool" about things like crushes, and are able to contain their excitement. Terry, however, was unable to handle the energy caused by his emotions. Karen, on the other hand, was so afraid of having her excitement show that as soon as she liked a boy, she poured all her energy into pretending that she didn't. She was simply too afraid of her excitement, and her fear of being controlled by the boy, to show anything real.

Finding Self-confidence

When we reach for something, when we attempt something that is out of our normal grasp, such as wanting that distant person who is so attractive to us, we need self-confidence. The experience can be pleasurable if we are not preoccupied with the outcome. However, for someone who is pain-avoidant, the natural frustration that occurs from trying to do something difficult is translated into negative self-assessments: "I am not attractive enough and that's why she won't go out with me," or "I failed this time. I'll never be able to do it."

Healthy people can manage and tolerate frustration, allowing them to persevere, despite negative thoughts that undermine others' efforts. The result is positive self-esteem, grounded in the understanding of one's limitations, and in the pleasure of having given one's best to meet a challenge.

The Lessons of Adolescence

When all the opportunities adolescence offers are supported within the family system, and the teenager is strong enough to take advantage of them, difficult life experiences can help in maturation and the development of a positive sense of self. As we mentioned earlier in this chapter, no matter how painful one's childhood was, adolescence can offer a way out of a pattern of pain avoidance. In an environment that supports this, a number of truths are learned and carried into adulthood.

• *Healthy pleasure is not* for *anything, and it is not a means to an end*. As we've discussed in previous chapters, healthy pleasure cannot be measured or compared between people, and it is always highly personal. It comes from the heart, and it is a worthy focus in life.

• *Healthy pleasure is not chaotic, it is safe.* It leaves one satisfied and not hungry for more immediately. Healthy pleasure leaves one in a peaceful and guilt-free state, because healthy pleasure is based on harmlessness.

• *The satisfaction from healthy pleasure leads to love and desire for the gratification of the other person with whom you have shared a pleasurable experience.* Our society believes love and commitment are prerequisites for sexual pleasure. Pleasure then becomes the reward rather than the focus. It is no wonder that so many adolescents ignore society's attempts to repress their sexuality; they see how easy it is to have sex without love.

Love and commitment have their place; they are the healthy products of pleasure and gratification. When one enjoys the pleasure of another's company, sexually or otherwise, the healthy response is to do it again. Pleasure then becomes the horse that pulls the cart of romantic love and commitment.

• *Healthy pleasure is a "being" state rather than a "doing" activity.* Many of us have lost our ability to feel pleasure naturally, and find ourselves drinking, smoking, or eating in order to feel good. This frantic pursuit of pleasure often has little to do with our innate capacity to enjoy ourselves. In the area of sexuality, many pain-avoidant people find the excitement of the chase invigorating and addictive, and too many of us are hooked on the pseudo-pleasure we derive from a conquest, rather than on the gratification that can be found in a loving relationship.

The Storm of Adolescence

Teenagers have all the resources to learn these truths if they have a healthy family foundation. Many ACOAs did not have the foundation a healthy home provides to see us through. Instead, we found ourselves using our coping mechanisms to steer us through adolescence, because the feelings and emotions associated with our emerging sexuality were too much for us to handle. Adolescence became a storm that blew us around, fueled by our fears and insecurities.

Perhaps the greatest fear of the ACOA is the fear of being injured. If as a child you were so often hurt, why would you expect things to be any different as you experimented with intimacy and independence? If the fear of hurt is so great, the teenager may withdraw completely and essentially have no adolescence at all.

We have met ACOAs who as teenagers hardly ever left their rooms at home for fear of what was out there. Nancy, twenty-five and a student, is one such person, a woman who had lost her ability to trust anyone.

> **Nancy:** I guess my strongest memory of that time is of my alcoholic parents constantly yelling at me and getting angry because I never had a date. "What's the matter with you?" they yelled. "The only time you ever act at all friendly is when you play with the cats and dogs." I was terrified of life at that point—it all seemed so out of my control. My parents had no idea how I really felt, and thought my silence was smugness and my loneliness was because I refused to try.

What did Nancy's parents want her to try? Maybe to open up to them and her peers and share what was going on. Nancy had trusted her parents when she was small, and had learned the hard way that they were the wrong people to trust, and she didn't want to risk being hurt again. Instead, she decided that she preferred to be alone.

Abby is another example of someone who learned in her adolescence how scary it can be to try to change things. She learned early on that her efforts to help her family caused too much pain and guilt. As a pretty, thirty-five-year-old recovering alcoholic, Abby had never had a steady relationship with a man. As she told her story, what emerged was a scared little girl, still waiting for the warmth and love that she never received from her parents.

> **Abby:** My mother was so hardened and bitter that she never let anyone in or out of her life. Despite that, I felt an overwhelming loyalty to her, and convinced myself that we were close, even though we weren't. I remember as a teenager doing something that no one else in my family ever did: I stood up to my father. Instead of responding to me and what I had said, he took it out on my mother. It was as though my feelings were not worthy of a response, and because of what I'd said, my mother ended up sobbing in the corner. Even though I knew what would happen when I stood up to my father, I couldn't stop after that. I was just too angry. But later I did decide not to stand up for anything in my life, because I just caused trouble when I did, and ended up hurting those I loved.

As Abby told her story, she cried. And as she cried and talked about it, she was learning to bear the devastating guilt she felt about her mother suffering for her confrontations with her father. Abby learned to act out her father's view of her, a nonperson who caused pain to innocent people. She did her best as an adult to keep her anger a secret and never rock the boat, but gradually in her therapy she was able to embrace the feisty adolescent within her who was finally ready to face the world and make the changes she wanted, and find pleasure in a relationship. She was able to learn that there weren't always disastrous consequences when she asserted herself.

Ed, a housing contractor, told us how his father had forced him to avoid anything painful in his life. His father had a frightening temper, and wanted Ed to be a "big man" like himself, and he would taunt and tease his son mercilessly. If Ed responded to his father's aggression as a child would, his father would continue the attack with even greater cruelty. Ed remembers that even in his adolescence he would chant to himself at those times, "Don't cry, don't cry, don't choke, don't choke, don't show it, don't show it. Cry and you're going to get it."

Remarkably the technique worked for Ed as a child as a way of containing his feelings, but tragically, as an adult, he was still telling himself not to feel, not to risk, not to show anything. His therapist responded to Ed by telling him that he was crying then, even if there were no tears. He did not know how to cry because all the force of his adolescent energy was set against ever having to feel humiliated again. It had worked to protect Ed for all those years, but it also prevented him from being able to share himself with others, and that was a terrible price to pay.

Another pain-avoidant mechanism that may occur in adolescence if the family is unhealthy is the use of sexuality as a means to feel valued. Both boys and girls spend a lot of time and energy making sure they are attractive to their peers. By being sexually attractive, they can feel that they are loved and appreciated. By touching and being touched, and by simply being involved with another, they can relieve some of the tension and unhappiness they feel at home.

Emily's homelife was a depressing scene of empty beer cans littered by her father and brother. She found a way to use her own sexual involvement as an escape.

Emily: From the age of fourteen on, I found comfort and closeness in the arms of a steady stream of older boyfriends. In return for sexual favors I would give, I demanded that they treat me like a princess. I enjoyed the sex, and think that actually some of those relationships were loving for a while. But it always happened that a boyfriend would disappoint me, or I would make him angry, and we'd break up. I felt alive during this time, though, very wanted, very feminine. At home, my father and brother would make nasty comments about my sex life, and my mother never said a word, although I know she disapproved.

Somewhere along the way, repeated disappointments in relationships and her family's derision and scorn of her brought an end to Emily's dream of finding a satisfying, permanent, and intimate relationship. She began to believe that her search for love had failed, and one day she simply decided to change.

When we met Emily, she was twenty-seven and out of work, and she had just emerged from six years of self-enforced celibacy. She was lonely, scared of men, and very confused about her sexuality. She was torn between her fear of sexual involvement and her longing for an intimate relationship. Her coping persona of hopelessness and depression told her things would never work out and there was no sense in even trying. Certainly, deciding never to touch or be touched again was an unhealthy conclusion for Emily to have drawn from her adolescent experiences. We tried to help her resolve her identity as a woman and work though the pain she had always steered away from.

We can look at Emily's situation and wonder what would have happened if she had been just moderately sexually active and had devoted herself to a more balanced life: school, friends, sports. Would she have had such a dramatic switch later in her sexual life? Emily's family needed help, but since that was an impossibility, she took advantage of her only available resource—her sexuality.

Eddie, our sexually compulsive client described in Chapter 3, had an opposite experience from Emily's. He spent his teen years isolated from his peers for the most part, and due to a childhood head injury, was forbidden to participate in sports. His isolation postponed his sexual awakening for as long as possible. When he eventually did become sexually active, it was to such an extent that he had little sense of his self-worth unless he was with a woman. Sexuality became for him an access point to a very immature but an extremely important part of his identity, a part that asked, "Do I exist?" rather than a healthier, more adult "How can I love?"

When there is an unhealthy family environment, the teenager is often forced to rely on self-aggrandizement to lead him through the storm of adolescence. When your self-esteem is fragile, it is easy to make yourself feel better, and bigger, by being cruel and bullying to others, pumping yourself up at someone else's expense. The adolescent who has seen this at home will learn to control and dominate rather than love and cooperate. At Terry's all-boy school, this was called hazing.

> **Terry:** I remember when I was in the seventh grade, I stood up to the school bully in the locker room, the only person who had ever stood up to him. Even though I was pushed hard, no fists were thrown, and I came away with a sense of pride. I had faced the giant and survived. Years later, I ran into the bully's sister, and as we talked, we discovered that we both had alcoholic fathers.

Using Power as a Way of Avoiding Pain

As ACOAs we experienced little sense of our own power or control at home, so our drive for dominance over our peers was strong. Without a strong foundation of love that accepts you as you are, muscle power for boys and physical beauty for girls become pain-avoidant weapons that demand attention, rather than part of your gender identity that spurs you on to the pursuit of pleasure.

Often a boy's self-esteem is built on how successful he is with girls. On the other hand, a girl's self-esteem is often related to how attractive she can be to a boy without actually giving in to her sexual desires. Boys and girls in this way are not taught to take pleasure from each other, but rather to manipulate the opposite sex. Ideally, healthy sexuality comes from the heart and does not involve competition and self-aggrandizement. Boys and girls may initially see each other as potential sources of pleasure and excitement, but they learn quickly that to get sexually involved is to risk attack and humiliation from parents and peers. They learn to deal with each other with strongly conflicted emotions.

If a teenager does not witness a healthy sexual relationship between his parents, he will often equate and/or confuse sex with caretaking and nurturing, or see it as a power game. Using sex to feel valued is not a loving exchange. If the teenager sees dissatisfaction between his parents, he will form an idea of what a relationship is about based on the behavior he witnesses. Without the positive guidelines implicit in a healthy sexual relationship, the teenager has little hope of becoming both sexual and loving. Fulfilled parents model fulfillment to their children, and teach appropriate pleasure-seeking.

Adolescence is a time of exploration and experimentation, a time of learning through trial and error, and some adolescents think they are grown-up when, in fact, they have very little adult experience. Take, for example, Andy, an attractive man who ran his own architecture and construction business. When we met him, he had been divorced twice from women who tired of his frenetic energy. He wasn't fun to be with, and his relationships were always in conflict. He was unable to relax and take pleasure in his work or relationships, but above all, he was unable to face the anger and grief he had been carrying around inside since he was a little boy.

> **Andy:** I grew up in a small town, the youngest of three children. My father was the fire chief and was very popular, and was an enthusiastic outdoorsman. We shared an interest in "man things"—fishing, hunting, sports—but we never talked about anything personal or emotional. We never discussed the fact that my mother was a barely functioning alcoholic and we didn't need to because when she was drunk my sisters filled in for her and my father just stayed busy. I was very attentive to my mother and all her needs, and was constantly frustrated by the fact that I couldn't get her to stop drinking. I think I was pretty anxious and hyperactive, but no one could tell because I let a lot of

it out in sports, or at school, or with my father hunting, fishing, or being with the dogs. Things went well for me—that is, until I fell in love with a woman. I soon realized that I had no idea how to be with a woman, as I'd never seen my father be with my mother.

In spite of this, women were attracted to Andy and his energy, but he was unable to be really attentive to them and his own needs at the same time. He felt that if he slowed down and felt his anger, especially at his father for leaving him to care for his mother, he would be faced with too much feeling. He was truly afraid of going crazy with rage. Instead, he held on and squeezed the life out of his relationships by being overprotective and unreasonably jealous. Eventually his second wife left him, and at this point, he sought help.

Learning From Our Parents

A child learns from his parents' behavior, and in Andy's case, he learned that whenever his mother's needs became apparent, his father would disappear. As long as Andy could remember, he'd never sensed any sexual feeling between his parents. He modeled their behavior, and grew up thinking that relationships are based on dependency rather than mutual pleasure. Andy had seen both ends of the spectrum—his giving in to his mother's needs, and seeing his father ignore them. He didn't know that there was a middle ground where he could satisfy a woman's needs without totally sacrificing his own.

In Andy's case, there was no role modeling from his parents about what his sexual behavior should be. Some parents, on the other hand, become obsessed with their child's sexuality, and can threaten the emergence of healthy sexual feeling.

Karen: When I was a teenager, my mother became overly involved in my sexual life. She always thought that I was out with a boy even if I wasn't, and inevitably accused me of having "gone too far" with him. My mother was convinced that I was having intercourse at least three years before I actually did. She made me feel guilty and confused. The fact was that because my mother was so unresolved about her own sexual feelings, she projected her fears and anxieties onto me. By accusing me of excessive sexual activity, she may have thought she was providing limits for me. Instead, she was shaming and wounding me deeply.

For Karen, it eventually got to the point where there were all sorts of things she couldn't, or wouldn't, talk about with her family. Certain topics were off limits because they were simply too volatile and painful for the family to address. As she got older, conversation with the family was like walking across a mine field. At any time there could be an explosion. For example, if Karen was hurt or sad, her father couldn't stand it, probably because it reminded him of his own pain and unresolved feelings, and he reacted with anger instead of comfort and understanding. It became so difficult that Karen could never say what or how she felt, could never disagree with her parents because they would get so angry, as if to assert herself would threaten the very fragile family system. Karen was not encouraged to think for herself, and was sent the message that unless she complied with her parents, she would be rejected. It seemed to Karen that all she ever heard was criticism and that her parents didn't have the slightest idea who she was.

How could Karen trust her parents when this was the scene of her homelife? How was she to feel about being a woman when her mother accused her of being a "slut"? So often, the sense of shame a teenager feels is enough to divert him from acknowledging his sexual feelings. Or it may be that the teenager responds by fulfilling the parents' fantasies and accusations, thinking, "If they think I'm bad and loose, why shouldn't I just be like that anyway?"

In Terry's family, there was an additional, and confusing, dynamic. His father was severely homophobic and expressed it whenever he was on the receiving end of warm feelings from his sons. He probably thought he was sending his sons a helpful message, but he sent them a mixed one: I want your love, but I'll humiliate and shame you for it. It was a destructive sexualizing of the playful and honest affection of his children.

With or without the guidance that healthy parental behavior provides, the teenager must still venture into adolescence with everyone else. There is a chronological growth, even though emotionally there may be no forward movement. The intensity of sexual feelings in adolescence, combined with feelings of vulnerability that intimacy entails, can expose the shaky foundation of the teenager from the unhealthy home for all to see. What emerges is the needy child who is trying to get from others what he did not receive from his parents. Initially this needy child might find what he is looking for, since there are, of course, other people looking for the same thing.

> **Terry:** My memories of this period are dominated by the image of myself as not being cool enough with girls. I developed ways to behave, such as saying "you know" and "sort of" to provide my free-floating anxiety with a structure. In my mind, my first heartbreak with a girl proved to me what my needy child had always feared, that my mother was the only person in the world who didn't want to hurt me, and that everyone else was just out for themselves. In fact, my mother had hurt me, but the child inside me had safely buried those memories.

Terry had some confused ideas of what relationships were all about, but like most adolescents, he thought he knew exactly what he was doing. As an adolescent he began to draw away from the stifling closeness of his mother. Unfortunately he found that the more aloof and cold a girl was, the more attractive she was to him. In pulling away from his mother, he also pulled away from, and devalued, the positive warmth of their relationship. Some of his adolescent relationships had been warm to an extent, but the warmer the girl was toward Terry, the more he withdrew and the less he valued the relationship. Something inside him longed for the sexual aliveness that closeness brings, but he simply could not settle down and enjoy it.

It was only much later in therapy that Terry realized that he had mistaken his mother's neediness as warmth, her dependency on him as closeness. The good feelings associated with his mother were additionally conflicted, because when he tried to make her happy, he also became anxious about his father's reactions and accusations of childishness and possible homosexuality. His father's alcoholism had slowly destroyed what Terry was willing to value in his relationship with his father. As a result, he was always on guard to never again be humiliated because of love for either a man or a woman. The needy child inside was determined to protect himself.

Eleanor's story is another example of the needy child that emerges in adolescence. In her case, the needy child coped through compliance. Eleanor loved her parents, but wanted independence that could only come about through rebellion in this controlled and secretive family. This presented a dilemma for her. Either she could fulfill her parents' expectations for her, thus satisfying her wounded child, or she could go against them, establishing an independent adult identity. Rebellion meant making things even worse at home, as well as risking punishment and humiliation. Given the conflict between the needy child and her need for autonomy, Emily chose to withdraw.

> **Eleanor:** I was the youngest of three children. Our family was wealthy and everyone thought we were happy. To the outside, my father appeared bright, successful, and entertaining. But the father we knew at home was completely different. At home he was

moody, dissatisfied with my mother, and quick to criticize. He was an alcoholic who sometimes passed out drunk on the living room floor. I never confronted my parents and just did as I was told. All my friends liked my parents and wanted to spend time at my house, but I never let anyone stay late, and I never let anyone spend the night. After 6:00, anything could happen.

When she entered therapy, Eleanor did not present her painful childhood as a problem. To her, it was all in the past, and her relationship with her parents was smooth and they were now supportive of her career as a graphic artist. Her problem, as she saw it, was that while she could easily attract men and could become initially intimate with them, the more she became excited, the more she felt her identity disappearing. She felt like putty in a man's hands, and it wouldn't be long before the man would lose interest in her. Her way of coping with excitement was to become compliant and lose herself. It was as though she had no idea of her own desires and wishes, just as when she'd been a child interacting with her parents. She found herself, again and again, just wanting to be close and to do as she was told.

It is at times of sexual excitement that all of a person's pain-avoidant mechanisms are set in motion. Eleanor's automatic impulse was to disappear, to be a passive participant in her life. When she attempted to correct her behavior, her self-criticism was so severe she destroyed her own self-esteem. In therapy, we were able to look at her experience in terms of her inability to tolerate excitement. This meant looking back at her childhood and adolescence when the avoidance of pain—in her case this was through compliance—was the only reasonable reaction to what was going on. When she thought back to painful incidents and explored her feelings about them, she learned to tolerate anger and sadness that came up in therapy without letting herself disappear. Her self-esteem gradually increased as she opened up to her past, and her ability to function as a sexually mature woman with her next boyfriend was the tangible reward for embracing the pain of her childhood.

Feeling Too Good

If a teenager has the foundation that a healthy home provides, he can face the pain of sexual rejection with the faith that ultimately there will be acceptance and love, because it had always been there through childhood. If an adolescent does not have a healthy foundation and has learned instead to deny and react with pain-avoidant mechanisms, the possibility of rejection becomes too great a risk to take for the chance of future pleasure. In these circumstances, it is difficult to sustain a healthy pursuit of sexual fulfillment.

In a men's group that formed during one of our workshops, Stuart, thirty-two, discovered that he was one of those people who had given up on pleasure.

> **Stuart:** At first I was reluctant to even join the men's group. I thought it would be boring and superficial, but I came out of it with a new appreciation for my masculinity and a sense of pleasure in being powerful. I realized that even if I try to hide my power, other people can sense it in me. What I learned to acknowledge is that my power isn't going to kill anyone, and that there is love in power and love in men. For the first time in my life I feel supported enough to acknowledge and enjoy my manhood.

Stuart's highly aggressive and physically abusive father set an example to Stuart of how to look and act like a man. Horrified by his father's cruelty, Stuart developed a deep sense of guilt and anxiety about his masculinity, fearing that being manly constituted a danger to women. Although for years he had tried to suppress it, he discovered in the men's group that his sense of himself as a man was, in fact, particularly important to him. The real issue in his recovery turned out to be exposing himself to the anxiety and guilt surrounding pleasure and feeling good. At the workshops, he tried to devalue his positive feelings and became haunted by thoughts that he was going crazy, as he was enjoying himself so much. He was afraid he would "crash" when he got home and began to pull away from the people he'd come to know and like, telling himself that they didn't really understand or care about him.

Teresa shot up her hand when Stuart was finished talking. She said: "I've been looking around and seeing people I care for, and all I could feel was that I wanted to get away. Somehow, I don't feel safe here. Since I'm feeling good, I'm waiting for the hurt to come. I keep telling myself to be quiet and private so I won't get hurt." Teresa was willing to talk herself out of feeling pleasure, rather than face the possibility of rejection that participating and opening up might involve.

What can people like Stuart and Teresa do when feeling good feels dangerous, when feeling pleasure causes anxiety and guilt? They must learn to know the depths of their confusion. Teenagers are often so afraid of admitting their confusion that they don't know how to ask for help. Teresa didn't suddenly decide to be quiet when she was scared. This was what she had been doing all her life; it was her coping mechanism of withdrawal in the face of both pleasure and pain.

What happens is that the fear of a painful experience overrides the pursuit of an experience that could be pleasurable and positive. Learning is by trial and error, and many children who grew up in alcoholic or abusive homes were too scared of the errors they might make. Stuart and Teresa were simply afraid to explore and experience. They were unable to develop enough self-confidence and reliance to tolerate their feelings and to keep them going forward in spite of their mistakes.

Pseudo-pleasure is a substitute for the natural pleasure of loving another person; it is the action without the heart. When one stops pursuing real pleasure, one turns toward the pursuit of pseudo-pleasure instead. Loving, by nature, requires risks and sets one up to be vulnerable to rejection and disappointment. Pseudo-pleasure requires no such risks. It only requires a certain effort, but does not leave the individual so exposed or vulnerable if it fails. Pseudo-pleasure allows the individual to organize his life in a way that protects him from pain. The goal then is to avoid being hurt, not to attain pleasure through love and intimacy.

Pseudo-pleasure in intimate relationships is derived from controlling oneself and others, and it is the pleasure of power, not love. In this situation, one's will takes precedence over the desires of the heart, resulting in the use of sex and seduction for achievement rather than physical or emotional gratification.

In pseudo-pleasure, a person can derive a certain pleasure from being in charge and from feeling other people's dependency and respect, or this power play can be explicitly sexualized. Pseudo-pleasure is learned in childhood from parents. Healthy parents do not use their sexuality or physical power to manipulate their children, but this is virtually impossible for those parents whose own intimate sexual life is not vital and fulfilling. These parents turn to their children to give them the pseudo-pleasurable feelings of power and "special" intimacy.

As we've mentioned before, people in the field of psychology often call this kind of behavior "covert incest," because the seduction is seldom actively sexual or acted out. Rarely do the victims of covert incest have memories of actual physical seduction by their parents. But all of us who grew up in alcoholic or abusive homes, as part of our recovery, need to explore the ways in which sexual boundaries were set by our parents, and why we may at times feel uncomfortable when we are in close or intimate contact with them.

It is almost inevitable that there will be some instance of covert incest or power play when the parent is drunk or unhappy much of the time he spends with the child. Intoxication dissolves one's awareness of boundaries and appropriate behavior. Even after a few drinks, the parent can respond to an excited child in ways that are inappropriate and inconsistent to the roles of parent and child. Chris's relationship with her father is an example.

> **Chris:** My father and I adored each other and were very close. When my mother had another child, I had to take on a lot of her duties, and it seemed that my relationship with my father grew closer and more important to me. He was an alcoholic, and I saw his drinking get heavier and heavier. My parents' marriage wasn't good—there was always a lot of blaming and fighting going on.
>
> My father always made me feel that I was very important to him and very special. The older I got, the more I saw that I could make the difference between his being happy and depressed simply by the way I acted with him, and the reverse was true. I often felt hurt and betrayed by him when I begged him to stop drinking and he wouldn't. I was angry when he didn't show up to watch me play sports, and I actually quit dancing because I was so upset that he didn't come to watch me compete in a statewide competition.
>
> When my parents divorced, it was really difficult for me, and I felt vulnerable and very sensitive when my mother accused me of being selfish and cold. My father died when I turned twenty, and I was devastated and without direction. After his death, I just couldn't be with a man. Their sexual desires and demands disgusted me.

Chris learned through her relationship with her father to confuse love with power and manipulation. Her relationship with her father was stressed further as Chris grew up to be an extremely attractive young woman and her mother became overtly jealous, both of her looks and of her relationship with her father. Unaware at first of what was happening, Chris became a sexual object to her parents, appreciated and resented at the same time. As she grew older and some of her natural innocence faded, she felt tremendously guilty about her family situation.

In the end, Chris's father had commanded such a high position in her life that no man could ever take his place. They all seemed like needy little boys to her. Through extensive therapy, Chris realized that her sexual feelings were devoted to the father image. It was an impossible fantasy that she had maintained. Once a man fell in love with her she lost interest, because her sexual excitement was still tied up with the unavailable fantasy man, and not with the real one. The pseudo-pleasure she had derived through sexual manipulation and control over her father was no longer enough for her. In order to heal, Chris had to come to terms with her relationship with her father.

> **Chris:** I was thinking about all the pain I had with my father and how much I really do love him, but it is really kidding love. I'm confused between real love and kidding love. The guys I go out with take the rap for the criticism that I was never able to give my father—to be a father rather than a flirter—and I know it's not fair to them. I want to love. I find men both scary and fascinating, just how I felt about my father. It's time to stop.

Terry's relationship with his mother was similar.

> **Terry:** When I was a kid, my mother and I adored each other, and without actually saying it, I think we promised each other that we would do everything we could to make life better for the other, and we would always be supportive of what the other did. We would always fill each other's needs. Now I see that her needs, not mine, were being fulfilled by the promise.

Without being aware of it at the time, this promise created in Terry a grandiose self-image that was constantly being tested and eroded through his experiences in adolescence. When things got bad, though, he simply had to go back to his mother for her seemingly unconditional love and reassurance. Eventually Terry was forced to see that he was involved in the pseudo-pleasure of seduction for self-aggrandizement, and though he thought he loved, he really didn't know how to. He had lost his sense of identity in his overinvolvement with meeting his mother's needs. He had unconsciously confused meeting her needs with adult intimacy and sexual affection. It took the breakup of his first marriage for him to realize that he could not meet his wife's needs no matter what he did, and to realize that this pseudo-pleasure was not really satisfying. Like Chris, Terry always returned to the idealized image of his mother, because he believed that she could fulfill all that she had promised. Victims of covert incest still struggle to accept the unreality of such a promise.

When the Heart and Sexual Feelings Diverge

As adolescents Terry and Chris did not have experiences of healthy sexuality because they were simply too busy coping with the difficult events of their lives. They experienced excitement like any teenager, but the difference is in what they did with their excitement.

The key to healthy sexuality is that one's heart and loving feelings are aligned with the sexual interest. In other words, the healthy individual does not have to force real love toward the object of physical affection—it flows naturally as a product of the pleasure of their interaction. If you have learned to avoid pain, the heart is defended and not able to experience love, and the natural flow is blocked. The focus then is on getting love and affection rather than on the pleasure of loving in and of itself.

Adolescents may learn to separate their sexual feelings from their heart feelings. One example of this is Susanna, the youngest child of four in a highly patriarchal family. When she was five, she was selected by her father as the "sexy one" among the children. She quickly matched the sexual sophistication of her older sisters and pursued her brothers' friends at an early age. As is common among many teenagers, Susanna and her friends told each other that it was stupid to wait for "true love" to have a sexual experience. Like many parents who try to discourage their children from this kind of behavior, Susanna's parents constantly chastised her for her sexual behavior. With the support of her friends, she simply ignored them.

In the long run, Susanna was probably better off to get out there and get hurt rather than cling to a romantic notion of "true love," because this notion is really rooted in trying to satisfy unmet childhood needs. To the extent that we as adults still have our hearts hitched to this romantic ideal, we are unconsciously marrying our opposite-sex parent so he or she can fulfill our childlike needs. It is as if two people say to each other, "You take care of my needs and I'll take care of yours." It is an intimacy based on dependency rather than pleasure and satisfaction, and it involves the heart and not the genitals. Susanna's problem went the other way.

> **Susanna:** My mother was supportive in many ways, but when I think about it, I see that she didn't protect me from my father's very seductive behavior toward me. When I entered therapy I was a junior in college. I had had a good time as a teenager and now in college my work suffered because I couldn't ever pass up the opportunity to have a good time so I could stay home and study. It was obvious to me that my heart wasn't really in anything I did, and I was lonely. Only sex seemed to make me feel better.

Toward the end of her therapy, Susanna went to visit her brother in another city and found herself very attracted to one of his friends, who she went home with for the night. As she recounted this experience she said, "Everything was going along nicely and then I said the dumbest thing right after we'd made love: 'I feel like I'm in love with you.'" It was one of those moments when the client is mortified but the therapist is delighted. Her therapist explained that a healthy thing had occurred: Susanna had had a healthy sexual response. He suggested, with a smile, that she better get used to her heart and her genitals functioning as one. It was as though a light went on for Susanna then, and she discovered that her ability to love was tied up with her ability to be sexual. Until that point, the promiscuity of Susanna's past had provided her with a weapon to ward off the possible pain of rejection.

Promiscuous men (and sometimes, though rarely, women) that we meet in our workshops have to hear an equally hard message about their immaturity: that they avoid intimacy. These are not men who are out to break hearts, but they are heartbreakers. Many of them complain about not being able to find the "right woman." Often they blame the failed relationship on their partner's neediness, rarely acknowledging their own needs. What seems to be helpful for these men is the realization on their part that they are a "danger to women," because they set up an impossible situation. Once a woman becomes sexually available to them, her intimate self-disclosure is perceived as critical, demanding, or needy, and the men are forced to drop these women for something "better." As they begin to face the fact of their inability to love, they begin to acknowledge their own neediness, and there is hope for change, although it can often be a humiliating and painful experience.

Like Susanna, these men are deeply disillusioned with intimacy whether they know it or not. To get close is to get clobbered. As one heartbreaker in the workshop put it after we had talked about taking responsibility for our adult lives: "I'm angry. I feel like I'm sabotaging my own recovery, because I'm still looking outside myself for someone to give to me freely without my having to manipulate them. That's not healthy either. I feel a resistance to parent myself. I feel as though I've always had to do that."

Our response was to tell him that taking responsibility for

yourself is not "re-parenting" ourselves. It is believing ourselves when we hear the cry of disappointment in our hearts.

The Disappointment of Fantasy

The truth of our adolescence was that, as much as we wished, no prince or princess was going to come and sweep us away. We maintained a fantasy that things would get better to help us cope with our daily disappointments. When you combine these fantasies with unrealistic expectations about the perfect mate, you begin to understand why it is so difficult for an ACOA to have a successful relationship.

The experience is different for men and women because of the double standard that persists in our culture. Boys want recognition for their power but are terrified of being humiliated. Many boys are frightened by female sexuality and are afraid of being controlled by it. Adolescent girls are encouraged to appear sexually vital and attractive but are shamed and humiliated for taking pleasure in themselves. They are cautioned against appearing needy or openly warm toward boys they are attracted to. Both are terrified of rejection. With all these concerns, it is hard to see how anyone manages to get close to another person. Often the sexual urge is so strong that people get involved despite all the hurdles, but they often get involved with the wrong person, as Celeste did.

Celeste, an advertising executive, grew up in a family that talked about sex openly. She began masturbating when she was six, and several years later was sexually assaulted by her brother. Although she had no memory of her father's sexuality directed at her as a child, his alcoholism, her early masturbation, and his later sexual behavior toward her suggest otherwise. Although she was quite pretty and had an active fantasy life, she did not date until quite late.

Celeste: My mother used to caution us about sex, but it was never really very direct or personal. She would

tell us that sex is wonderful but dangerous so we
should be careful. We would roll our eyes at each
other when she talked like that. I already knew sex was
dangerous because of the experience with my brother,
but I didn't know if it was wonderful or not yet.

Celeste later fell in love with a man she found intellec-
tually stimulating and very caring. She chose a man who was
uncomfortable with his sexuality, though, and he cultivated
her dependency on him so as not to expose his own insecurities. It was only after they had married that the mutual lack of
sexual feeling was addressed. Closeness and sexual feeling just
did not go together.

Since her divorce, Celeste had relationships that were
either full of passion or full of caring, but never both at the
same time. She said: "I am freer sexually with men who are
unavailable, and I end up feeling ashamed, like my sexuality
is a dirty secret." When she allowed a man to get close to her,
she only felt needy and inhibited. Back and forth it went, from
one to the other, and she didn't know how to change.

For Jamie, the fear and humiliation associated with sex
began when he was expected to know things he knew nothing
about.

Jamie: My parents were devout Catholics and certainly
weren't the people to go to, to learn about sex. I asked
our parish priest, and he made sex sound like a
horrible, degrading experience. I got the message from
him that if I wanted to avoid being humiliated, I
shouldn't touch a woman until we were married. I had
a girlfriend who told me that she loved drive-ins, so I
took her to one. I didn't touch her—I had completely
missed the point—and she dumped me. Another
girlfriend was a cheerleader who used to kiss me
whenever I did something good on the field, and it
was thrilling, but I never knew what to do next.
Looking back, I think she would have married me—if
I'd only gotten around to asking her for a date.

Perhaps Jamie's story is extreme. His parents were alcoholics and he was ashamed of them. They embarrassed him
often, but to the outside, they looked like a nice stable family.
By the time Jamie was a senior, he was so obsessed with sex
that he felt controlled by it. He had no mentor in his life to
help him understand what was going on.

Jamie: I just wanted to touch a girl, just gently maul
her a few times. Just about any girl would do so long
as she wasn't in my school, but I didn't know any well
enough to ask. I thought you would have to get
married first before you could touch, and I had the
impression that it would offend them personally if I
tried anything. I was afraid that I would be caught
staring at a girl's chest, and sometimes I was so
transfixed it would have been easy to catch me.
Getting close was dangerous—she might run off,
screaming down the hall that I had looked at her
bosom. Certainly seeing a naked girl and touching was
too much to ask for. Playing with yourself meant you
didn't have the guts to play with girls. I was always
aware of my desire but never lost control. I was a
nervous wreck.

We might easily question whether or not Jamie had lost
control. Having no choice but to bury himself inside, Jamie
came to hate women for the effect they had on him. The
tragedy for Jamie and others like him is that they become so
paralyzed by the contradictory feelings of excitement and
frustration, they end up in a relationship with someone they
have little sexual feeling for and remain depressed for years to
come. The additional tragedy is when their children begin the
same cycle again because no one breaks the connection
between excitement, guilt, and depression.

Without the support of family, friends, and mentors, pain
avoidance is really the only choice in reaction to the surge of
feelings in adolescence. To face the pain inherent in growing

up, and to feel as though there is no one to talk to, are simply too much to bear alone without support.

Without focused attention from a role model, the teenager is left with feelings of guilt for failed actions, and there is no one there to say, "Sorry it didn't work out , but these things happen. Better luck next time." Without support and attention, the teenager feels shame for what he is or is not. At the core is the problem of adolescent sexuality and a society that has yet to figure out a good way to deal with it. Ultimately it must be the family that deals with it, and if there is no caring and support, but only pain, it cannot happen.

The dreams of the adolescent are too often shattered and damaged in the environment of the unhealthy home. As we'll see in the following chapter, the coping personas are standing ready to take hold when the flame of teenage courage burns out in its vain attempts to find pleasure. The coping personas provide the young adult with a way out of the predicament of having so many feelings to deal with, while still needing to get on with life. The coping personas, in effect, provide a way of life.

CHAPTER 6

Reaching the Turning Point: Adult Burnout

Tracy: When I first met Karen and Terry, I was scared by all the feelings that were coming up, because I'd held them in for so long. I had a job I found tedious, and although I dated a lot, I never let anyone get very close to me. I knew I needed help but I was too afraid to rock the boat. I wasn't getting along with my sisters, my father was badgering me about my lack of ambition, men wanted more from me in terms of commitment, and I was consumed with guilt about not being able to help or understand my mother, who died of alcoholism. I was a pretty face to the outside world, and no one, not even myself, could understand why I couldn't make things work.

As in thirty-year-old Tracy's case, there comes a time in the lives of many ACOAs when the old behavior patterns just don't work anymore. Things begin to fall apart—relationships, jobs, families—and the usual coping mechanisms become less and less effective in handling difficult situations and stress. Eventually the individual becomes burned out from trying so hard and reaches a breaking point where things become too much to handle. While painful and disruptive, the breaking point can also be an opportunity for remarkable and significant change. When life is at its lowest, new possibilities exist to make the switch from a life of pain avoidance to one geared toward the pursuit of pleasure.

A Life of Struggle May Be All We Know

As we discussed in Chapter 4, each of us has developed a unique way of responding to life's events so that we feel as little pain as possible and suffer the least amount of stress and anxiety. As adults we continue to hold on to these behavioral patterns and characteristic stances—our coping persona—that have become our way of coping with life. Tragically our coping persona has committed us to a life of disappointment, depression, and isolation, because, when we hide behind it, we become removed from our true inner selves and from real contact with other people. Many of us have spent all of our energy trying to cope with and control our lives, and even today, we may not realize how hard this has been to do. We've spent years of effort trying to cover up and deny anything that is painful. It may be difficult for us to admit that we are tired and that things seem to get a little harder each day but change is only possible when we finally own up to the fact that our lives are not working.

What does burnout look like? As we become increasingly burned-out, we begin to sense that our lives are a struggle each day and that things are not working out. We tire easily and push away people who try to help, telling them that they don't really understand. Eventually, we reach the breaking point because we can no longer fight so hard. The breaking point is a time of surrender, a time when one's will collapses under the increasing weight of anxiety, stress, and pain. The burned-out person must admit at this point that there are parts of life that simply are not controllable. Sometimes this realization is brought on by a shock or a painful experience: the death of a loved one, the end of a relationship, the loss of a job, the onset of serious illness. It is a painful time of accepting the ways and mysteries of life.

The breaking point can lead one to make the switch from the avoidance of pain to the pursuit of pleasure, because it is at this time that the pain is no longer avoided but is finally accepted. The individual no longer has to hide his pain and appear invincible, but he can finally say, "I am injured. I need help and I can't handle this one all alone."

There are times when this breaking point leads to an emotional breakdown in the clinical sense. Too often, there is an insufficient support system around the individual, and he must depend on traditional mental health systems to help him through. Rarely, though, is the approach of mental health professionals oriented toward helping the individual make the switch from pain avoidance to the pursuit of pleasure as we have described it. To support the switch, the therapist must focus on what pain the individual can bear, rather than, for example, immediately offering medication so that he feels no pain at all. The therapist must help the client understand the failures of his coping patterns (rather than reconstructing them to work again). Of course rest and medication can be helpful in some circumstances, but dependency on drugs or therapy to help us simply cope day to day is not the solution.

In an ideal situation, breakdown leads us to find the support of those who have been through the same experience. It is the initial experience of fellowship with other injured people that is often the first taste of real pleasure after a burnout and breakdown period. We feel we are no longer alone with our pain, and we experience a pleasure that healthy children get to experience in the dependent relationship between parent and child. As children in dysfunctional families, we were forced to rise above that relationship, because it was so confusing, conflicted, and full of pain. As adults, when we reveal our pain to those like us, the pleasure is an experience of collective strength and recovery, rather than a re-creation of the negative dependency we personally experienced in our own families. The empathetic contact with others is immediately energizing, and it is this resource that the "Anonymous" traditions have tapped to benefit so many.

Identifying Burnout

How does burnout manifest itself in our lives, and how can we recognize it? Let's look at the example of a workaholic who does not yet recognize that he is burned-out. Moving toward burnout, he has buried himself in his career, a place where his coping persona can really shine. He may have bought and fulfilled the American dream and found that he is consumed by his work, when he actually derives little pleasure or satisfaction from it. Burying himself in his work takes up all his free time, and enables him to avoid confronting his feelings and those few people who are close to him. Work becomes the place where he can demonstrate his power and show people that he has everything under control. But the control he exhibits in work often matches the amount of denial and lack of control that actually exist in his personal life. His career success gives him (pseudo) pleasure derived from a false sense of self-worth, and while he may be tired of working so hard, the pseudo-pleasure is the reward for such dedication and sacrifice, and keeps him on track. His job began as an exciting challenge but it has turned into an addiction.

Control may be effective on the job, but it rarely works well in relationships. As we find ourselves increasingly burned-out, our relationships are beginning to suffer. Since the message we grew up with was "to get close is to get clobbered," many adults now live in fear of being hurt by the ones they love. Marriages that were "made in heaven" are falling apart as old resentments pile up and communication breaks down. We avoid spending time with our mates, and when we do, our interactions are predictable and repetitive. We may feel isolated in our own home and do our best to steer away from any possible conflict, resentment, and guilt. Some of us steer away from all intimate interaction.

Daniel, a salesman in his thirties, took up running in order to hide from himself and everyone else the fact that he was burning out and that his life was falling apart. Daniel didn't notice that his marriage had reached a point where all interaction was polite and only touched upon "safe" topics.

> **Daniel:** I couldn't have been more surprised when I was laid off from my job in favor of someone they'd just hired three months earlier. I'd been feeling so good ever since I started running, and I was unprepared for anything to go wrong in my life. Now when I look back, I see that I was bored to death with my job, going from customer to customer. My wife had been upset at how little I was around, but was proud of my running. When I lost my job, her lack of support floored me. I felt betrayed by her, but I guess I'd gotten to the point where running was the only thing that brought me any pleasure, so I guess I shouldn't have been surprised. I kept saying to myself, though, "How could she kick me when I'm down?"

For those of us who are not in an intimate relationship, we wonder if there is really anyone out there for us, and if there is, are they worth all the pain and aggravation? When we feel defeated and discouraged by the course of our relationships, we blame ourselves and effectively deflate our already weak self-esteem.

As our life begins to fall apart, our children, once the pride and joy of our lives, now irritate us by the way they talk, the way they dress, and what they think. We begin to notice that they and their problems remind us of ourselves at that age, and when we talk to them, we remind ourselves of our alcoholic and abusive parents in our responses and frustrations. If our children are using drugs or alcohol, we feel hopeless and desperate as we see the addictive cycle repeating itself all over again. When we try to intervene in our children's lives, to give advice and support, things just seem to get worse. Seeing our own coping persona develop in our children may be the ultimate heartbreak for us. Even though we have tried so hard to be different from our parents, we have failed, and we now see our own children becoming like us, as in Marva's case.

> **Marva:** My children's teenage years shocked me into the reality of my mother's alcoholism and the denial of it that was still so much a part of me. Even though I was determined to be different from her, and I'm sure I was, my kids seemed to be responding to me in the same way I responded to my mother. My oldest son was taking the arrogant position I had taken that no one knew better than him about anything. My eldest daughter went into a several-year sulk, which was just what my sister had done. My youngest daughter's learning disabilities and quiet demeanor were an amazing repetition of my brother's difficulties. It was at the point that I realized this that I broke the family pattern and sought help for all of us.

What happened to the dreams we had when we were young, of what we would do and how life would be? Where are they now? For most of us, the dreams are buried under the weight of trying to cope day to day, and distanced by our continual attempts to deny the effects our parents had on us so long ago. Too often, when we feel the disappointment of shattered dreams, we turn to addictive behaviors. We can tell ourselves that a drink at the end of a day is what we need to feel better, just what we need to melt away the pressure and stress we've had to put up with. We won't tell ourselves that we drink because we are tired and disappointed with the way our life has turned out.

We have been waiting for tomorrow for a long time, thinking that the future will finally bring us what we want. But now the future is here, and it may be that we still don't have what we want—the right family, job, friends, success. We continue to attract people who aren't good for us, and we haven't yet experienced the joy of a committed, loving relationship. If we've had therapy, and we may have had a lot, somehow it hasn't worked as we hoped it would, and we are still struggling with our pain.

Welcoming the Breakdown

The key to changing our lives is to burn out on our coping mechanisms, have them fail us, usually in a painful and profound way. Then we become ready to make the switch. If we are forty, or even thirty, successful or not, we have come to the realization that life will not go on forever. Whatever magic we've been waiting for may not come at all, and we cannot know if it will come in time to save our lives. This is our life, and we have only one chance to live it right. We look back at our life and realize that so far it has been a bust. We reach the breaking point when we simply cannot go on as before, exhausted by the struggle, ready to admit that all our efforts and all the strength of our coping persona have not brought us happiness. This is when we are ready to switch. As we mentioned before, this can be precipitated by a serious illness, a loss, or a crisis, or simply a nagging dissatisfaction we feel with life. Our coping mechanisms finally cave in to the pressure.

As we tell our clients, from our point of view the burnout and breaking point are welcome events, because it is the crisis they create that gives us the opportunity to begin to look back and say, "Yes, my childhood really was that bad."

Let's look at how burnout and breakdown manifest themselves in each of our coping personas. As you study these personas, remember that each one is a model of one style of handling the pain of childhood. Rarely does one find pure types of personalities in real life, and of course, these coping personas are not pure types either. Imagine them as well-worn riverbeds in a delta through which the water flows easily in a number of directions. Water flows through all of them to a greater or lesser degree; together they constitute our coping persona. Most people are made up of combinations of various characteristics we describe, usually with one dominant coping persona that emerges most clearly under severe stress.

The John Wayne: Pride

Burnout

The primary indication that the John Wayne is approaching burnout is the fact that he is getting tired. He has put so much energy into taking care of himself and others, to making sure things run smoothly, and relying only on himself, that he is exhausted by his efforts. He is frantic at the pace of his life. He is strongly dedicated to his work but it no longer brings him the satisfaction it used to. Activities that used to bring him pleasure, such as sports, are now compulsions, and he is running on empty.

He is dissatisfied with his relationships. He doesn't always want to have to be the one everyone depends on, and longs for something more equal. Worse, his spouse or loved ones are disappointed in him, and his children are becoming an annoying strain as they assert their individuality. They aren't turning out the way he planned and he has trouble relating to them. His ego is so tied up in their success and an ideal image of how they should be that if they aren't perfect, he cannot feel any pride in them.

Deep inside he knows that there is falsehood in his posturing. Often there are cracks in his facade that hint that everything is not right underneath, and he often exhibits signs of this—high blood pressure, frequent illness, and continual conflict with colleagues and friends.

Many John Wayne types come to our workshops so they can patch their crumbling facades, like cracked walls that need some plaster to look as good as new. Ginny, a nurse, is one such person, a woman who looked great on the outside, but inside was falling apart. When we met her, Ginny's sense of pride was barely sustaining her, but she still looked and acted as though she could take care of herself and everyone else, just as she had always done before.

> **Ginny:** I had cancer for twelve years. People always told me how brave I was, and even the hospital that I worked in asked me to talk to other cancer patients and their families about facing death. I guess to everyone I was some sort of pillar of strength and people always seemed to be calling on me for some kind of help or support.

Ginny was an exceptional person, a model of strength and a fountain of generosity, but she never allowed herself to be vulnerable and never asked for help from anyone. Her coping persona of pride was overly developed while her sense of mortality and vulnerability and, most important, her sense of self-worth were underdeveloped. She had always believed that everything in life was up to her, and she had allowed her pride in the good work she did to nurture her and motivate her to do more. It was all she could do, because she didn't believe that she could be loved simply for who she was, but only for what she did.

Then Ginny had a recurrence of cancer, this time in her spleen, and her pride began to fail to provide her with the support and satisfaction she needed to sustain herself. One might have thought this would be a breaking point for Ginny. She had reached a point where she was too tired, too sick, and too burned-out from being the brave one and the one who held everything together to manage her life the way she had before. But Ginny was too strong to give in quite yet. She was, however, ready to consider a change in her life, but even how she came to our workshop was a sign of the extent to which her coping persona still had a grip on her. Instead of admitting to us, to her employers, and to herself that she was joining the workshop for her own needs, she told everyone she was doing it so she could learn how to work with ACOAs at the hospital. Her pride at this point was still so powerful and protective that it would not even allow her to ask for help.

Breakdown

The John Wayne type's emotional breakdown is often accompanied by a physical breakdown as well, because this is the kind of person who will push ahead until he collapses, and in the example of Ginny, her breakdown almost looked more like a meltdown. As our workshop went on, and Ginny found that she couldn't maintain her aloofness and self-protective stance anymore, she told the group of her recurring cancer. Her emotions at that point revealed to her a secret conflict she'd been carrying around inside herself for years, and she began to tell her story.

As a child Ginny suffered from the abuse of her mother. Her father's alcoholism had been the visible family problem, but there were others: the terrifying punishments that occurred behind closed doors, and her mother's obsession with search-ing her children's genitals for infection. These were well-kept secrets. When Ginny attempted to tell a teacher at school about what went on at home, she found herself being accused of lying by the principal, the teacher, and her mother that afternoon when she returned from school.

As Ginny began to cry, she softened and opened up a little, and admitted that even her own children had never known how crazy and cruel her mother had been. As she faced her pain, this dramatic breakdown gave her a vivid glimpse of the flooding of warmth that emerges when one lets pride dissolve, and one's frailty is met with compassion and under-standing. Her pride had isolated her, and now she allowed people to hold her as she cried, and stopped being the one who always had to comfort other people. Ginny began to give in and discover parts of herself through love. She gave up her pride to let life in instead.

The James Dean: Resentment

Burnout

The primary characteristic of this coping persona heading toward burnout is an overwhelming expression of resentment, dissatisfaction, and bitterness. The James Dean type uses his anger and resentment toward the world to deny grief and sadness. Anger and resentment have permeated every aspect of the James Dean's life, and people who stick around him are liable to be attacked without warning. There are fewer and fewer people in his life that he feels happy to be with, and more and more people are avoiding spending time with him.

Work is dissatisfying for the James Dean and he feels angry and unappreciated most of the time. He is disappointed at the way his life has turned out and he resents everyone but himself for it. No one wants to be on his team because of his attitude, and since he is so judgmental and thinks everyone else is inferior, he doesn't want to play on their team either. Instead, he sits on the sidelines alone and watches everyone else have a good time.

The James Dean has blocked off his heart. If he has a spouse or a lover, he is not open to her and receptive to her love. Anger is such an automatic response for him that he has forgotten how to be tender and gentle with his family and may even be abusive to them. Probably the James Dean's children are angry, too, and he may be locked into a pattern of conflict and confrontation with at least one of them.

Even as an adult the James Dean has not forgiven his parents for what they did to and have done to him, and he still carries around anger toward them that comes out at all times and is directed at all people. He may have broken off relations with his entire family but still feels a great resentment toward them.

As the James Dean becomes increasingly burned-out, he finds less satisfaction in the things he used to enjoy. His anger blinds him to his addictions and self-destructive behaviors, and he may end up following in his parents' footsteps. Only when the James Dean is burned-out to the point of breaking does he feel his isolation. Usually at the breakdown point, there is a dramatic incident in his life—a broken relationship or a death—that leaves him with nothing and no one toward whom he can direct his anger and resentment anymore.

Diane was a woman whose deep anger closed out the possibility of pleasure in her life. When Diane began therapy, she had just begun to accept the fact that a boyfriend who had left her two years earlier was not interested in her. She had sustained a relationship with him in her fantasy of hope and reconciliation. Diane thought of herself as a caring and considerate person, but the reality was quite different.

She was successful in her administrative job at a college, but she had very sharp edges, and during the two years we worked with her, Diane alienated almost everyone close to her. She was filled with despair over the fact that she seemed incapable of having and maintaining a close relationship with anyone—friend or lover. Although she was a gifted teacher, she had lost several jobs because her anger had gotten out of control and was misdirected. She was desperate to be close but she had blocked off her heart, and only presented a hardened, uninviting exterior to the outside world.

Diane was furious with her mother for all that had happened in her childhood, but she also continued to be overinvolved in her family's affairs. Much of the time that she was in therapy was spent expressing how angry she was at the various family situations she found herself sucked into. She claimed that she was the model of thoughtfulness when she was with her family, but somehow always ended up being attacked by them. She resented the fact that she was the scapegoat for them. Her hostility toward everyone and everything was out of control, and repeated rejections from her friends broke her heart time and time again. Diane found herself protesting to her friends, "I thought you cared about me!" Whatever her friends were willing to do for her was never right, according to Diane, and never enough.

Breakdown

The breakdown for the James Dean type usually occurs when he has succeeded in fully isolating himself so that he is finally forced to take responsibility for his vulnerability and needs.

In Diane's case, she was tired of feeling that her life was awful, and was more than ready for a change. For this to happen, though, she had to allow herself to feel her pain and let other people experience her vulnerability without biting their heads off. Because she distrusted people so deeply, giving up her coping persona was a drawn-out, step-by-step process. She would have small breakthroughs and feel the feelings underneath, but would soon respond with anger again, as was her old habit. It was hard for her to stay with the wounded child inside, because the needs of that child overwhelmed her, and she often returned to the imagined safety of her coping persona, the one that pushed people away. Her childlike needs had always been responded to with criticism in the past, and she expected it in her present life as well.

Eventually she was able to have interactions where there was no anger, and as her natural sweetness and sensitivity came out, she was able to make some new friends. At first, her new relationships were rocky, as she would feel hurt or imagine an affront, and she would react with anger. She spent a lot of time talking with friends, trying to straighten out hurt feelings, but sometimes things couldn't work out, and she would be deeply wounded again by the loss of yet another friend.

As her coping persona began to break down, Diane observed how she interacted with people, and she promised herself that she would only be with people she felt were right for her. To do this, she had to face her fear of rejection and choose to be alone rather than be in the endless drama of relationships in which she would find herself provoked and angry. Diane eventually realized how her angry outbursts kept her involved in bad situations, endlessly struggling to straighten things out rather than enjoying herself. She had been too busy telling people what she didn't want instead of what she did want, and at that point, she hardly even knew herself.

The more she was able to remain with her pain, the more she was able to develop responsibility for how she treated the problems in her relationships with anger, and for her tendency to blame other people for what went wrong. Because she had been very injured as a child by her family, Diane still had a lot to be angry about.

The breaking down of the coping persona of resentment would occur when she could see that her anger at a current insult was exaggerated by old baggage and feelings. It was a big step for Diane to apologize the first time she was aware that this had happened. It became easier after practice and receiving a compassionate response in return. To learn to stand by her anger that was fair, legitimate, and real to the situation was a truly empowering achievement for her. It took a very self-conscious attempt on Diane's part to focus on what her heart's desire was—to love and be loved.

The Marilyn Monroe: Depression, Hopelessness

Burnout

Always present in the Marilyn Monroe type is a feeling of deadness and a severe lack of energy to do anything about it. Unlike the James Dean, the Marilyn Monroe is all too aware of how isolated she is. The Marilyn Monroe's depression is very real, but it acts like a narcotic. If the Marilyn Monroe stopped covering her feelings with a mask of hopelessness and depression, she would be forced to face the pain and anger that lie underneath. Her attempts to take control of her life, to express her anger and state her own needs, are often met with resistance from family and friends who do not want to respond or do not know how. Often people consider her feelings inappropriate and out of proportion, because they don't realize what's been building up inside her for years. Those who do try to help eventually give up when they realize that they have no effect on Marilyn, and gradually her friends drift away.

As she becomes more burned-out, the Marilyn Monroe is so wrapped up in her depression that she has little energy for anyone else, and she may have given up on relationships and sex. In her work life, the same cloud of hopelessness and depression hovers over her. Her children haven't turned out the way she hoped; they didn't fulfill her dreams and now they are beginning to exhibit problems of their own, and she has no idea how to deal with them or herself. Everything just seems too hopeless to her for her to even try.

The Marilyn Monroe prays that her parents will come around someday and finally give her what they couldn't when she was a child. She doesn't understand that it is too late for that, and she unconsciously pins her hopes on an unlikely event and a better tomorrow. Because the Marilyn Monroe doesn't take responsibility for her own pain but is waiting for someone to fix it for her, she is locked into a trap of hopelessness forever.

Manny is a classic example of someone with this kind of coping persona. As a medical school dropout, he believed that he knew more about medicine than any doctor who treated him, and while he was able to respect us because we are nontraditional therapists, he was cynical about how much we could really help him. He began in group therapy because he liked the social aspect it provided, and he felt safe talking about his depression in a large group.

Manny: I was an only child, and except for being in school, where I was very competitive, I don't think I ever had an opportunity to learn how to work cooperatively. When I went into engineering, it seemed like I had made the perfect choice because I could work alone and at my own pace, and treat everyone else as potential competition. That way I'd never have to be close to anyone. If anyone tried to give me some criticism, even if it was constructive, I felt insulted and depressed. I never took anyone's advice. I was an island unto myself.

Group therapy was able to lift Manny from his isolation somewhat, and he became interested in dating again and soon met a woman who was very open and forceful with him. Shortly after their marriage, she became pregnant and decided to keep the baby against Manny's strong wishes. He couldn't handle the conflict and pressure it was causing in his life, and he was pushed toward the breaking point. He felt that his wife's pregnancy was a fulfillment of his nightmare of having to care and provide for a child. It disturbed him so deeply and disrupted his life to such an extent that he soon realized things were out of control. He was then able to start facing the pain of having lived an isolated and removed life for so many years.

Judy, thirty-three and unemployed, is another example of a person burned-out and trapped in isolation and depression.

Judy: After a long series of really disastrous love affairs, I decided to have nothing more to do with men. I also hadn't had a steady job in six years and was supported by my parents. I had tried just about every single kind of therapy there is, and nothing seemed to work for me, so I just about gave up. What happened was that I'd start something with a burst of enthusiasm, and things would seem to be working. I'd have this amazing period of health and energy, but then it would sort of fade away and I'd be as bad as I was before.

Judy was convinced it was the therapy that didn't work. In reality, she was too afraid and depressed to expend the energy necessary to make a change in her life. Gradually Judy's friends became aware of the hopelessness and depression that surrounded her, and seeing no results, became tired of helping her. Judy had an attractive and bright side to her, though, and did manage to make new friends from time to time, but the friendships rarely lasted. New friends could sense something desperate about Judy and pulled away as if her depression was contagious. Judy felt unloved as usual, but rather than feel the associated pain, she became angry and blamed other people, and soon sank back into her depression.

Judy was also overinvolved with her family and flew to them whenever she thought they needed her help. She was extremely attentive to their needs and saw her involvement as something they required from her. As she became increasingly burned-out, Judy began to resent her family for not appreciating all that she did for them. She talked with them about it but felt that no one ever really understood what she was saying, and she began to think of herself as the family martyr, ill-used and misunderstood. Her family, in fact, was often irritated by her unhappiness and suffering, and they didn't appreciate her nosing her way into their affairs. They simply wished she would work on her own life instead. They complained that she didn't listen to them when they tried to talk to her, and they thought Judy was very out of touch with what was going on. They were beginning to lose patience with her.

It is almost as though the Marilyn Monroe has to be pushed to the edge before she burns out. The danger that this will lead to suicide is very real, as it was in Judy's case.

Breakdown

The Marilyn Monroe type seems to live in a state of perpetual breakdown, but the true breakdown occurs when she begins to take her pain seriously and admit to herself and to others that her childhood wounded her. It is not enough to feel sorry for yourself. Depression is a serious problem and when it is the primary coping persona of an individual, the episodic assault of the feelings of lack of energy and helplessness is inevitable.

The breaking point for this coping persona involves grasping that however difficult and dysfunctional depression is, it is the pain-avoidant solution to covering up the dark secrets and painful memories of a distressed childhood.

Manny's breakdown obviously occurred in his reaction to

his wife's pregnancy. His seething and inappropriate rage about becoming a parent helped him stop mouthing the words of an injured person, and finally feel what it had been like to be the target of similar rage when he was a child. He had denied it for so long, constantly making excuses for how his parents had treated him. The depression lifted soon after, and what was exposed was an image of himself as the "unwanted" child who was supposedly the fulfillment of his parents' marriage. He was an only child, and this is the message he'd heard so many times. His parents simply were ill-equipped to open up their hearts and home to a child, and they had had a child because they thought they were "supposed" to. The burden of this illusion of a happy home had been heavy on him, and the contempt his parents had always had for his "childishness" had left him emotionally dead.

At the depth of his breakdown, Manny felt as though he was being pushed toward rebirth, but for a while he had no energy to move to it. "I feel as though I am at the bottom and I am just a piece of shit," he said. He said life had turned on him again, this time in the form of his wife. It was the force of the support of fellow group members involved in their own recoveries that carried Manny through this difficult time.

Judy's breakdown occurred when her depression reached extreme levels. When we met Judy, she was already full into the burnout phase, but she was still too afraid to break down. She was so terrified of confronting the feelings of the wounded child inside herself that she preferred to stay in a fog of hopelessness and depression. In order to break through her coping mechanisms, she would have to face her feelings of vulnerability and her fears of being unloved. But Judy was too scared, and instead of taking her pain seriously, she simply became more uptight with everyone around her. She became angry if people didn't respond to her in the way she wanted them to, and she was very difficult to be around. Judy was incapable of seeing that the complaints she had about other people were projections of her own behavior. In order to break down, she would have to stop trying to cope and admit that her life wasn't working, but until she did that, she continued to vacillate between depression and discontent, a drama that distracted her from her intense childhood pain.

Finally suicidal thoughts began to creep into her thinking. When she was asked to consider hospitalizing herself, she found herself in a dilemma: Are these people trying to help me, or are they simply tired of my problems? It was this dilemma that helped her begin to remember the hatred she had felt from her parents, and the messages that her needs were not legitimate and that her mother would be happier if Judy wasn't around.

Joining an ACOA group was the step Judy chose next, and certainly one preferable to hospitalization. She found fellowship there, and support for telling the truth about her childhood. She still had a long road of recovery ahead of her, one that included several severe bouts of depression requiring medication. She did have a circle of friends who believed and supported her, not only with encouragement but with their own parallel stories of struggle and recovery.

The Greta Garbo: Withdrawal

Burnout

The primary feature of this coping persona is a quiet reserve that is shown to the outside world, one that belies turmoil and depression. Internally, the Greta Garbo feels lonely, isolated, and misunderstood. She may derive some satisfaction from her work and the interpersonal contact, but she participates with others without ever really sharing or being completely there.

The Greta Garbo's love life is most likely unsatisfactory, and her partners are often angry with her. She doesn't understand why they feel that way and tends to think they are a little crazy because of it. Her family life is not going well. Since closeness makes her anxious, she is estranged from her mate and children, but is still dedicated to having a "nice" family, even if it isn't a "real" one.

Any anxiety makes the Greta Garbo withdraw even further, and whenever she feels tension, she hides further inside herself for safety. The burnout thus occurs when there is no more safety inside herself. The isolation she has made for herself becomes all too apparent, the frustration of being alone all too intense.

Randy, a physical therapist and the father of two, is a good example of how long the burnout period can extend in a Greta Garbo type before reaching the breaking point. In Randy's case, he was able to absorb huge amounts of personal disappointment and simply withdraw when anything went wrong. Randy believed that there was no conceivable way to successfully confront the issues that frustrated him, so he chose to hide his true feelings in almost every instance.

Randy had been told by his parents that "it doesn't help to get angry," and he believed it. The little boy in him was terrified of being abandoned, and as an adult his biggest fear was that if he spoke up and said what he felt, his wife would leave him. By the time we met Randy, his wife was on the verge of leaving him out of frustration with their relationship, and this discord had been going on for several years. She said that Randy didn't listen or respond to her, and she saw herself as the only adult in the family. She was tired of having to be in charge of everything.

Even Randy's children didn't take him seriously and saw their mother as the boss of the family. Randy knew that something wasn't going right, but instead of trying to figure out what it was, he withdrew into himself so he wouldn't have to deal with it, and inevitably his wife, feeling abandoned and disappointed by her husband, reacted with anger.

The burnout period was painstakingly slow for Randy. In couples therapy, Randy talked mostly about his wife and almost never about himself. Randy needed to look at the feelings that existed underneath his calm and remote exterior. He needed to feel his anger and fear instead of ignoring it, but as the therapy progressed, and his wife got clearer and clearer about her own needs, Randy just listened, was unable to respond.

It took the departure of Randy's wife from their home to force him to face up to the fact that it was just an illusion that his marriage was working and his wife was happy. He had to let go of it. His worst fears had been realized, and this time there was no safety. It was hard for Randy to acknowledge that his coping persona had never really worked at all, but it had been his only option. All other options were just too painful.

Breakdown

The necessary ingredient to the Greta Garbo's breakdown is a reexperience of childhood longings that were repressed for reasons of survival. These longings are crucial to a healthy adult sexual life and the focus on pleasure that sexually alive people possess.

If the Greta Garbo always withdraws when there is excitement in the air, she will be left alone waiting for Prince Charming to come and sweep her away. The Greta Garbo's fantasy life is filled with these sorts of notions, including the notion that continues to tell her she is doing everything just right. She justifies her withdrawal with ideas such as "Only loose women approach men" or "I am being a lady." For men, this is justified with, "I have to be cool" or "I'm being a gentleman." Longings, especially sexual ones, are crucial to adult fulfillment, because pain-avoidant people would never come out of their shells if it weren't for the forceful push of their desires.

The Greta Garbo must find out what "turns her on" and follow those feelings, but until she breaks down the barriers of her coping mechanism, this isn't possible.

In Randy's case, the breakdown did not occur until a long and grueling burnout phase of his life where he continually withdrew. His friends had given up any hope that he would ever change, and he said in therapy, "I realize now that I don't trust anyone with my true feelings. I don't know if it's fear or mistrust or just an idea that things will never turn out right. I'm sure I won't be good enough anyway."

His wife's departure turned out to be the breaking point

for Randy, and he recognized that his fear of abandonment was at the root of his problem. He finally faced the panic that her leaving had stirred in him, and saw that he feared for his emotional survival. Unconsciously he did not believe he could take care of himself, and so had been willing to make himself seem small so someone would take care of him. He had learned as a child to be a "good boy" so his parents would take care of him, and a "good boy" as an adult so his wife and friends would attend to him. He was good at never rocking the boat, but he wasn't so adept at getting his own needs met, especially the need to love as an adult.

After his breaking point, Randy slowly learned that being himself was a reward in itself, and he began to love the feelings of excitement and immediacy when he confronted and shared his feelings. He came to hate the feelings associated with his withdrawal and found it was becoming increasingly easy to give up his coping persona. When Randy saw the price he was paying for his withdrawal, he spoke out and said what he felt, and asked for what he needed. He discovered that he could take care of himself. Randy's wife returned several months after her departure, and he was able to relate to her as an adult, not as a little boy.

The Frances Farmer: **Confusion**

Burnout

The Frances Farmer's behavior and perceptions are always unpredictable as she enters the burn-out phase. At work, the Frances Farmer does not do well. She feels persecuted and misunderstood, and frequently finds herself in conflict with her co-workers. Often she overinvolves herself in other people's problems and affairs and has no sense of appropriate interaction.

In her love life, the Frances Farmer is so often spaced-out that her partners are frustrated by her. She is suspicious of those close to her, particularly if she is also dependent on them.

In the process of the burnout phase, the Frances Farmer begins to pull away from everyone. She has been overinvolved in her family drama and she begins to realize that it is making her crazy and taking away her sense of self and autonomy. This pulling away is not a withdrawal into herself, as it is with the Greta Garbo. Instead, it is stepping back to take a good long look at her predicament. As she does this, she begins to focus on her life, and with work, finds her own path while she stays in contact with herself. Most often, though, the Frances Farmer is not able to do this without significant outside help. The point is that she needs to withdraw to herself, not away from others. Usually the breaking point occurs when there is some major traumatic event that she cannot rationalize or escape from. An illness or the ending of a relationship can be the brick wall that stops Frances Farmer. It is during the burnout that Frances Farmer comes to an awareness, and an acceptance, of how erratic and disconnected she really is.

This awareness emerges slowly, and at first is barely noticed. Trusted friends repeat the same message over and over, and eventually the Frances Farmer is able to listen, because her coping persona that tells her that everyone else is crazy is beginning to wear thin. The family of the Frances Farmer almost destroyed her perceptual ability, but as she reaches the breaking point, she is able to discriminate between the crazy-making and highly confusing messages she received from her parents, and the consistent and loving feedback from friends and loved ones.

In the case of Victor, burnout came in his late thirties when he began to feel that life was passing him by. He was a very skilled woodworker with many talents, and a hard worker who was appreciated on any job, but his emotional life was as sparse as his work life was varied. As the youngest of five children from a midwestern family, Victor had adopted craziness and confusion as his coping mechanism to survive in an alcoholic home. Victor's memory of himself was that he had always been "a little weird" and that he played the role of mascot in the family. He moved East to get a college degree which he didn't complete, and never moved back home. He was smart but inattentive, curious but headstrong.

At thirty-four, Victor fancied himself part of the counter-culture, and he lived in group houses that shared meals and provided a steady social life. He was physically attractive but never seemed excited enough about anyone to make a commitment or be affectionate for any extended period of time. He came to our workshop on the recommendation of a friend who knew of Victor's family circumstances.

Victor didn't feel that his disassociation from family and friends was very significant. He did notice, however, that there was a steady turnover of roommates in the houses he lived in and he had eventually become the oldest. Nothing in the future seemed to excite Victor very much anymore, and he was beginning to view his life with a certain nostalgia. He had been steering himself along his own path for so long that he was out of touch with the world around him. Then a crisis occurred when he went home one Christmas.

> **Victor:** I hadn't seen my family for a while and during Christmas dinner we all got into a big fight. My father had said something to my younger brother that I thought was very mean and unfair and so I said something about it. Immediately the whole family ganged up on me and said things like "He didn't mean it" or "He said it because he loves your brother." They were really very condescending to me and told me that, as usual, I had no idea of what was going on and that I had misread the situation again. All of a sudden I felt as though they had set a trap for me, and because all the dynamics felt so familiar, I began to see that this is what they had been doing to me all my life. They were trying to drive me crazy. I don't think they meant to, but they did it just the same.

His family taught him to doubt his own perceptions. After the incident, he realized that conflicts over "what really happened" were not limited to his nuclear family. He soon noticed that he often had arguments, just like the one with his family, even with his closest friends. With this realization, he decided to slow himself down and accept that sometimes he did misread situations. By paying closer attention to what was going on around him, he was also able to be more aware of how he affected people.

Eventually Victor was able to see that underneath the confusion and craziness he projected was a reservoir of anxiety. The anxiety had made him so uncomfortable all his life that he had "checked out" to do "his own thing." A supportive relationship with his therapist was important at this time to keep him moving forward into deeper and deeper feelings. It frightened him and made him angry, but he learned to talk about his pain with people he trusted.

Breakdown

The key ingredient to the breakdown for Frances Farmer is not only to see that everyone thinks she's crazy but to admit that she really is confused as to what is real and what is her imagination. In that sense, she has become "crazy," and by crazy, we mean that she doesn't really understand herself and the things she does. Breaking down means facing the remarkable inconsistency of her life. It is frightening because of the fear that everything will fall apart if things are opened up. The opposite is true, but it is a hard thing to trust.

Victor's breakdown was initially not as dramatic as he had feared. When a person admits to himself for the first time that there may be something seriously wrong with his mental health, it is truly a terrifying moment, and he feels powerless to do anything about it. It cannot be done in one giant moment; problems must be addressed slowly, one at a time.

Victor began by allowing himself and a few trusted others to see that he was aware of his "craziness." This helped him to stop believing that everything he did was correct and to stop being so defensive about it. He learned to take a more inquisitive position in looking at his actions and feelings. This led him to discover, with great relief, that people did not depend on him to be right all the time. Their affection for him was not dependent on his ability to be "right," but rather on his ability to be a warm and open person.

The next part of Victor's breakdown was more difficult, because as he slowed down, he was aware of a tremendous amount of anxiety inside himself. If there is one clear breakdown point, it was the family incident described earlier. To be aware of his anxiety helped him withdraw from the drama his family created. Solving the family problems was not his task, and his anxiety became a better point of focus than the addictive excitement of being with them and trying to have them see his point of view—a hopeless and destructive agenda for Victor.

The Charlie Brown: Chameleon

Burnout

The Charlie Brown often functions very well in adulthood, dancing to whatever tune is playing. His deep fear of abandonment and conflict makes him a sympathetic and understanding friend and partner. His behavior always appears to be correct, and while this may earn him respect and admiration, it also earns him contempt and derision. Because he is seen by many as spineless, he is also often not taken seriously.

The Charlie Brown wants everything to run smoothly, but since the world is full of conflict, he finds he doesn't have the skills to do anything other than be accommodating. Whenever he attempts to assert himself, he becomes anxious, and thus the pain-avoidant stance of accommodation takes priority over self-assertion.

As the Charlie Brown begins to burn out in his job, he feels the bitterness and resentment he hasn't ever allowed himself to acknowledge. He feels unsafe and unsure as to who his real friends are and sees a lack of real communication in his intimate relationships. He has put little energy into defining himself as a separate entity, paid little attention to his boundaries, rights, and desires. His relationship with his mate may be static and habitual, and both partners may want more space. If he is single, people may see him as "nice" and attentive, but rarely is "nice" sexually attractive.

Becky is a good example of the Charlie Brown type. She always had a lot of energy, was good-looking and successful in her business, but was unable to sustain an intimate relationship.

> **Becky:** I've always done my best to try to fulfill my father's dreams for my success. My mother was very shy and withdrawn, and while we wanted to help her, she found that drinking gave her the most comfort. Her drunkenness was a private matter and we didn't talk about it, but my father started to spend more and more time away from home. When he left for good, I tried to help out, and I'm still trying. Now when I'm with a man, when I'm angry, I get so anxious about it, I stew quietly or play with my hair or leave the room. I always avoid confrontation. The men are always shocked that I've turned into this little girl who only wants to please.

Becky attracted men with her high-powered career and her attentiveness, but eventually the needy and scared little girl in her would begin to show.

Breakdown

The breakdown for the Charlie Brown might never occur if not encouraged by friends and loved ones. As long as he is appreciated and rewarded for being so accommodating, he can avoid asserting himself. It is only when the Charlie Brown feels enough trust in the people around him that he can listen when someone points out what he is doing.

Becky finally met a man who would stay with her long enough to allow her to let down some of her defenses. The breakdown occurred for Becky when she began therapy. She would start the session in a cheery mood, but as she discussed what was going on in her life, she began to feel anxious. When she found the strength to feel what was going on, she realized how sad she was.

With her grief revealed, she was better able to feel a genuine warmth inside, rather than depend on her ability to make other people feel good to get her through the day. With this warmth also came a greater ability to be genuinely warm and responsive to her boyfriend, both sexually and emotionally. As she cried in therapy, she became less afraid.

Identifying Burnout and Breakdown in Your Own Life

Do these stories sound disquietingly familiar to you? At this point in your life, do you see your old behaviors and pain-avoidant mechanisms failing? The irony about coping personas is that we learned to adopt them because they protect us from our underlying pain. However, they do not work forever. They simply trap us in a way of life that eventually ends up harming us more than if we had begun earlier to face our pain, anxiety, and grief. Facing our pain hurts, that is sure, but it is a healing pain. The harm we do to ourselves when we act under our coping persona saps our strength to love and live. It is a degenerating pain we experience as well, because the longer we live with it, the more it alienates us from our true selves, others, and our yearnings for fulfillment through healthy pleasure.

Are you feeling tired of the same old story in your life and wish that you could change but you can't seem to find the way? Has much of the vitality and excitement in your life disappeared? Do you find yourself unable to enjoy things and participate in simple pleasure? Is your marriage on the rocks or has it ended? Are you unable to sustain a relationship past the "honeymoon" stage? Do you feel that you are beginning to resemble your parents in your behavior? Are your children responding to you the way you responded to your parents? Are you dissatisfied with your career and have low self-esteem? Are you committing "social suicide" by overeating, drinking, drugging, gambling?

If you have answered yes to even one of these questions, chances are you are burned-out by your current way of life and are approaching, or are past, a breaking point. Maybe now, as you read this book, you are at that point when change is possible, ready to face the feelings you've been denying for so long. Maybe you are ready now to live your life instead of trying to cope with it, to make the switch in your life from the avoidance of pain to the pursuit of pleasure.

There are steps we follow that may help you through this difficult time. You may feel that you are at a place in your life when you are ready to make the switch from pain avoidance to the pursuit of pleasure, but you have no idea where to begin, and the prospect of it seems frightening and makes you anxious. Many of you can't do it alone and will need the help of a therapist. The close fellowship of some very good and trusted friends who will support and encourage you is essential. Many of us, particularly men, feel that we must do everything on our own and that asking for help is a sign of weakness or self-indulgence. This is a tragedy, because being able to ask for help is truly a human and loving gesture, and it marks the first step of the switch. When we make the decision not to "play God" with our lives anymore, not to try to control and squelch all our problems, we take a giant human step.

① After this first step of reaching out to others, you won't be alone as things become difficult. Someone else will be witness to your progress and will support your healing. You were alone with your pain as a child, but that doesn't have to be true for you now as an adult. There are subsequent steps to take that will help you reach this crucial point in your life.

② • *Stop trying to "fix" everything.* Many of the coping personas we have discussed share the characteristics of being overinvolved with their original families and attempting to fix every problem that exists within it. Focusing on everyone else's life but our own is just a way we avoid facing our problems, and in order to make a switch, we need to begin to focus on ourselves. We must admit that some things are not fixable and simply can't be changed. We cannot fix or change the fact that, for example, our father was abusive, that our mother abandoned us, that they were both alcoholics. All we can do is grieve about it and get on with our lives.

3 • *Admit to yourself that your life is not working.* Admit to yourself that you have reached a burnout stage in your life. You need to stop masking your pain and begin to feel it, admit that it exists and that you are hurt. When you are able to redirect the energy that has gone into denying your true feelings into accepting yourself as you are, your life will begin to change.

4 • *To make the switch, you must admit that your life is not manageable in its current form.* It is amazing that our coping persona, in the face of so much contrary evidence, continues to believe that relief, and all the answers, are just a minute away. In continuing to protect ourselves from the full extent of our disappointment about how our lives have turned out, we deny the depth of our pain. We avoid seeing the truth, we pretend that things are not so bad, but the truth is that things are out of our control and we don't have any idea about how to find happiness for ourselves. This admission, while extremely painful, contains the seeds for a new life. Only when we admit that there is a problem can we begin to address it and look for solutions.

5 • *Let go of your illusions and finally tell the truth.* When we deny our feelings, we often deny the facts of our lives as well. Many of us cherish and protect our illusions—that we have a loving family, that our marriage is ideal, that we are proud of our children—and we'd rather die than admit how we really feel. But we must be honest with ourselves if we are to make the switch, because illusions cover up the truth, and until we face the truth, our energy is directed toward suppressing it.

6 • *Give up the idea that "things will be better tomorrow."* The truth is, today stinks. If you live in your life today, you can

make some changes now. A mountain climber doesn't get up the mountain by telling himself it isn't steep or by blaming other people for how difficult it is. He only makes it to the top by being fully attentive to where he is and each move that he must make.

When we look back at the six coping personas we've described, we can see what burnout and the breaking point for each looks like. The unifying feature in each instance is that the old way of life ceases to produce the motivating pseudo-pleasure and energy that are necessary to carry on as before. As the examples illustrate, facing the pain and feeling its impact is the crucial element of breaking down and ultimately letting go of your coping persona. To make the switch toward the pursuit of pleasure takes a few more steps, though.

• *Tell the stories of your life, reveal the truth, and speak the words.* Until we begin to tell our stories, we may not even be aware that they exist. The combination of denial and natural memory loss often leads to minimizing the pain of childhood.

It is very difficult to break through the wall of denial and share the secrets behind it. We may still maintain a fierce loyalty to our parents, and by telling what happened, we break a strong family rule—never tell anyone! Jennifer, a childhood friend of Karen's, came to our workshop because she believed Karen's knowledge of her parents would be helpful. Out of her sense of loyalty, it was important to Jennifer that she not reduce her parents to simply a couple of alcoholics. It also turned out to be important because Jennifer was full of illusions about the way things had been, and Karen, who had been there, was able to help her look back with a sharper eye to reconstruct the truth. Jennifer's breaking point occurred during our workshop.

> **Jennifer:** When I went to Karen's workshop, I had recently separated from my husband of fourteen years, and I had chosen to have my two kids go with him. I was a basket case and felt that I could no longer be a good mother to my children. I felt that sometimes I got so angry that my temper became violent and I

didn't want to hurt them. I had no idea where this anger came from and it upset me very much. I had only recently gotten close to my mother again when she died, and I was at a point where I didn't want to talk about anything bad about my childhood because of my loyalty to her. But Karen had spent a lot of time in my house when we were growing up and said she knew exactly where my anger came from.

For years, Karen said, Jennifer's mother had been very mean to Jennifer. While she doted on her other children, she often lost her temper and screamed at Jennifer. As Jennifer listened to this she was stunned, but it was important that she hear the truth. Only then could she break the illusion and find the source of her anger. When she understood her anger, she could control it. Instead of believing in a fantasy past, she felt the reality of it. For Jennifer, the truth set her free.

• *Join a community of supportive friends who are going through the same switch in life.* ACOAs are not the only people who deny the past and prefer to live under illusions. It is important to be with a group that understands just how difficult and painful it is to confront the past. As you dredge up the past, you need to be surrounded by patient people who are willing to listen to you and believe you, even if it makes them uncomfortable. We have spent our lives suffering alone and now we need to feel the support of fellow seekers. As we make the switch from pain avoidance to the pursuit of pleasure, we learn that we don't have to cry alone anymore. There is a point when we can honestly say "it hurts good" because we are believed.

• *Get information about what it means to have grown up in an alcoholic or abusive home.* Just knowing the facts can help us break through some of the denial. We can see that it wasn't only us that got hurt, but that everyone else who grew up in similar situations was hurt, too. We need reassurance to face the pain because of our tendency to think that we overdramatize or exaggerate what happened. It helps to have others corroborate our stories. By reading this book, you have begun this step. To inform yourself more, visit your local bookstore. Many bookstores now have sections on adult children of alcoholics. If you want more information, or help finding a therapist in your area, you can call or write:

> The National Association for Adult Children
>   of Alcoholics
> 31706 Coast Highway, #201
> South Laguna, CA 92677
>   (714) 499-3889

> Children of Alcoholics Foundation
> 200 Park Avenue, 31st floor
> New York, NY 10166
>   (212) 351-2680

• *Get in touch with the wounded child that is within you, because this is where the original pain lies.* We must convince this child inside that it is okay to take down the walls and feel the hurt. Only when we stop the pain-avoidant denial of the child within us can we begin to pursue pleasure. We must allow the independent voice of that child to speak from the heart, for above all else, that child longs to live and be loved.

• *Use your will where you can and ask for help where and when you can't.* As we begin to understand our coping personas, we also begin to see when they start to take over. Jennifer, for example, becomes aware of how her coping mechanism of anger protects her from the pain she feels. She learns that when she starts yelling at her children, she can use her will to stop, and ask herself what it is that's hurting instead. Jennifer has a lot of crying to do, but once she is willing to stop ignoring the pain behind her tears, she will begin to experience the pleasure of inner peace. When she cannot stop herself from yelling at her children, she can ask for help.

We've discussed steps that are the beginnings of making the switch from avoidance of pain and an addiction to excitement to a pursuit of healthy pleasure. What we strive for is a way to get off the roller coaster and live emotionally sober lives. We are tired of always being in extremes and we search for the middle ground where we can feel peaceful and safe.

We know that it is possible to switch, because we have done it, and are still involved in the ongoing process of recovery. As we have made the switch, we have identified, and continue to work on, areas in our lives where we tend to be pain-avoidant and emotionally unstable. In the following chapters, we'll present to you our program for recovery and the attainment of an emotionally sober life.

PART
III

THE
ROAD
TO
EMOTIONAL
HEALING

CHAPTER 7

Toward Emotional Sobriety: Discovering Contact and Boundaries

Christie: Sometimes my life still looks sad to me. My father drinks, although we can't discuss it, and my mother, with her drinking, is no help. I'm sad and angry about this, but now when I refuse to get drawn back into all the family problems, I feel as though I'm helping not only them, but myself as well. I don't give in to them anymore, and I don't allow myself to become the scapegoat for their problems. It's a wonderful feeling to have this boundary behind which I have rights and faith in my life. It's a relief for me to know what's me and what's them, and it's not my responsibility to make everything right.

Introducing Emotional Sobriety Into Your Life

As in Christie's story, Emotional Sobriety is more than a state of mind—it is a way of living, a way that leads to health. Like alcoholic sobriety, Emotional Sobriety is not achieved simply through a decisive act of will, one that says, "Today I will stop drinking" and "Tomorrow I'll change." Each day, Emotional Sobriety means focusing on a target which is easy to see but sometimes very hard to hit. Finding Emotional Sobriety in your life comes from having faced the pain and gathered the courage to accept all that life has to offer.

Achieving Emotional Sobriety means stepping off the roller coaster of emotions and sitting still while the storm continues to rage around us. It means using considered judgment instead of an immediate response, and recognizing our excitements and fears for what they really are, without getting caught up in them. It means finding gratification in a relationship, rather than reenacting an unhappy childhood. Some aspects of Emotional Sobriety which we are about to discuss may already be present in your life, while others may seem foreign and barely attainable. As you work toward making changes in particular aspects of your life, focus on those things that you can achieve now. When you succeed in one area, you'll find the increased strength and self-esteem to succeed in others.

As ACOAs so much of our energy is tied up in pain-avoidant behavior that when we shift to the pursuit of pleasure and sobriety, we sometimes find ourselves confused and full of anxiety. In our exploration of Emotional Sobriety in this and the following chapters, we present techniques to use to combat this anxiety. We will also explore Emotional Sobriety as a way to anchor yourself against the storm.

Perhaps you have already begun to take a step toward Emotional Sobriety by being honest with yourself, and you have admitted that your childhood "really was so bad," that you "didn't make it all up," and that you aren't blaming anyone when you tell it the way it really was. Maybe now you've realized that your childhood not only hurt you, but injured you as well, and that this injury remains with you to this day.

Many people in our workshops spend hours exploring the question "How did your parents hurt you?" but will close up when we mention the word "injury," because "injury" has more severe implications. They would still like to believe that their parents' effect on them was insignificant or temporary. This is a continuation of denial on yet another level. It may still feel disloyal to say that our parents injured us, but unless we admit this, we continue to deny that we need to make a switch in our lives now. It is hard work to explore the memories, and often it hurts and brings out our anger. Sometimes the pain and anger seem so overwhelming we are afraid these feelings will control us or make us do something we'll regret. To make the journey through the storm to Emotional Sobriety means taking the time and doing the work to allow the storm to move through our bodies and our hearts at a pace we can handle.

Once you've admitted that you are injured, you can make a more realistic assessment of how that injury is affecting your life today. To continue to say about your past that "it wasn't so bad" clouds over the reality of the present. When you are not honest, you are out of contact with yourself. It is important to be in contact with a strong sense of self and to have an understanding of personal boundaries. When these things are in place, we are able to be in contact with ourselves and with others and we resist being drawn back into the storm of repetitious, self-destructive behavior.

We have broken our program for Emotional Sobriety down into four major components, which we discuss in this and the next three chapters. This chapter focuses on contact and boundaries, Chapter 8 explores learning moderation, Chapter 9 addresses discovering faith, and Chapter 10 concentrates on forming intimate relationships.

Defining Contact and Boundaries

When we talk of contact, we mean an emotional touching or a connection—two people meeting each other at their boundaries, the point where one person ends and the other begins. When we refer to contact with yourself, we mean the relationship of your ego to your feelings, knowing who you are, what you feel, and where your boundaries are. Through our hearts, we can also make contact with a sacred and profound part of ourselves.

Contact has many levels. There is a superficial level of contact that most people operate in, and there is a deeper level of contact where the heart is involved, open, and vulnerable. We are not suggesting that it is necessary for you to always be at the deepest level of contact with yourself. We only recommend that you become capable of the various levels of contact, and be able to feel the full range of your emotions: fear, anger, sorrow, joy. To be in contact with someone else means being aware of how that person wants to interact with you, and making a choice for yourself as to whether you want to join him or her at that level. Interaction with others occurs at boundaries—yours and theirs—where you end and they begin. The easiest way to understand healthy functioning of boundaries is to think of the role of cells.

The cell wall is a semipermeable membrane. When it functions correctly, the cell wall keeps poisons out, lets nutrients in, and excretes waste. It also defines the existence of the cell by separating it from other cells. Healthy cells have an intelligence that knows whether to be a stomach cell or a brain cell.

Healthy cells demonstrate good contact at their boundaries by discriminating between nutrition and poison, and by positioning and duplicating themselves. The healthy person must do the same. To have a semipermeable membrane, to know when to allow in and when to keep out, means you have a choice in your life, and means you will be an active rather than a passive participant in it. To manage contact well is an expression of self, integrity, and freedom.

When one has a clear sense of boundaries between the inside and the outside, one is able to develop healthy self-esteem based on a sense of autonomy. Unfortunately parents in alcoholic and unhealthy homes do not have a clear sense of where they end and where their children begin, and they are more interested in controlling their children than in respecting their individuality. Closed doors and the privacy of mail and diaries might be ignored as parents barge into any realm of their children's lives they wish to invade. They may keep their children up into the night sharing adult confidences, and often accuse them of behaviors that are simply projections of the parental turmoil. As a result, these children either don't have a sense that it is okay to say "no" to people infringing on them, or they become so rigid in their need to defend themselves that they are unable to let anything in.

As ACOAs both of us felt at times so pushed and pulled by contradictory parental needs and rules while we were growing up that by the time we were supposed to act autonomously, our personal boundaries were too ill-defined to function well. We were therefore always dependent on what other people thought of us, and our lives were roller-coaster rides of ego boosts and personal attacks.

Boundary Violations Continue to Haunt Us

To have a healthy sense of one's boundaries is more difficult for humans than it is for cells, but both share the need to define their physical sense of boundary as a first step to the defining of the self. Touching and other forms of sensual pleasure take place at one's boundaries, and require respect for the boundaries of the other person involved. The ability to say "yes" or "no" helps develop the sense of self. Alcoholic and abusive parents often rob children of their right to decide what sort of touching they do or do not want.

Overt physical and sexual abuse is an obvious and all too common violation of boundaries in children, as well as in adults. Lisa is an example of one such victim whose boundaries were violated in covert ways, but this violation still greatly affected her adult life. She was the eldest daughter in an extremely chaotic family, and she was sexually abused by her father during her adolescence. She never told anyone about what happened, partly out of loyalty to her father, partly because she felt no one would believe her. Although her father never touched Lisa genitally, he seduced her with talk, inappropriate touching, and a fascination with her sexuality. Although he was gentle with her, Lisa was left with a tremendous fear of her own sexuality and the sexuality of men. She was repelled by the idea of closeness, and despite years of therapy, she was unable to maintain relationships. At one point, she had a dream she recounted.

> **Lisa:** I think the dream relates to my difficulty in letting go and opening up to people. In the dream, I was carrying stacks of newspaper to the fireplace, and I was putting the papers in the fire. The fire was turning them into hot lava that was flowing out of the fireplace. The fire screen was completely ineffectual, and I felt responsible for what was happening because I'd put the papers in. I was terrified. I had a kitchen spatula, which I was using to try to keep the lava from flowing out. I kept scraping and backing up. I was thinking, "I'm not doing this right," and "I'm not doing a good enough job." When I think about the dream, I'm sure the newspapers have to do with my boyfriend, who is a reporter. The lava must be the feelings we have for each other, and I guess I'm afraid of how intense our relationship has become, and how I can't control it.

In order to protect herself from her father's violation, Lisa had constructed boundaries so rigid that she couldn't let anyone in. His inappropriate behavior had led to an impairment in her contact with herself, so that she was unable to accept love from another person. Lisa did not feel that her sexuality was her own. While many girls are taught that men are uncontrollable, Lisa directly experienced this lack of control in her father, a man she loved and had trusted. In order to protect herself from the pain and confusion of the situation, she learned to close off her own sexual feelings and desires. When men attempted to be intimate with her, she felt violated and self-protective.

Violations to our boundaries traumatized us, and our capacity for contact diminished, because we now see life through those negative experiences of the past. We continue to expect bad things to happen over and over when we get close to someone, and we lose the ability to see that contact can be pleasurable, instead of an experience that compromises us or makes us unhappy.

This history of violations to our boundaries causes our pain-avoidant mechanisms to kick in and reduce our ability to have good contact with others. People need contact for survival—a hug, a smile, words of affection. When we withdraw from these things, we often suffer the consequences—depression and anxiety. When we are depressed, it becomes even more difficult to be in true contact with ourselves, because our energy is drained by the emotion. For example, when things became too much to handle, Karen often sought refuge in bed. Her depression sapped her of energy and made her life seem gray and dead.

When we are anxious, contact with others makes us so uncomfortable we withdraw. It's as if we can't tune in a clear signal from the radio because our anxiety is jamming the system. Anxiety can also create its own signal, so that we are unaware of how tuned-out we really are to reality. Instead, we listen to our own channel, believing that we are in contact with the world.

Terry often fell victim to this when he was in his twenties. Bright, energetic, and willful, he often got caught up in his own drama. Sometimes he would enforce his own perception of reality by convincing those around him that things were as he saw them. When the truth of a situation eventually revealed itself, his self-esteem suffered a blow, but this simply fueled him further toward the same behavior. The next time, he believed, he would get it right.

Components of Contact and Boundaries

There are four important components to healthy contact and boundaries, each of which is necessary for the development of full Emotional Sobriety.

1. *Healthy "self-consciousness."* When you have a sense of your boundaries, you also have a realistic, positive sense of self-consciousness. Healthy people *do* feel shy, uncomfortable, and self-conscious in new situations. If you are meeting someone for the first time, it is healthy to go gently and make contact slowly, not push yourself onto the other person. Gradually you find a level of contact that each of you feels comfortable with. When you have a positive self-consciousness, you are aware of what you need and what you want. As a result of negative responses to us in childhood, we now associate self-consciousness with discomfort or shame. To be in contact with yourself, however, means bearing the temporary stress of this uncomfortable "self-consciousness," while you allow the possibility of rejection as well as the possibility of acceptance. The task is simply to "hang in there" and be as self-aware as you can.

Healthy people go slowly with people they are getting to know. They collect data about the person that enables them to act accordingly. Terry always had trouble with this. He prided himself on being "open" and allowed himself to get used all too often. He was unable to "read" other people, seeing them only in terms of himself. By learning to be more self-conscious, Terry learned to take the time to check his own feelings and accurately assess the other person before plunging in.

2. *Healthy excitement is held with boundaries.* When we have an awareness that we can make choices in relation to our boundaries, we are able to experience healthy excitement *inside our own selves*. When we lose contact with our boundaries, our excitement becomes the addictive experience

of pseudo-pleasure. This excitement is fueled by fantasy and adrenaline, rather than by reality and clear messages. For example, when our fantasy is one of achievement and conquest, our boundaries melt away in the heat of our desire. In this state, we cannot judge what is really going on, and we often act impulsively and destructively. When our fantasy involves only failure and disappointment, we focus on our bad experiences of the past and lose sight of the possibility that we may find pleasure in the reality of the present. When we are involved in a fantasy, we are so caught up in it that we often lose sight of the fact that there is another person involved in the equation. When our boundaries are weak, fantasy takes control over real excitement. When we can enjoy the feeling of being sexually attracted to someone without getting caught up in a fantasy, it is a sign that we have healthy boundaries.

June is an example of a person who did not have the protection of good boundaries. As the younger of two daughters in a very repressed and troubled family, June never received the focused attention from her parents that she needed to develop a clear sense of her self and her boundaries, and in her late twenties, she sought help.

> **June:** I was a good child and always did what I was told. It was my sister that stood up to my parents and their abuse. When I was ten, something very crucial happened, and I still get scared when I think about it. My sister had sneaked out to meet a boy, and when my father found out, he beat her badly. I still remember the crazed look on his face, and I think I decided right then that I'd never be able to go after what I wanted because of what I'd seen.
>
> My parents wouldn't let us take any chances, and I felt like I had to accommodate their needs if I was to stay safe and have a home. My parents couldn't deal with anything sexual, so my attempts to become a woman were met with scorn. They always had to know everything we were up to. I didn't hide any secrets from them like my sister did, and as a result, I didn't

dare have much of a life either. Now I see that I don't really have the skills I need to deal with men. When one comes near me, I freeze. I can hardly breathe, much less have a conversation. I have two choices: either I do exactly what the man wants, or I run away from him. Either way, I don't feel like I exist at all, especially when I really care about something.

June's problem with excitement is that she never learned to tolerate it. As an adult she suffers from severe depression and lives with the fear that she will always freeze up if something positive or exciting happens to her.

3. *We have a right to determine our own boundaries.* The third component of healthy contact and boundaries is the issue of privacy, our right to have it, and the responsibility for it. This includes having an awareness of and a respect for the boundaries of others. In June's story, for example, her parents did not respect her or her sister's boundaries, nor did they allow their children to have a private world where they could be independent and autonomous. For June, getting along with her parents meant being owned by them in a way, and as an adult, when she became sexually interested in a man, the same held true. She had not learned that her body, her desires, and her sexuality were private, precious, and above all, hers.

June achieved almost immediate results in her recovery when she accepted the principle of her right to privacy. No longer did she give in to her automatic sense of responsibility for another's well-being, ignoring her own out of a sense of worthlessness and fear of what would happen if she put herself first. Within the privacy of herself, June became more confident about what she wanted, needed, and deserved.

Modesty is an expression of privacy involving the body, and has often been devalued by our society's obsession with being sexy and appearing available and active. Modesty, however, is a healthy expression of sexual self-consciousness. It is a message that says, "My sexuality is my own and it is too important to put on display." Modesty can also be an indication of self-respect and self-possession. It is common in our clinical work to find patients who are quite able to act immodestly and be sexually appealing, but who in reality are suffering from orgasmic inhibitions or premature ejaculation.

4. *Becoming the author of your own life.* The fourth component of healthy contact and boundaries emerges naturally out of the development of the other three. It involves creating an integrated sense of self which is differentiated from other people. This means respecting your individuality, both your strengths and your weaknesses, how you are different from others and how you are the same. Out of this individuality you can claim and determine an independent life for yourself. Alcoholic and abusive families make it hard for a child to get on with his own life, and many ACOAs still find themselves under pressure from their families to be involved in the family drama. The message is clear: If you love us, you will stay involved with us. When, as adults, we are still overly involved with our families, and still feel responsible, it is evidence that our boundaries have been dissolved. It is then impossible to develop an independent sense of self.

Withdrawing entirely from the family drama is sometimes necessary and crucial to becoming the author of your own life. This choice has a price, the loss of these highly emotional relationships. As we say in our workshops, "This is the only mother, father, and sibling you will ever have," and your identity was developed through significant interactions with them. Whether we see these people or not, whether they are still living, does not diminish their importance. Ultimately, healthy family members must find a middle ground between involvement and distance, and each situation is unique.

Finding a comfortable degree of closeness was a depressing struggle for Wendy, twenty-seven, who was searching for a life of her own. When we met Wendy, she had just terminated therapy with a man who had sexualized their relationship, and it brought back feelings she had of being used like an emotional football between her parents when she was a child, and suffering through their separation, manipulations, and bitterness. Although Wendy was very interested in men, she had never been sexually intimate with one.

Wendy: It's as though I don't dare let my interest for a man show. When I'm around an attractive man, I simply disappear. I now see that's what I had to do as a child to deal with my anxiety. I'm very angry at my parents for everything that's happened, and I don't know how to deal with that. I tried not seeing them for two years, but that only hurt them, and we didn't get anywhere, and the only involvement I had at that time was with my therapist. Now I see my parents once a month. That's still too much, but I can't bear to hurt them. They just don't seem to be able to let me be my own person.

Wendy clearly needed help sorting out her needs and wishes from those of people around her. For Wendy, staying away from her parents was hardly any better than being with them.

When we have a mature sense of self, it is at our boundary that we learn to experience pleasurable contact with others. When we are in contact with others, our definition of self further emerges. When you define your boundaries, you discover what pleases you, and you develop a deeper sense of yourself as a unique individual. As you find more pleasure in your life, you build up self-esteem and are better able to accept all that life has to offer.

When you have a firm sense of personal boundaries, you can begin to ask yourself some questions about how you define yourself. How am I similar to, and how am I different from, other people? When is it safe for me to disclose information about myself and when is it a good time to maintain my privacy?

You can ask yourself, "What is it that I want? What is it that the other person wants? Am I willing to sacrifice for that other person or do I need to say 'no'?" Remember that when you say "no," you are not rejecting that other person, you are simply saying that you exist as a separate person with free choice. When you are in contact with yourself, and act within your boundaries, you can make these choices in a personal and fulfilling way.

Developing Contact and Boundaries to Achieve Emotional Sobriety

In our program for Emotional Sobriety there are four items relating to the development of contact and boundaries that can be a focus for your recovery. Each item begins with a slogan, and is followed by an explanation. We look at what life can be like when these items are absent, and what it looks like if they are functioning well for you. Finally we offer some specific techniques for developing each of these items for yourself through suggestions and exercises we use in our workshops.

Item 1. *Mind Your Own Process*

As ACOAs work on their recovery, this may be the most important—and also the most difficult—guiding rule to remember and implement. ACOAs are so accustomed to being enmeshed in the family confusion and craziness, and are often so addicted to it, that we tend to involve ourselves in every problem that comes along.

We have grown up feeling responsible for everyone in the family—taking care of our siblings, protecting our parents—and we were often involved in inappropriate situations when our parents should have been responsible. Our families have been overly involved with us as well, further confusing our sense of responsibility and importance.

Karen: I remember that I used to talk to my father late into the night after my mother had gone to bed. Often my role in these conversations was to get him to understand my mother, or my sister, or my brother. I wanted the anger in the family to stop so much that it seemed that if I could just explain it right to him, he'd stop being mad and our house would be peaceful again. The first conversation must have happened when I was as young as five or six. There is a picture of me and my little sister in the family scrapbook taken when I was five. I have my arm around her in a protective way, and I have the most worried expression on my face. It looks like I felt responsible even then. Why was I behaving like a parent? I was just a kid.

With feelings such as those Karen had, we grow up with a deeply ingrained sense of being responsible for everyone around us. As children we learned to be involved in everyone's "process," and as adults we don't know how to stop.

Our overinvolvement with other people's problems serves as a salve for our own pain. As long as our attention is taken up by someone else's troubles, we don't need to focus on our own. In our workshops, we meet couples who have made a habit of paying much more attention to their partner's process than their own. As long as we make our happiness dependent on our partner's recovery, we are sunk. If we wait for our partner to make the first move, we may wait forever.

Merrill was full of sadness when she finally realized all the opportunities she'd missed waiting for her husband to go first. She was so busy "minding his process" that she didn't mind hers.

Merrill: I wanted to go away for a three-day weekend, and I decided that my husband, Merv, should take the initiative and make all the reservations. I didn't tell him this is what I wanted, and I just waited. When he didn't do it, I got mad. But it was so stupid. I was the one who wanted to go away, and I knew if I'd suggested it to Merv, he would have been perfectly agreeable to it. I really am the initiator in our relationship, and I wish I could just accept that. I feel sad when I think about how many opportunities we've missed because I've waited for him.

It's probably hardest to learn to mind your own process in intimate relationships. The boundary between partners can often become so blurry that the relationship takes on a life of its own, and may move in a direction neither person likes. When the two people start talking about the relationship as if it were a separate entity, that is a signal that they have lost contact with themselves and are very busy examining each other's process. They lose sight of the fact that they are dealing with a real person who thinks, feels, and acts independently.

Karen: Minding my own process has never been one of my strengths. Gifted with a heightened sensitivity to what goes on in other people, I was always minding someone else's process and never my own. Most often I focused on Rick, my husband. I knew all his shortcomings, all his failings, and the problems they caused in our relationship. No matter how he might try to hide them from himself, or from me, I always knew best what direction his growth should take. And I had a real stake in addressing it. Unable to bear my own pain, I was certain that my unhappiness was caused by him. I insisted that he change, believing that if he did, our relationship would improve. All of this emphasis on him meant that I never had to look at my own behavior and feelings.

Even in less intimate circumstances, the problem is the same. When we become so enmeshed with another person, we lose contact with who they are. The result is that we interact with our projection of who we see them as, and we end up playing both parts in the relationship. When this happens, we leave little room for understanding and satisfaction.

Terry: Learning to mind my own process has resulted in the most important growth in my life. I now have faith in the capacity of each individual to heal, no matter how great the damage. Not surprisingly, many of my lessons came when I was in training to be a psychotherapist. I realize now that I was unconsciously trying to make a career out of minding other people's processes. I had to learn that it was my job to *understand* my clients, not *fix* them, or convince them that doing things my way would make their lives better. As I discovered my own boundaries, I was better able to help my clients find theirs.

As Terry was able to learn to mind his own process, he found a way to contain his feelings that worked for him. Another client, Edwin, like Terry, had to fight against the impulse to always mind someone else's process.

Edwin: I had to learn to mind my own process, and it wasn't easy. I have always felt that it was my job as oldest child, as a man, as a boss to others, to mind everyone else's process. I rationalized it by saying I was being helpful, and I could see their problems more clearly than they could. I'm still interested in helping people, but now I don't presume to know what is best for them. I see that the other person is separate and has a life of his own.

This is most difficult for me with my wife. I have always made the effort to accommodate the needs of women, while unconsciously believing that they are manipulative witches that may eventually take over my life if I'm not careful. This makes me see-saw between being nice and erupting with rage when I feel pushed. Once I start paying attention to my own process instead of my wife's, I become aware of when I am allowing my boundaries to be violated and am more able to negotiate instead of getting angry when she asks me to do something.

The cycle of the nice guy turned monster does not happen so often when I mind my own process. While

I act within my own boundary, I can be more fully attentive, because I am not so caught up in someone else's problems. I am listening without assuming that my way or my experience applies to them.

By staying within his own boundaries, Edwin stopped turning himself into a monster and picking fights with his wife. The ensuing calmness and lack of anxiety were Edwin's rewards.

Exercise I.
Witnessing

We help people learn to mind their own process in our workshops with a simple exercise we call Witnessing. Find an uninterrupted hour to do this exercise. Sit opposite someone you trust and feel comfortable with. As you face each other, one person in the pair will act as a "witness" and say, "Tell me how you feel inside." The other person answers with what he is aware of feeling. Sometimes the feeling that emerges is historical and the witness can provide a face to speak to about old hurts, griefs, angers, or joys. Do this as if it is happening in the present, with time and space suspended. This allows feelings to come more directly to the surface. After a few minutes, you reverse roles. Taking several turns in each direction tends to deepen the experience, because each person stimulates and inspires the other to deeper feeling. In the context of a workshop, many people are able to tap deep feelings of pain, anger, and fear.

The witness has instructions to give no response, but to simply give concentrated attention. Usually the impulse of the witness is to console quickly, be overtly and visibly empathic or withdrawn. Sometimes the witness also jumps in and becomes "therapeutic" and offers suggestions. As the witness, try to see that you are being unhelpful when you respond this way. First, you are being impatient with your partner and want him to do more than he is doing. Second, you are communicating to your partner that you don't believe he can bear the feelings that he is expressing.

We then invite you as the witness to consider another way of listening, which involves minding your own process. In giving simple focused attention to your partner, you are providing a context in which the partner can bear his own feelings. Your job is to disengage yourself and simply "witness."

In the less structured time that follows this exercise, minding one's own process gets more difficult. Consider the problem that emerged for Ted and Elaine in one of our extended retreats. Ted, thirty-nine, was a gentle man whose alcoholism surfaced in the Navy. In the early part of our workshop, we saw how angry he was at his absent father and inattentive mother. Mostly he felt sorry for himself, and this drove Elaine up the wall. To us, it seemed that Ted was doing some positive work, expressing his grief publicly for the first time. Elaine, forty-two, found herself seething and wondering why we weren't pushing Ted to take responsibility for his own life. "Isn't he just being a victim and moaner?" she asked.

We responded, "It seems like it, but what's it to you? Isn't Ted telling his story the way it happened?" When she was pushed to consider that she wasn't minding her own process, she felt like a scapegoat. It wasn't that we thought Elaine was wrong, but we felt that Ted's boundaries and pace needed to be respected. When Elaine began to mind her own process, she became aware of the fear she experienced when Ted cried. What she was really afraid of was her own weakness, and as soon as she stopped focusing on Ted, she was able to begin confronting this.

In an intimate relationship, giving yourself and your partner time to express thoughts and feelings without responding can be a valuable exercise in learning to mind your own process. Both people will discover that a deeper closeness can develop from expression and attention—not always immediately, but with time.

Item 2. *This May Not Be So*

> Afraid of confronting the residual childhood confusion, ACOAs invent stories to define their reality. When we consider the possibility that we may not know what's going on in any given situation, we create the opportunity to be open to new experiences, including the wonder and delight in life.

Many ACOAs are very sensitive (as children we had to be for our survival) and can pick up subtle clues. We are often aware of what other people around us feel. The habit of assigning a meaning to events also survives from our childhood, and we constantly explain and make logical the information we pick up, although we aren't always aware that this is what we are doing. We also continue to have the belief that what we don't understand will hurt us, thus increasing our desire to find meaning in events. There is, however, a tendency and danger of becoming too self-assured and overconfident about correctly reading a situation when in fact we might be wrong. These misjudgments can get us into trouble. Learning to question yourself and sometimes say, "This may not be so," is designed to temper this tendency and offer a model of humility and healthy self-doubt with which to approach any given situation. Humility does not mean telling yourself that you are less. It means telling yourself that you are human, fallible, and may not always be right.

In working with this, we must keep in mind that there is a thin line between sensitivity and paranoia. At the same time, if you think that something is going on, it probably is, given your sensitivity. It is the explanation you give the situation that may be wrong or exaggerated.

A woman in a workshop told us a story of just how wrong we can be when we blindly assume what things mean. One night she came down the stairs in a new dress to find her husband looking at her with a strange expression on his face. Immediately she assumed this meant he didn't like the dress or that it made her look fat. She didn't ask him what his look meant, getting mad at him instead, and she felt bad about it for days. In fact, we suggested, couldn't her husband's look have meant: "She's wearing a dress. Maybe I should put on a tie?" She was flabbergasted. It had been so important for her to assign meaning because it was better than not knowing what was going on. She had believed what she wanted to believe without even questioning that it "may not be so."

As children our lives were dependent on knowing when danger was near. But as adults why do we still always expect the worst? Why don't we allow ourselves to be humble and curious sometimes? It is because we feel safer when we prepare for the worst. We were so often criticized as children, we now believe that we always have to know what we are talking about and be right, if we are to be valuable people. This makes it nearly impossible for us to be easygoing when we are unsure, because our self-esteem always seems to be at stake. To accept that "this may not be so" is to lean back and relax within the safety of your boundaries, letting contact come to you. When we say, "This may not be so," we ask questions, gather data, and reserve judgment, instead of instantly assuming that we know just what's going on. This is a good goal to focus on as you make the switch from pain avoidance to the pursuit of pleasure, because you will quickly discover that many of your conclusions about situations are pain-based rather than trust-based.

When we first met Andrew, a thirty-seven-year-old Spanish teacher at a high school, he was tortured with conflict about his wife's very active sexual history. He loved her dearly, but her past haunted and repelled him. It was as though Andrew had no boundaries, and his wife's previous lovers were in the bedroom with them. Andrew couldn't help but think that his wife compared him to previous lovers and was sure his judgments and feelings were correct. His obsession with this finally brought him to therapy. Andrew had decided he didn't love his wife anymore and wanted support for leaving her.

In therapy, careful questioning of Andrew and his wife revealed that he really did like his wife's interest in sex and her availability to him. His assumptions that she was comparing him to other men simply were not so, and he discovered that what his wife's sexual history was reminding him of was his childhood memories of his father's weekly, drunken poker game where pornographic movies were shown. As a young boy Andrew had been torn between his desire to be with the men and his desire to honor the loyalty he felt for his mother. His fantasy was that his love for his mother was of a higher order. Under examination, this turned out not to be true, and Andrew admitted that his mother had been dependent upon him and often seductive as well. Andrew had been emotionally torn apart until his parents divorced. He discovered with amazement that he had been re-creating the same conflict in his own life by thinking that a sexual woman was a bad woman, and a nonsexual woman was a good woman, like his mother.

It is important to develop a sense of humility and wonder about the way things are. It is not by accident that the great mystics in almost all religious traditions talk of states of consciousness where they don't know anything or can't speak about what they know. There is much in the human experience that is impossible to describe and classify, and there is much in life that is mysterious and full of wonder. When we tell ourselves, "This may not be so," we open ourselves up to discovery.

If you find yourself drawing conclusions about your loved ones and others, stop and ask yourself, "How can I be sure of that?" You may think it is your intuition speaking, but we caution you against acting as though your intuitions are always correct.

Exercise II.
Challenging Your Internal Dialogue

This is an exercise that you can do anywhere. It involves noticing the story you have about everyone around you. If you are on a bus or in a restaurant, give yourself a couple of minutes to hear what you are thinking about these people. Have a conversation with yourself about what you think these people are like. What does the expression on a person's face tell you about his life? What is the story you think of that expresses this person's childhood relationships? What do you imagine are this person's current intimate relationships? Then stop yourself and think, "This may not be so." Notice how that makes you feel. Are you still convinced of the validity of your intuition, or are you reconsidering? Notice the anxiety that arises in not knowing.

Now consider your closest friend in the same way. Notice the story you have about him or her for a few minutes, and then stop yourself, as before, with "This may not be so." The closer you get to someone, the harder it is to maintain a sense of wonder and curiosity about who that person is, or is becoming, but for a relationship to grow, this wonder must be present. Healthy lovers support each other to grow and look forward with confidence to discoveries ahead.

Item 3. *I Give to You and You Give to Me*

ACOAs have been so hurt in the name of love that in our adult lives we avoid equal, intimate relationships. Being receptive to love and learning to give love in return are important parts of recovery. The key word here is "equal." We focus on the problem of intimacy in terms of equality because historically, when we got close (to our parents), we got clobbered. Intimacy that is unequal will always have this shadow hanging over it by introducing the question of power in the relationship. Fear takes the place of intimacy and trust.

Karen: Terry and I have been friends a long time. Years ago we were sitting at the table when my husband, Rick, said, "Karen, I love you." I imagined that he'd just hurled a ball of vomit at me aimed right for my gut. "Yuck!" I said, almost without thinking. "I think," Terry said, "that you two need to find a new word for love."

This was good advice. So much hurt had been done to me in the name of love that I wanted nothing to do with it. "I love you best of all," my mother said, "because you're the oldest." What her loving meant was that I had to give myself up and do it her way. If this was love, I'd rather be hated. When people express their love to me, I think, "What do they want?" I know better, but I still have trouble convincing myself otherwise. I still sometimes have the suspicion that love isn't something you share, it's something that's demanded of you.

As ACOAs we experienced so much emotional and physical pain from those we loved most that it is now difficult to accept love into our lives today. The way the pain-avoidant person deals with this fear of love is to cultivate relationships at either end of the dependency spectrum. Either we become overly dependent in our relationships, acting out the impossible desire to have our mate be a parental replacement and make up for our childhood betrayals, or we move through the world sending out the message "I need no one," politely acting grateful for acts of kindness and the willingness of others to put up with our various inadequacies.

As most of us have learned, each time we suffer a heartbreak, it becomes harder to get the courage to try again. What seems most difficult when we look at our past relationships is finding one where the giving and the receiving were equal. In these past relationships, if we had not established a pattern of interaction with clearly stated expectations of who takes which role when, we felt out of control. By contrast, an emotionally vital relationship is characterized by open definitions and freedom, and commitment grows out of joy, not dependency.

Many of us would prefer guarantees in our life, because knowing what will happen, even if the outcome is bad, is preferable to taking a chance on the unfolding of an adult relationship. Many of us are afraid of people we can't control and bored by people whom we can control. Johanna is an example of this kind of person. According to Johanna, her sexual relationships developed with strong emotional fervor on both sides, but would eventually fall into a pattern of the man needing to control her. When she refused to give in and be controlled, he would leave her.

> **Johanna:** I'm just not attracted to nice guys. I may be able to see that they are perfectly appropriate for me, but sexually they leave me cold. I've now been in enough relationships with men to know that when I choose them, they will do me wrong. Whatever it is in me that gets turned on can't be trusted. I've been without a relationship now for four years, and I'd rather be alone than hurt again.

What is going wrong in Johanna's relationships? Why is she always attracted to men who want to control her? Because she would prefer to engage in the game of struggling for control rather than take her chances with true intimacy. The next step for Johanna is to learn to find sexual feeling for the man who wants to be kind to her. Although it will feel frightening to let herself be receptive, she must learn to say, "I give to you and you give to me."

As in Johanna's case, sexual urges can over and over again draw one into self-destructive situations that are not easy to break out of. Learning to give and receive love on an equal basis is a trial-and-error endeavor, and you have to be out there and take your knocks like everyone else. We must teach each other what brings us joy. The cornerstone of the success of "I give to you and you give to me" is the switch to pleasure as the focus of your life.

> **Terry:** When I met Gale, I was still shocked by the barrage of criticism I had received in my first marriage. I felt like I could do nothing right sometimes. The one commitment I had made to myself after my first

marriage was to find a woman who was easygoing and relaxed. I had had my fill of intensity and passionate arguing. I felt, somewhat self-deprecatingly, that I wasn't up to that again. I think I thought that had I been a "real man," I could have worked out my first marriage.

I now see that I was stumbling, quite unconsciously, down the road of maturity, choosing companionship and respect over control and the pursuit of unavailable women. Once I made the choice to pursue the available woman and not the woman who was always a challenge, I never looked back.

Exercise III.
Opening the Heart to Another

In our couples workshops, we do an exercise that was developed at Arica, a psychospiritual training center, which allows a couple to investigate their issues of equality. Find a partner you feel you can trust and with whom you are willing to be intimate. Sit facing each other and look into your partner's left eye. Breathe deeply and slowly, emptying yourself of thoughts and feelings. Sitting empty allows each of you to experience the connection between the two of you. At its essence, we believe the connection to be of deep and unconditional love. In order to feel this connection, both partners must be "present," and the experience must be uninterrupted. If one partner is dependent on the other, or is full of resentment, or feels superior, these feelings will block the opening to love. Unconditional love happens between equals and is an experience of equal give-and-take. Be honest with yourself about whatever thoughts are coming up. It is all "grist for the mill."

After a few minutes of eye gazing, we ask the partners to take turns sharing honestly about what feelings, thoughts, or images are causing them to hold back. Often, buried resentments emerge, feelings of not being loved resurface, that may have little or nothing to do with your partner in this exercise. After several rounds of eye gazing and sharing with each other what thoughts or feelings you have, we invite you to add a variation which will counter any negative images. Take turns saying the words "You love me" to each other, listening closely to the various ways you might utter these words. The goal, of course, is to believe that this is possible: you are lovable.

Ultimately, by working on "I give to you and you give to me," you'll develop a clear sense of your boundaries. Through this you can also learn to give and receive without any greater expectation than one of pleasure.

Item 3. *Recover From "Don't Mind Me"*

ACOAs are not good at setting limits that are appropriate to their own needs. Even if we can say "no" without hesitation, we doubt our right to say it and feel guilty for asserting ourselves. We need to learn that it is okay to have boundaries and useful to specify what they are.

When you live life saying, "Don't mind me," you make it difficult for others to respond to you in a healthy fashion, because the underlying message is always "I don't really matter." If you can't say, "I do matter," then you can't say "I exist." When you are willing to take a stand and say, "I am here and I do matter," you are setting your boundaries for others to respect.

Why is this so hard for us? For many, the issue is unresolved guilt. We grew up thinking that we were responsible for the family, and because the family fell apart, we are to blame, and we carry that guilt with us still. Perhaps our parents were right all along—we are selfish, mean, and wrong. We think that if we don't assert our needs and opinions, no one will notice the problems we cause because of our inadequacies. When you say, "I have boundaries," you run the risk of being rejected, because you have asserted yourself. We do not want to be seen as needy or selfish, and avoid this by never expressing our desires.

At a recent couples workshop, we gave the instruction that when each couple went home, they should exchange twenty minutes of pleasure. The next morning Mickey, one of the participants, reported that she had been too tired to do the exercise and just wanted to sleep, but because we had assigned her a task, because she had been told to do something, she did it anyway.

> **Mickey:** Both Kevin and I wanted a back rub. I insisted that I give first, because I was close to falling asleep, and I was afraid that if I lay down, I'd conk out. I got out the clock and watched it carefully, and it seemed to me that twenty minutes was an incredibly long time. It never occurred to me to ask Kevin about making the time shorter, because I was told twenty minutes and I would do twenty minutes. When it was my turn to be rubbed, I was still conscious of the time, and was worried that Kevin was getting tired. I wanted to tell him it was okay if he stopped early, but I was too embarrassed.
>
> I learned a lot from that pleasure exercise. What I hope is that someday I can be my own authority, and not do things just because they are assigned and someone tells me to do them. I also saw that I wanted to give the back rub first, because I am willing to be disappointed, but I can't stand my partner to be.

Mickey has trouble with her boundaries, and in this story, both the instructions from us and the feelings she imagined her partner had took precedence over her needs. Her partner, in fact, was amazed when he heard Mickey tell this story, because he had no idea that this drama had been going on the whole time. Just as Mickey hoped, he "didn't mind her."

The difficulty in trying to correct this boundary problem in ourselves is that we so often feel guilty when we stand up for ourselves. We believe that people will be disappointed and angry if we assert ourselves, and we've had to bear so much of that all our lives, we don't want any more of it now. We would rather give up on what we really want than have people be dissatisfied with us. We stay stuck and say "yes," when what we really want to say is "no."

Nowhere is this problem more pronounced than in the area of sexuality. Sandra grew up in a highly structured family where there was abuse and punishment. She, in turn, became a dutiful and obedient wife and mother, still maintaining her "Don't mind me" stance.

> **Sandra:** For the first three years of my marriage, whenever my husband wanted sex, I'd say "yes," even if I wasn't in the mood. I thought it was my duty and I didn't want him to be angry or disappointed in me. I also accepted it when I didn't have an orgasm (which was most of the time), since I couldn't ask him to touch me the way I wanted, and it was just too embarrassing. If he didn't have an orgasm, I'd be very concerned and try to do whatever I could. I don't know why I let it all be so unbalanced. I guess I didn't think my needs really counted, but I was sure his did.

When Sandra did finally ask her husband for what she needed sexually, sure enough, he became angry. His expectations of her as wholly accommodating had been shattered, and he felt criticized by her requests. No matter how hard you may try not to rock the boat, asserting yourself for the first time can often cause trouble.

The person who says "no" all the time finds it equally difficult. He is so afraid of having his boundaries violated that he protects them overzealously, alienating those who would be close to him. Paul, twenty-seven, a computer operator, is a good example of someone who had to fight the impulse to close himself off, even to those he wanted to let in.

> **Paul:** I met a woman I really liked, and at one point, I made a conscious decision to relax my boundaries,

allowing a little inconvenience from time to time, and letting someone else in. The problem was that when I relaxed my boundaries, I felt as though I was making myself completely vulnerable, opening myself up to my abusive mother all over again. I had fought so hard to have my rights, to be able to assert myself without feeling guilty, and I thought I'd lose it all. Opening up felt like giving up my power.

Paul wasn't losing his power, he was simply getting close to a woman he liked very much. He found that he had to force himself not to react to the woman as though she was his mother who would try to control him. Karen had to learn the same thing.

Karen: Whenever Rick became sick, I got scared that it was going to be a repeat of my mother lying in her bed demanding attention and service. First she controlled us through alcoholism, and then cancer, and by the time she was really sick, I was so resentful about how she had dominated me that it was hard to be compassionate and caretaking. Later in my life when Rick became sick for a day or two, I'd find myself doing only the minimum for him. My fear was that if I said "yes" to his needs, he'd never get out of bed, and I'd be swamped, just like I was as a little girl by my mother's needs.

When struggling for an awareness of your boundaries, be prepared for friction and resistance, not only from others but from yourself as well. The better contact you have with yourself and with another person, the more fluid the interaction will be. Remember that friction is part of life, however, and be wary of trying to minimize the friction that occurs as you assert yourself.

Conflict is not always bad. The problem is that we are so afraid of conflict that we lose contact and don't function as we should. Learning to negotiate a mutually satisfactory solution can be exciting and creative. When we feel confident about our ability to say "yes," "no," or "maybe," we become relaxed about whether we will or will not do something after all.

In leading our extended workshops, there are times when the two of us disagree about the direction in which we should take the group next. Often we play out our disagreement in front of the participants. When we first start disagreeing, the tension in the room is so thick you can feel it. When ACOAs have seen authority figures in conflict in their past, there has been a real danger to them. Many of us have come to believe that when people are healthy, they do not fight. Combine this fear of conflict with our open disagreement, and you have a genuinely wonderful learning experience for everyone. Participants are able to see authorities disagree, and say, "Do mind me!" without anything terrible happening.

Since we respect each other's judgment, the direction we ultimately choose to go with the workshop is mutually agreeable and reasonable. The key to reaching this kind of satisfying resolution is for each of us to assert our point of view and listen to the other do the same. What we hear often from workshop participants is that in this kind of situation, they either want to bulldoze their way through a conflict or back down entirely. When conflicts arise, we teach people to get a sense of their "ground" from which they can speak. By "ground," we refer to the basic right each of us has to a place in the world, as a place where we can stand and say, "Do mind me." To do this, the illusion that "if I had been doing it right, there wouldn't be a conflict" must be broken. The truth is that sometimes we do hurt others when we assert ourselves. However, when we maintain the intention to be compassionate and to maintain harmlessness, and put it into practice, we can assert ourselves with confidence.

Finding your own "ground" cannot be accomplished without good contact with yourself and a sense of your own boundaries. There is enough resiliency in the human spirit to recover from damage done to one's boundaries in childhood, but it takes work and attention. As we will see in the following chapters, achieving Emotional Sobriety can be a struggle. When you finally cease to struggle with your life, however, you'll find calm and fulfillment within your self.

CHAPTER 8

Toward Emotional Sobriety: Learning Moderation

ACOAs often have little sense of moderation. Our moods swing violently from one of the spectrum to the other, and we tend to see things in black or white, either/or terms. Our addictions and other pain-avoidant behaviors keep us on a roller coaster of excitement and make moderate and normal life look boring. But once we have broken our addictive patterns, moderation begins to look much more attractive. No longer does it imply a dull life to us. It is appreciated for the simplicity, sense of reality, and pleasure it can bring to our lives. Moderation is an important part of living an emotionally sober life.

Learning moderation does not come easily to ACOAs. When we have not faced our pain-avoidant way of life, we are afraid of the quiet and peace that moderation can bring. We may also sense that when we let go of the drama in our lives, the pain and anxiety underneath will surface. Since we can only cover it up for so long, the only way to deal with this internal anxiety is to stop and face it. Next, we must learn to adjust to the simple pace of everyday life instead of the chaotic pace of a life filled with crisis. We must learn to make an adjustment in the way our lives operate: to switch from involving ourselves in the storm that surrounds us to focusing on the quiet center within ourselves.

Moderation must be learned—it does not come naturally to the ACOA. This chapter will help you to introduce moderation into your life. In our program for Emotional Sobriety, we offer methods that are designed to help you live a life of moderation instead of a life that is based on addiction, pain avoidance, and pseudo-pleasure.

In the previous chapter, we looked at how to develop contact and boundaries as part of the program for Emotional Sobriety. When you have established a firm sense of boundaries and developed good contact with yourself and the world around you, you have provided yourself a context in which to find Emotional Healing in your life. Without a good sense of boundaries, the storm around you will draw you in and sweep you away. Without a good sense of what to let in and keep out, you will cut yourself off from the pleasure life offers.

Having personal boundaries allows us to be moderate and in control of our emotions. We are able to make a better choice about when to act assertive and when to act tender. When we know that we can protect our boundaries, we no longer feel that we have to guard them so zealously. When we live a life of moderation, we become more relaxed, and we can be vulnerable when we choose. We are confident in our ability to know when it is best to open up and when it is best to close down.

Some of us make the same mistake over and over of disclosing too much about ourselves, and we must learn that it is important when, and to whom, we reveal our inner thoughts. There are times when it is best to hold back. Others of us need to learn to disclose more of ourselves, since self-disclosure is important in keeping intimacy alive. Each of us needs to learn where our own middle ground of self-disclosure lies.

Learning to Take Your Time

As we learn more about the subtleties of negotiating the appropriate levels of self-disclosure, we must also learn to slow down and feel the truth of a particular moment. When we live in the moment, we no longer respond out of past programming and confuse now with then, but respond out of feelings that are current, that belong to the moment. We begin to see that we don't really need to make an immediate or impulsive response, but that it is okay to take our time and think about an appropriate response. There is moderation in the use of our time; it is not always a matter of "now or never."

> **Karen:** Whenever I was asked for a decision about anything, I always felt rushed. The fact was that until I was alone and quiet, I really had trouble being in touch with how I felt about a decision, separate from what people wanted me to feel. I was so used to trying to discern my parents' preferences from their facial expression or tone of voice that my attention was always focused outside myself. I thought my task was to guess what the other person wanted—I was good at that—and there were always rewards for being so accommodating and cooperative. I was also familiar with what would happen if I did not "go with the program." The problem with all this was that as soon as I was alone, I would begin to feel what I wanted, and then I'd be full of conflict about whether I could change my mind, whether I could disappoint people, whether I could live with a decision I didn't like.

What can we do when we find ourselves leaping into promises and commitments we later realize we don't want to keep? First we must learn how to create the necessary time and space for ourselves so that we can ponder our decisions. We must learn to say things like, "I need time to think this over." We must then take that time to think about our decision, to think about similar instances in the past, and to ask for feedback from our friends. It is our sense of obligation and our addiction to the excitement of immediacy and crisis that force us into premature response. If someone pushes us hard for a decision, we need not let that become our problem. If we find ourselves abandoning our own desires because of pressure from the outside, we need to think about our boundaries and the level of contact we are interacting on.

> **Terry:** As the oldest child in a highly verbal family, I was always encouraged to say whatever was going through my head at any given moment. It both relieved my anxiety and gave me the excitement of "airtime," even though no one in my family really listened to what anyone else said. As I ventured out into the world, I found that I was often having to account for things I'd said that I really had very little interest in or feeling for. Learning a sense of moderation in this area came from learning to listen carefully to other people and slow down in my habit of responding to someone before they'd even finished what they were saying. I am more careful now about what I say, and I get myself into many fewer misunderstandings and embarrassments this way.

Moving Toward Moderation

The part of Emotional Sobriety that introduces moderation into our lives entails focusing attention in a number of different ways.

Item 1. *Emotional Sobriety Means Facing Our Addictions*

> The addictive part of our personality is a strong one, and in order to liberate ourselves from its grip, we must face into the struggle that surrounds it, and be willing to tolerate the turbulence that comes from withdrawal from an addiction.

As we've discussed before, addiction means not being able to stop a particular behavior, even if our minds and our hearts beg us to do so. For addictive people, the price we must pay—hangovers, loss of friends, job, money, health—seems small compared to the euphoric effects we derive from our addictions.

We've seen that growing up in an environment where there was addiction greatly increases our chances of being addicted as well. Our tendency to become addicted may also have a biochemical component and be passed down genetically from generation to generation. But genetics aside, what is it that we learned in our families that led us to become addicted in the first place?

We learned that certain feelings are intolerable, that anger cannot be resolved and sorrow cannot be worked through. We saw people fighting about the same things, year after year, that they held grudges and were unable to forgive and move on. We saw our families grieve over the same things time and again, and from this we learned that sadness is a permanent fact of life that can never be resolved or eased.

Because things never change, and there was no growth in our families, we learned to adopt a sense of hopelessness about life, about things ever being resolved and improving. In fact, our fears were most often confirmed—things often did get worse—and to cope, we turned to addictive behaviors to find relief for ourselves.

It is often very hard to admit that we are addicted. At the

heart of the nature of addiction is the inability to see that one is addicted in the first place. "I can stop anytime I want to. I just don't want to right now" is the addict's greatest rationalization. We tell ourselves that one more drink or one more pill isn't really going to hurt. Some of us may not even realize that our drug *is* addictive. Many of us who grew up in the sixties and seventies may find it hard to admit that marijuana is an addictive drug. We worried about alcohol, but marijuana was a seemingly harmless and necessary part of our personal spiritual growth. The problem is that when we look back, we see that for twenty years we have been using a substance to alter our consciousness, and that's a long time. We must ask ourselves what it is in our lives that is so stressful or so horrible that we need to alter our perception of it time after time.

Fritz, a thirty-three-year-old plumber, is an example of someone whose recreational use of marijuana became a habit he could not kick.

Fritz: I remember when my father used to say his best ideas came when he was drunk. When he realized that things had gotten out of hand, that he'd become an alcoholic, he begged me to be careful. By the time you realize you're addicted, he said, it's too late. I vowed to myself that I would not fall into the same trap as my father, and decided absolutely to avoid alcohol. I liked the smell of marijuana, though—it reminded me of fall and burning leaves—and by watching my brother and his friends, I saw that it didn't make you crazy or grow fangs, but it made you calm and smile, and it was a protest against the drug of alcohol.

By the time I was fourteen, I had started to experiment with smoking myself. I wanted a way to change my perceptions, to lessen my feelings of displeasure and confinement. I wanted to be creative, heard, and respected. For a while, smoking was experimentation, a game of seeing how high I could get. Now it is far from that.

The physical painkilling effects of marijuana are why I smoke. Nothing makes me feel better than getting stoned, and I can relax and ignore my injuries. I wouldn't call it euphoria, but when I am high, I often am filled with the energy to work on projects I might normally not. Marijuana lets me cope with my physical and mental pain. But now it's not doing as much for me as it once did, and it's time to stop. I can stop for a few weeks and the desire to smoke seems to go away, and then the first time I get stoned, I don't like the feeling—confusion, paranoia, increased heartbreak—but soon the desire to smoke takes over, and I find that once again I am getting stoned every day. I know that I need to quit to have my self-esteem. At this point, I don't know how to take this step, and I am too proud to ask for help.

Fritz does need help and is aware of his predisposition toward addictive behavior. Clearly his use of marijuana is no longer recreational, and as Fritz realized, his task was to reestablish his self-esteem and goals, making his achievements and excitements his high in life.

Certain patterns of sexual behavior can also be labeled addictive. There is a compulsive quality to certain sexual behavior that seems to have little to do with the pleasure and joy of sexual feeling and even less to do with the reality of the situation. It begins with anticipation and a fantasy of how this will be the romance to end all romances, how this will be the love to change everything. Often it involves a level of distortion, where one views one's object of affection to be equally desirous of the union, despite a lack of evidence to the contrary. This part of the cycle—the fantasizing, the stalking—may be drawn-out and highly exciting. Then the conquest occurs, inevitably followed by disappointment, boredom, and remorse, and soon the cycle begins all over again. The continual emotional up-and-down that this behavior provides, as with all addictions, is a way to hide underlying pain.

As ACOAs we believe that our parents allowed themselves to become addicted, and for many years we have said that we will never allow that to happen to us; yet sometimes our addictions creep up on us so slowly we don't even realize what's happening. And because our addictions have at times given us the rare feeling of wholeness, and have increased our awareness, opening us up to a sensitivity we didn't know we had, they have relieved us of much of our pain. ACOAs find it hard to identify their addictive patterns because it often takes a while before these habits turn on us and become ugly and destructive; they simply seem to be a way of life.

People who are ready to face their addictions come to see their actions as self-destructive and recognize that things are not working. They must become humble in the face of the substances and behaviors that rule their lives. There are several guidelines we offer you to protect yourself against deepening your involvement with an addiction:

1. *Don't indulge in the addictive behavior when you are in pain or feeling down.* Call up a friend instead, take a walk, cry, punch a pillow. Embrace your feelings and you'll embrace your life.

2. *Accept that it's okay to be a "cheap drunk."* If you can get high off one beer, feel it, enjoy it, and stop there. If you particularly love the taste of something, eat it slowly and savor each bite. If you cannot set limits for yourself, stay away from that food or drink entirely.

3. *Vary your habits.* If you insist on eating or drinking the same food and drink every day, you may have a problem. Attempt to break some seemingly innocuous habits.

4. *Be mindful.* Be aware of what you are doing and when you are doing it. Give your friends permission to point out your behavior to you. Allow them to say, "You've already had a drink" or "That's your second slice of cake."

5. *Replace a negative addiction with a positive behavior.* Exercise can replace worrying and anxiety and can actually make one feel euphoric. Meditation can also ease withdrawal from certain habits such as smoking, drinking, and caffeine intake.

6. *Consider abstinence.* The best protection against addiction is abstinence, the second best is moderation, and the third is allowing friends to intervene and help you deal with your problems of addiction.

As we consider moderation in our lives, we also find that some AA guidelines are helpful: "One day at a time," "Easy does it," "Keep it simple." These slogans remind us to slow down, to not expect that we can change ourselves overnight, and to keep focused and on track.

As we begin to change our lives, it is helpful to keep in mind some more items of Emotional Sobriety.

Item 2. *"It's Not All Up to Me"*

> Our feelings of responsibility are deep and extend to everything that happens around us, and we blame ourselves when things go wrong. We need to learn that we are not in charge of everything.

We grew up in families where blame was assigned without justification, where action and reaction bore no relationship. Our parents told us that they drank because of us, couldn't sleep because of us, abused us because of what we did. They told us that we were the source of all the pain and turmoil, and we believed it. No wonder we now think that we can affect everything around us.

Karen: I had a very powerful lesson about how it was not all up to me when I was seventeen. I ignored it then but can look back on it now. One day I was driving my father's car when a suitcase from the car in front of me fell out onto the road. I could have pulled around the suitcase and continued on, but instead I stopped the car and got out. Then I saw that there was a long line of cars behind me, and the feelings of responsibility for the suitcase suddenly switched to the cars behind me, and I threw the suitcase to the side and got in my car. Then I saw that the people who had dropped the suitcase in the first place were backing up in my direction. I tried to get out of the way as fast as possible, and I drove over the suitcase! As I drove off, the owners of the suitcase were shaking their fists at me, and I was overcome with remorse at the whole situation.

Because we often feel that life is all up to us, we worry about the future and become immobilized when we think about what might happen. Our worrying becomes compulsive and fills us with a feeling of pessimism and negativity. A traditional Hopi leader named Grandfather David once said: "Worrying is praying for what you don't want." This is particularly true when we find ourselves dwelling on our fears as though we were waiting for them to come true, rather than expending our energy on making our dreams into reality. Worrying is a way we can protect ourselves from being surprised. If we anticipate disaster and disappointment, we feel that we will not hurt as much when it occurs. The fact is, however, that all we can really deal with is today, and if we take one day at a time, we can manage our lives effectively.

Recovery means having the freedom to choose, and there may be times when we choose to take responsibility and be in charge, and there may be times when the healthy choice is to sit back. For example, one of the very positive aspects of the ACOA movement is that by getting people together to work on the project of recovery, we are introducing them to a middle ground where an individual's success at recovery depends on other members' sharing and sense of community. We see that when we cooperate on something, the weight of responsibility lessens but the satisfaction of having done a good job does not, and we discover that there are others around to share our joys and pains.

Item 3. *A Feeling for Every Thought and a Thought for Every Feeling*

As we introduce moderation into our lives, ACOAs need to learn that there is balance between thinking and feeling. We need to reconnect with our true feelings, understanding, accepting, and expressing them in appropriate ways.

There are three components to any moment: the physical data (words, gestures, glances, etc.), the thought or story we tell ourselves about the data, and finally, the feelings we have about it. For ACOAs, the connection among these three components is not always there, because perceptions are often distorted, stories are often fantasized, and feelings are often distanced or denied. Much of what we feel about any given thing or circumstance has less to do with the reality of today than it does with our past. Feelings that have not been dealt with in the past have a way of creeping into everything in the present. Separating what belongs to the past from what exists in the present becomes far more difficult.

Karen: It's as though I've lived my whole life through my nervous system. My husband, Rick, used to say, "Why don't you *listen* to what I have to say?" In fact, I did listen, but only peripherally, because it was much more important for me to register what I *felt* as he spoke. Growing up in a family where there was such a distance between what people said and what was going on, I learned to distrust words and rely on my feelings and reactions for the truth. The problem with this was that I was often unable to discriminate among all the feelings that were swirling inside me at once. Much of the time when I was with other people, I wasn't sure if I was picking up their feelings or my own. All the emotions that I wasn't acknowledging made me very vulnerable to crying jags and depression. Perhaps at times I needed to feel other people's feelings in order to experience some of my own.

In contrast to Karen, some people protect themselves from feeling by living life from their heads. People who do this are scared out of their intuitive and spontaneous feelings. They can't cry deeply even when they are in a safe place, and they simply cannot acknowledge certain feelings. Jordan, a thirty-five-year-old lawyer, protected himself from the confusion he felt growing up in this way.

Jordan: My father was rich, successful, respected, and an alcoholic. He functioned very well during the day, but every night he got drunk. The family coped with this through denial. I don't think my siblings and I ever acknowledged Dad's drinking problem to each other, and I'm not sure I ever acknowledged it to myself. In the workshops, I felt that I could only participate on the level of ideas. I know I was too scared to experience my feelings, that I could only go so far before I started analyzing and distancing myself from them.

Finding a balance between thoughts and feelings requires an accurate self-assessment. Jordan and Karen needed to move in different directions—they will never have the same psychological makeup—but each needs to develop interest and respect for his or her thoughts and feelings, and to bring the two together in a dynamic and meaningful interaction.

Whether we have too much feeling or too little, the way to begin to own our emotion is to be able to connect our thoughts with our feelings, because what we think, and how we think, affects how we feel. In order to avoid being overwhelmed by feelings, we need to stop and identify the thought we had that sparked the feeling. The thought "No one at this party likes me" may fly so quickly through our heads that we don't even hear ourselves thinking it, but find ourselves suddenly feeling shy and uncomfortable because of it. When we are aware of the thoughts we have, we can then have a more balanced response to the feelings we have. When we think, "No one at this party likes me," and become aware of how that thought is making us feel, we can then choose to think instead, "No one here knows me, but when they do get to know me a little, they'll like me." This thought produces a feeling of excitement and challenge, not inferiority and insecurity.

If, on the other hand, we have no feelings, we can use the same technique of attaching feelings to thoughts to discover our emotional lives. We begin by noticing thoughts we have that our intellect tells us we should have a feeling for. If you think about a parent dying, or being deserted by a lover, and you feel nothing, you might be suspicious about where those feelings have gone. When you are aware of feelings you think you might have buried somewhere, you support the emergence of those feelings. As you become aware of the kinds of thoughts you are having, you can then see which thoughts are shields against feeling. Becoming aware of this dynamic between thought and feeling can slowly help bring about a change.

Therapeutic situations such as workshops and therapy can provide safe environments for learning to bring out buried feelings. In such structured contexts, focused attention from another helps keep one on track, and makes it more difficult to fall back on old coping mechanisms. When first opening up to deep feelings, it can be frightening and sometimes seem humiliating, but over time, and with support, it begins to feel more familiar and welcomed. The goal in this is not a final or ultimate purging of feelings, but a confidence within that you can bear these feelings. As a child you were not able to, but as an adult you can, and it is the focused attention and the reassurance from others that help you develop the confidence to acknowledge your feelings without turning them into a problem or becoming overwhelmed by them.

Item 4. *Being Appropriate Works Better*

In our childhood, our parental role models were flawed. Bizarre and unpredictable behavior passed for normal, so that we grew up, not knowing what kind of behavior is appropriate in any given situation. As far as we are concerned, being brutalized and criticized is normal, so that we now don't know how to be good friends, lovers, or parents. The even greater problem is that when we don't know what normal is, when we are unable to see that things could be different and better.

Karen: After I married Rick, I told him what it was like growing up in my house and he was appalled. He told me that the chaos I had grown up in was not normal. It was hard for me to see it that way, though, see it from his point of view, because I'd always thought that things weren't so bad. If I remembered something about my past and began to feel emotional about it, I'd think I was just being melodramatic.

Once Rick was particularly outraged by the fact that my mother used to hit me across the face without warning. "Oh, no," I told him, "I always knew when it was coming." In my mind that made it all okay. "Most children," Rick said, "don't get slapped across the face. It's a very violent thing to do." The fact was, I didn't know that. I thought it was hard and unpleasant, but basically okay and normal.

The fact is that healthy parents, through their own behavior and through teaching, pass on to their children constructive and understandable rules for relating. In contrast, alcoholic and abusive parents force their children into rigid roles and arbitrary and inconsistent rules that constrict the child's natural development. Now as adults, our lives do not work, and we don't know what appropriate behavior is. In relationships, we find ourselves either overly dependent or too aloof. We have difficulty in jobs and with colleagues. We don't know what distance to maintain and we don't always know how to behave in different social situations. As recovering ACOAs we now have the task of learning about appropriate behavior.

We are often ashamed to ask about simple things we think we should already know, and admitting that we need help and guidance is not in our repertoire. We so often distrust authority that it is also hard for us to listen when we are being taught. But as adults we can surround ourselves with trusted friends whom we can ask advice from and articulate our fears to without humiliation or fear of criticism. One word of caution: Choose your friends and advisors carefully. Know in which areas they can advise you well, and be aware of when you should consult someone else. One friend might be great for career advice, but don't turn to him for help with your relationship when he's going through a divorce. Choose your mentors carefully, and ask advice from people who are role models rather than fellow sufferers.

When you develop a relationship with a trusted friend or friends, you can start learning by noticing what it is they do. This does not mean that you should look for someone to imitate, because you need to rediscover your own individual desires, quirks, and values. There is a tremendous range of what is considered appropriate behavior, and each of us must be exposed to the options, so look at the way different people act differently in various areas of life. The goal is to have a choice. The word "trusted" is important here. In life, we come across people who are not to be trusted. They may be envious of us, jealous, angry, or just not truthful, and they will not be able to, or want to, give us good feedback and advice. There may be plenty of people who are more than willing to give you advice, but there may only be a few you really should listen to. Having grown up being abused and accepting of criticism, we may now gravitate toward people who are critical of us, thinking that if they have an opinion, it must be an opinion of value.

Exercise IV.
Goal Setting: Your Circle of Friends

There is an exercise called Your Circle of Friends that we use in our workshops that will help you think about what we have been discussing. Draw two archery targets on a piece of paper. Represent yourself at the center of each target with a star. One target represents a circle of friends and mentors from when you were younger (choose a specific age). The other represents your current circle of friends and mentors. Place your friends and mentors on the target according to how much you attend(ed) to their advice and support. Each ring out from the center is a little more distant from you. Hopefully, in the innermost circle are a handful of your most trusted friends, and they are the people you really listen to. Perhaps your parents are in an inner circle on the target representing yourself at a younger age. Notice in the example from Terry's life that there are significant people who eventually disappear or are discredited, leaving important gaps in his support system.

This can be an opportunity for you to set some goals for yourself. Are you still listening to your parents as if their opinions are as important as your own or your friends'? Do they deserve the position you have put them in? Maybe the members of your family still occupy important places on your target without really doing their jobs. You may now want to make a third target of the goals you wish to achieve. Perhaps you see that there are too few people on your current target, or too many of them have the same problems you do, or the people you have included are not sufficient for all the significant areas of your life.

In our workshops, we say that if one person tells you that you are a jackass, you simply notice it and may question that

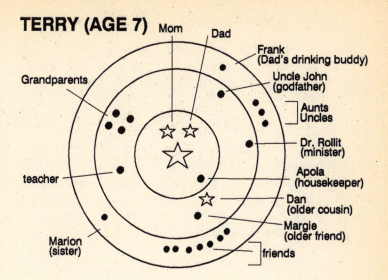

TERRY (AGE 7)

Mom
Dad
Frank
(Dad's drinking buddy)
Uncle John
(godfather)
Aunts
Uncles
Grandparents
Dr. Rollit
(minister)
Apola
(housekeeper)
teacher
Dan
(older cousin)
Margie
(older friend)
Marion
(sister)
friends

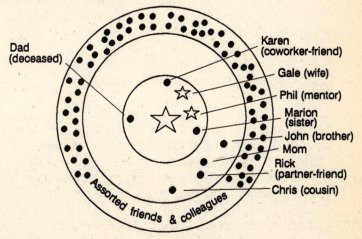

TERRY TODAY

Dad
(deceased)
Karen
(coworker-friend)
Gale (wife)
Phil (mentor)
Marion
(sister)
John (brother)
Mom
Rick
(partner-friend)
Chris (cousin)
Assorted friends & colleagues

Wish List:

- Closer male friends
- Letting my father's voice leave the target
- Finding the right spot for son, Evan
- Moving specific assorted friends & colleagues into my inner support system

person's judgment. If two people tell you that you're a jackass, you wonder if it might be true. If three people tell you, you get a saddle. What this means is that one person's opinion should not carry too much weight, but as the opinions begin to pile up, they carry more validity. Where the opinion comes from is also important to consider. If it's from someone in one of the inner circles of your target, you'll listen more carefully than if it's from someone you neither respect nor like.

Among a trusted group of friends, giving feedback is as important as receiving feedback. Learning to give feedback takes some practice, and we offer here some guidelines!

• When offering feedback, make sure that the other person wants it. The best way to find this out is by asking.

• Good feedback is specific and timely.

• Give balanced feedback so that it is not all positive and not all negative. Don't exaggerate the significance of your feedback and act as though it could change someone's life.

• Be gentle with yourself and other people. Giving and receiving feedback can often seem scary, but it is what makes having a trusted group of friends worthwhile.

Item 5. *"I'm Not Okay and You're Not Okay, and That's Okay"*

Developing self-esteem is a painstaking process of personal honesty that leads to the ability to assess oneself realistically. In time one learns to avoid the trap of feeling superior and its inverse, the trap of low self-esteem. This slogan that we use for the development of moderation in self-esteem comes to us from the expert on dying and bereavement, Elizabeth Kübler-Ross. We find the assumption that we are all injured in some way more realistic than the one that says, "I'm okay, you're okay." Being not okay is a relief and does not diminish our ability to recover from pain avoidance and pursue pleasure.

People who have healthy self-esteem value themselves but are not grandiose. They value the success of others, and when they can make another feel good, they feel good about themselves. Healthy people realize their limitations, and understand that having limitations does not curtail their essential right or capacity for fulfillment.

Too many people feel ashamed to ask for help, feeling that they should be able to handle things all by themselves. It is risky to admit that we have faults, and in a relationship this means we ask to love and be loved unconditionally, for our faults and failings as well as for our good parts.

People often make themselves feel better by comparing themselves to others. Fritz Perls, the father of Gestalt therapy, identifies two kinds of self-destructive self-esteem, Top Dog and Under Dog, one on each end of the same continuum. Top Dog arrogantly thinks that he is the best thing around and that he is better than everyone else. If we live our lives from the Top Dog position, it may be hard to give it up. What's wrong with feeling right? we wonder. The problem is that the superiority of the Top Dog does not represent a balance between strengths and weaknesses, but only a cover for uncertainty and self-doubt. Because the Top Dog attitude does not allow the possibility of failure, it is rigid and unrealistic, pompous and isolating. Under Dog, on the other hand, feels awful, believes he can't do anything right, and thinks that he is inferior to the rest of the world. Fritz Perls believes that no matter which side you identify with, the other side is right beneath it. The attitudes of Top Dog and Under Dog are opposite sides of the same coin, and one side is hiding from the other. A superior attitude, Perls says, is just a cover for feelings of inferiority, just as feelings of inferiority and insecurity are a mask for unacknowledged feelings of superiority.

The balance position is somewhere in between the two extremes. Sometimes we feel good about ourselves and sometimes we don't. Each of us has areas where we do well, and areas where we need to learn and work harder. Some days we feel "on," others we feel "off." ACOAs tend to overreact and go up and down to the extremes of this continuum of self-esteem, constantly being overwhelmed by Top Dog or Under Dog feelings. At the turn of a thought, we can feel terrific one minute and in the dumps the next. It is impossible in this great up-and-down of self-perception to get a clear idea of who we really are. Margie, twenty-seven, is an example of someone whose self-esteem went up and down in wild movements. In therapy, she struggled to develop a more secure and steady sense of herself.

> **Margie:** I was part of a circle of people who were playing instruments and singing songs. There was no established rhythm or tone yet, and it felt as though we were chanting the songs without much energy. It took all my nerve to do something, and I took over leadership of the group. I started a song in which everyone could join in, and soon we were sounding beautiful and energetic. I was really impressed with myself and believed that no one could have done what I did. When the singing was over and I was with my boyfriend, I suddenly became contemptuous and angry at how ordinary he was. He could never have done what I had, and since I felt so great, I had no way to relate to him. I started picking on him and then felt terrible for being so arrogant. A few hours later during a meeting I felt stupid and ill-informed, and I was soon back to hating myself and feeling like a slug. I don't know which feeling is worse. I hate them both.

When we admit that "I'm not okay and you're not okay and that's okay," we introduce humility into our lives. We say that sometimes we hurt, sometimes we are wrong, but our self-esteem stays intact. Self-esteem resides in our ability to love ourselves and feel as though we are making a contribution to the world in some way.

At the end of our workshops, we both ask the participants for written feedback. In the early days of our workshops, one positive statement and we felt good, one negative one and we would crash. As we would read through a hundred of these evaluations, we got a clear idea of how vulnerable we were to fluctuations in our self-esteem. We now find that even though what they say still has an emotional impact on us, our self-worth is no longer so dependent on what other people say. This we believe is an outgrowth of the Emotional Sobriety we've developed. Our self-esteem is grounded in our belief in our work, and not in what others say about us.

Once you have gotten off the roller coaster of ups and downs in your self-esteem, there is one more step: *take credit for your recovery.* Because ACOAs so often adopt the all-or-nothing stance, it is sometimes difficult for us to recognize that we are making progress at all. We tend to focus on our mistakes, and the mistakes become the whole picture. This is one reason why having a therapist or group of trusted friends can be so helpful. Because we can't see the positive things we have accomplished, they are there to point them out for us, to show us that, in fact, we are taking steps in the right direction.

Millie, a thirty-four-year-old graphic artist, had been working hard on setting limits with her family and finding the path of moderation in her reactions when things went wrong. Every time Millie was going to see her mother, she would become anxious and depressed, and she was learning how not to let her mother affect her so acutely. At the same time she was learning to distance herself from her mother, she was also forming friendships that were deeper and closer than ever before in her life. In the midst of this success, her grandmother died.

> **Millie:** After my trip home from my grandmother's funeral, I was beside myself with disappointment. My mother had started picking on me and I couldn't stand it, and I refused to go to the viewing at the funeral home. Then I had a fight with my sister, and despite the fact that finally I did go to the funeral home, the whole family was mad at me. My father accused me of being insensitive to my mother, who was under stress, and I began to feel terribly guilty about what I'd done.

I felt that all the work I'd done in therapy over the last year had just gone out the window. I thought I was a total failure, and I even began to doubt my friendships.

At this point, with the help of others in her therapy group, Millie was able to focus on what it was that had made her so upset. It turned out that she was particularly angry at her mother, because she thought she'd been cruel to her grandmother. Millie also blamed herself for not spending more time with her grandmother and giving her more pleasure. The combination of anger, grief, and guilt made Millie explode at her mother. At this point she also needed to be reminded of all the progress she had made. In her lack of moderation, she had thrown everything positive away. She needed to acknowledge that although there was still pain in her life, she was happier than she'd ever been, and that there was progress she could feel good about taking credit for.

Item 6. *Fun Is for Fun*

Feeling good and having fun don't come easily to ACOAs. Since we didn't learn how to nurture ourselves or be lighthearted, we feel guilty when we feel good, guilty when we waste time, and guilty unless we make each moment significant. We have to realize that it is okay to do nothing, to sit still and feel peaceful.

In many ways, our recovery itself leads to this very point, because it is the switch from pain avoidance to the pursuit of pleasure that will lead us there. "Fun is for fun" is another way of saying that pleasure need not have a direction or a purpose. We must use moderation here as well—"playing hard" can be pain-avoidant.

Karen: When my children were young, I thought the hardest part was having to get down on the floor and play with them. Feeding them, dressing them, comforting them was not hard at all, but just relaxing and hanging out with them was beyond me. I was the same relating to my friends. Socializing to me meant working on something—their issues, mine, or ours. If people were just hanging out and chatting, I got impatient and bored.

When I began therapy, my therapist asked me one day if I ever had fun. "Oh, yes," I said. "This weekend I was with two of my friends." "And what did you do?" Celia asked. "They talked to me about parts of myself that I haven't integrated into my personality. We identified them, and explored them. One of my friends kept notes." "That's not fun," Celia said. "That's work."

Until that moment, I don't think I'd ever really known the difference. If activities didn't have meaning, they seemed frivolous. If I enjoyed something, I quickly assigned a meaning to it instead of just letting it be plain old fun. Other people seemed to be able to just let themselves "be" while I never could.

ACOAs are serious much of the time. Believing that life is all up to us, we think that we are supposed to be solving problems all the time, and we feel guilty when we let up. As soon as we stop working, we open ourselves up to feeling those things we've been hiding for so long and we feel out of control. Fun—unplanned, spontaneous, energetic fun—frightens us, because we fear we'll be swept away into something dangerous. Growing up, we saw that fun meant getting drunk and being out of control. We saw that what began as good-natured fun ended up hurting people with cruelty and criticism. Teasing became character assassination, touching became abuse.

People who are able to have fun are relaxed and open to the adventure of new experience, and they throw themselves into it with as much enthusiasm as they throw themselves into their work. Quiet pleasures—a nap in the sun, a soak in a tub, a swim in the lake, planting a garden—require that you let go of the idea of accomplishment and allow yourself to experience the pleasure in your body. If you find that in order to have fun, you need to be competitive or take a drug, maybe you aren't having fun at all.

Above all, fun is a personal experience that only you can identify for yourself. It is not hedonist or selfish, and it is good for you in many ways. In order to recover our capacity to have fun, we need to learn how to hang out, relax, do nothing, and feel good about it. As you continue to explore your past, you will find that the intensity of the pain will lessen, and you'll be able to just be with yourself for longer and longer periods of time. No longer driven to escape the pain, you'll learn how to feel good. When you stop feeling that everything you do must be meaningful, you'll discover a new meaning: fun.

Until we learn moderation, we may feel that we need the big bang of excitement we find in addiction before we can feel anything. True pleasure is simple and often quiet. It can be found simply on the path of moderation, and we must release ourselves from our addictive patterns before we can feel it.

Betty, a woman in one of our workshops, expressed her discovery of simple pleasure this way:

> **Betty:** Last night, everyone in the group was dancing. My daughter and I went, too, but then she got tired and I had to bring her back to the tent and put her to bed. I sat there—she was asleep—in the dark, and I could hear the music and people having fun. At first I felt sorry for myself to be sitting alone, in the dark, left out. I wanted to be dancing with the others. But then I thought, wait a minute, I have a beautiful little girl here. I'll dance some other time. As I sat there listening to my daughter breathe, I thought about how blessed I really am.

Betty had learned the joys of moderation. She learned that life doesn't always have to be lived at full tilt; pleasure sometimes comes in small packages. She managed to find pleasure in the moment and in her sleeping child.

Learn moderation with moderation. Many of us view our recovery as though it were a project with a deadline. We drive ourselves by deciding to read every book published about ACOAs, and attend every meeting. We want to immerse ourselves so entirely that our recovery will become our focus—morning, noon, and night. Although focusing on your recovery can never be bad, it is always good to remember, "Easy does it." You don't have to do it all today. Recovery is an ongoing process and it takes time.

Both of us have been working on our recovery for years and continue to do so. We have learned fairly well now to stop riding the roller coaster of excitement and find moderation in all things—including working on ourselves. There will be times when you feel that you are making good progress, that it is tangible and obvious. Other times, you'll feel like you're plodding through a thick fog and you can see nothing behind you and nothing ahead. In learning moderation, you begin to realize that there is a natural rhythm of life, that sometimes things will move slowly, and sometimes you'll need to relax, to hang loose, to have fun. You learn to value the down times because they do not make you anxious and they allow you to gather momentum for the up times. The realization comes that there is not one place you are trying to get to and that the process of getting there is what counts.

CHAPTER 9

Toward Emotional Sobriety: Discovering Faith

Karen: I remember the day I first discovered there was a spiritual dimension to my life. Until that time, I didn't really have faith in anything except myself, and I thought the world began and ended with my consciousness. It was during a ten-day psychodrama group in which I found myself very open and aware of what was going on within me and with other people, and I found myself adopting the role of mother and problem solver for the group. I was beginning to feel very alone in the role and didn't know who would be there to support me. Feeling quite isolated one morning, I went outside to sit near the ocean, and as I meditated on how lonely I was, all of a sudden I could "feel" and "hear" a number of "beings" coming around me. I understood instantly that these beings were my "caretakers," that they were watching over me, and I was not alone. Two of these beings were in my life in bodily form—one was an old man who had befriended my family when we lived in Morocco, and the other was the man who would become my second husband.

The others were in spirit, but were around me nonetheless. Ever since this experience, I have had faith that I an not really alone.

Theologian Jim Fowler says that having faith is like "having a coat against the nakedness of finding ourselves alone in the universe." Carl Jung believed that the need for a connection with our own spirit is human instinct, and we know that faith and worship are common to people from every culture. But what exactly is faith?

As Karen described in her own experience in the above story, faith means acknowledging that there are mysteries to life and the universe, that there are realms and truths beyond our knowing. Faith means accepting the possibility that there is a plan, an intelligence, and an organizing principle beyond our understanding, one that governs our existence.

For so many ACOAs, having faith is a struggle. Without a direct experience such as the one Karen describes, we aren't sure what we believe; we are vulnerable to believing other people's "truths," and we misinterpret the teachings that we hear. ACOAs often believe that life is up to them and that they are responsible for everything that has happened and continues to happen. They attach themselves to various tenets of "New Age" or mystical thinking that encourage them to take on this responsibility and beat themselves up.

There are times in our lives, however, when spirit is very much alive. It happens in our workshops when we feel we have revealed a profound truth or witnessed a participant discovering self-love. It happens during meditation when we feel ourselves transported by an energy that is part of, but greater than, ourselves. It may happen in a relationship when there is a feeling of pure love, or perhaps while playing with a child, or walking by the ocean, or listening to music. There may be days in our lives when our suffering has a sense of movement and purpose, and we believe in ourselves and our path. On those days, when spirit is very much alive inside of us, it is easy to have faith.

Both of us, longtime seekers of self-awareness, have

searched in many different places for a relationship with Spirit. We have left the religions of our childhood and studied different systems and ways of living, opening ourselves up to many teachings. At different times, we have been attracted to Eastern religions and have discovered meditation to be helpful in our lives. At this point, neither of us adheres to any one system, nor do we belong to any church, center, or ashram. At the same time, we both consider our spiritual lives to be of crucial importance. We discuss our spirituality and explore it within ourselves and within others. We often feel the presence of spirit in our workshops in the love and unity that develop. What we are not particularly interested in for ourselves at this time is dogma of any sort. We've lived too long, and seen too much, to believe that there is one way that is good for everyone or that there are specific or correct answers to every question.

The spiritual path is not always an easy one to find. There are times in life when we feel overwhelmed by tragedy and sadness, and we are not able to be in touch with our spirit at all. At these times, there is a temptation to grab for easy answers. We would all like to be able to embrace a system that makes everything crystal clear for us. Ambivalence makes us anxious, and we are tired of confusion in our lives, and we make ourselves vulnerable to those who want to control us with their answers. However, it is out of the struggle of doubting, questioning, and ambivalence that we begin to explore and discover what is right for us in all parts of our lives, including our spirituality. We present our approach here in the hopes that you will not swallow it hook, line, and sinker, but that it will strike a responsive chord in you and will be a catalyst for your own spiritual growth.

Exploring Faith in Daily Life

Why is faith important to ACOAs? Without faith, we are like leaves blowing in the wind, a piece of sand in a vast desert. We are disconnected and isolated, relying only on ourselves to guide us through life. Without faith, the confusion, chaos, and arbitrariness that ruled our childhood are still present. When we have a strong sense of the interconnectedness and basic benevolence of the universe, we know that we are no longer alone. Life does have a plan, and although we may only be one thread in the weaving, we are part of the grand design. We find a meaning in our lives that gives us joy and satisfaction.

AA knows how important the component of faith is in the alcoholic's attempt to stop drinking. When a person is addicted, the addiction becomes God to him, and he uses his addiction to make him feel better, to open his heart and relax his inhibitions. Giving up that addiction is too great a loss and must be replaced with something else that can do the job. That something else can be faith and a relationship with one's own spirituality. AA calls this one's "higher power" in their twelve steps for recovery. They recognize the fact that in the bottle, the alcoholic is looking for a way to make himself feel whole, a way to connect with something greater than himself. The experience he seeks in alcohol can better be found in a personal system of faith.

Faith allows us to release control. When we believe that the universe has meaning and order, we can stop trying to run it, and we can accept the fact that some things are as they are. We can even begin to accept the times when we are in pain or distress, because when we have faith, we can let life be, and stop trying to fix everything all the time.

Faith allows us to let go of the weight of responsibility we have carried for so many years. Many of us feel a heaviness across our shoulders, and our minds are filled with worries about other people and the continual accounting of what, and to whom, we owe. We are often sorely out of touch with what we need, because we haven't found the internal quiet to sort it all out. We experience putting down the burden as an act of faith, because the burden is also our protector, our safety, and our addictive way of life.

With faith, we can make it through the pain. We discover that almost anything is tolerable if we feel a sense of purpose behind it. The idea that the universe is chaotic and arbitrary is truly unbearable to some, because it means that the crises that befall us are just chance bad luck and could not have been avoided. If the universe is arbitrary, things just happen. For example, if we had left the house three seconds earlier, then the child wouldn't have been killed by the car. We always seek to understand why something happened as it did, but sometimes the answer eludes us. When we have faith, we accept that there is some order to the universe, even though it may be beyond our understanding.

Sometimes things happen in our lives that are so difficult, and test us to such an extent, that we are forced to discover the limits of our faith. In the recent past, we both have dealt with great tragedy. But the experiences, while still painful today, were great teachers in that they pushed us up against life and demanded responses from us, based on our faith, that neither of us knew we had.

Terry: Several years ago, my wife, Gale, and I were expecting our first child. Gale's pregnancy had been healthy and uneventful, and we planned a home birth. But when Gale's labor did not progress after many hours, we went to the hospital. Still there was no sense of danger. At one point, though, the doctor could hear through the fetal heart monitor that the baby's heart was in some distress, but the baby recovered and Gale's labor appeared to continue normally. A cesarean section was suggested because Gale was getting tired and not making much progress in labor. Still there was no concern that there was anything wrong. The transfer to the operating room was leisurely, the fetal heart monitor was removed, and the cesarean was performed. Sometime during the ten or fifteen minutes after the heart monitor was removed and before the baby was born, he died. We watched in horror as the medical team tried unsuccessfully to revive our child.

In a few short minutes, our universe changed from a friendly place to a place of tragedy and grief. Our baby

Lee was healthy-looking and chubby, a ten-pounder. There was no explanation for why he died. In dying, he altered forever our view of the world. No longer could I take life's unfolding for granted.

Karen: About a year after Terry's baby died, I was routinely examining my breasts, when I felt an area of thickening. Because it didn't actually feel like a lump, I didn't worry abut it, but when it was still there a month later, I called my doctor. He was concerned enough to order an immediate mammogram, and the results were "suspicious." After the biopsy, we were told that because the cancer had invaded the tissue surrounding the tumor, there was a good possibility that the cancer had spread to the rest of my body as well. In a single moment, my life turned upside down, and I found myself, without preparation, facing the fact that I might be dying. I knew of course that we all die someday, but it always seemed so distant to me. Now here it was, and it might be painful and very soon. I was facing something that no one else could help me with. Although I received enormous support from family and friends, I was alone in my body, and the death I was facing was mine only.

At this point, I had a choice. I could have denied what was happening and collapsed into terror. I could blame myself and hate God. But instead, I faced what was happening and rode my fear. I resisted the temptation to escape through television and food, sleep and magical thinking, and stayed awake instead, acknowledging all the feelings within myself. I lived with the possibility that what had happened to me was arbitrary and capricious, that it had no meaning. It was then that I discovered that understanding the "why" of my cancer was not so important. What mattered was that I was becoming aware of an energy, a space, a presence inside me that felt comforting, one I believed would not desert me no matter what happened in the future. I realized I was finding a faith I had never known I had. This time of fear and pain became a time of growth and self-discovery. It was a time of learning to rely on a strength within, which was part of a power far greater than mine.

The events that pushed both of us into a greater relationship with our faith were tragic, but that is not always the case. Sometimes having an experience that allows you to discover your faith just comes, like a miracle. The death of Terry's baby and the fight against Karen's cancer forced us to make a leap in our thinking. We now see that the universe is more complex than we had imagined, and the easy answers we relied on before don't suffice in the face of so much pain. What allowed us to make this leap, to discover our faith, is an openness to the spiritual meaning of life. We have learned, as part of our recovery and move toward Emotional Sobriety, four important elements that help us cultivate a sustaining faith and develop a strong sense of self necessary to face all that life has to offer.

Item 1. *Be Here Now*

The phrase "Be here now" comes to us from Ram Dass's book of the same name, and it is an instruction that can be found in many Eastern traditions. Ram Dass tells us that life lived in the present—when we are totally in the moment—has a shimmering, larger-than-life quality. Time slows down and the cells in our bodies feel as though they are expanding out to meet the air. We feel a clarity in our bodies and our minds. Life just is and we are a part of it, and our memories of the past and our fantasies of the future do not stand up to the experience of the moment.

When we are so involved in yearning for what might have been, we miss what is at the moment. Once in a while, we are clobbered by great pain or pleasure, and we are thrust into the present. We remember those times as peak experiences, because when one is fully in the present, life has a thrilling and brilliant immediacy.

It is not always possible to "be here now." Because we are afraid of feeling, of not being in control, and of being surprised, we create a buffer between our experience and ourselves, and control how we view reality. We look at life from a distance, and compare what's happening today with what happened yesterday, closing ourselves off to new experience. We imagine that in this way we protect ourselves from being hurt, from feeling the intensity of things. We need instead to say to ourselves, "This may not be so," reevaluate, and open ourselves to life's unfolding.

We lie to ourselves about what's really going on, hoping that if we ignore it, it will go away. We turn on the television, take a drink, beat our children, fantasize—anything to escape the reality of today. When we aren't living in the past, we tend to jump into a fantasy future. Whether our forecasts for the future are accurate, full of pain, disaster, or glory, they take us out of our present, and we miss out on our lives as they are now.

We avoid the present moment because we feel safe doing that. We were taught to be ashamed of our unedited, spontaneous responses. We were told not to let anyone see our hurt, to pretend we don't care and aren't disappointed, to hide our pride when we are praised, mask our excitement when we care, to be diplomatic when we are angry, to be indifferent when we fall in love. We learned that to show ourselves is to be vulnerable and open to hurt. As adults we are covered with layers of padding which muffle our true responses and place a distance between us and the moment.

How can we teach ourselves to be here now? How do we crawl out from under all those layers of protective padding and feel what is real at the moment? We must develop a curiosity about what we feel, because when we explore our emotions, we can explore ourselves at great depth. There is no way *out* of our problems, only *through* them. Sometimes a shock or a loss is so great that there is no way to deny what's going on. When Terry and Gale's baby died, they had no choice but to grieve with all their being and realize that they couldn't control life. For Karen, discovering that she had cancer was a tremendous shock. At first, it all seemed like a movie about someone else's life and she wanted it to stop. She then began to see that each time she was willing to be with her feelings, the deeper into herself she got, and the more she thought she could make it through. Life took on a magnified quality for Karen, and her feelings were heightened. Her old habit of moving through life half asleep was destroyed in an instant by the diagnosis of cancer.

We must learn to accept ourselves and our own path, honoring our pace and direction. We feel so much to blame for what went on in our childhood that we tend to look at ourselves critically, and always doubt that we are doing, or feeling, the right thing. We also constantly compare ourselves to other people. Instead, we must learn to know when we need to accept ourselves and when we need to push and ask for help.

We must learn to notice which thoughts are real responses to the moment and which are "negative tape loops."

Karen: The first time I encountered the notion of negative tape loops, I was helping staff a workshop, and at the break I was criticizing myself for the mistakes I'd made. Someone said to me, "Karen, aren't you tired of that negative tape loop yet? You've been running it for years, always saying the same thing. You're always criticizing yourself yet people are pleased with your work." I thought I was making an honest evaluation of myself, but she showed me it was not grounded in the real facts.

Negative tape loops come from the past and are one of the things our minds play instead of being here now. It can be difficult to challenge what we are so used to assuming is true. We assign a truth to our thoughts, without realizing that we may be responding out of our past experiences. Asking friends, colleagues, or group members for feedback is a great way to work your way into the present. If there is a disparity between what others think of you and how you feel inside, chances are you are running a tape from the past instead of being in the moment.

We can learn to be here now by finding support around us. We need the support of someone who can recognize and understand our experiences and ways of thinking. One place to find support is in ACOA groups, because as we watch others do their work, we learn from them, and sense when they are truly present, and when they are being protective and in denial of their experiences.

Meditation can help us be here now. It can quiet our minds and allow us to tune into the truth of ourselves below the level of everyday worries and fears. We must give ourselves a quiet time to hear the whisper of our true selves. Developing a habit of daily contemplation creates a time for this. Meditation does not serve as a substitute for dealing with feelings, and it does not make our self-criticism and emotionality go away. Rather, it gives us a break so that our feelings and emotions begin to release their hold on us.

To be here now, we must develop an awareness of the moment. When we are aware of the physical—what we see, hear, smell, touch—we also become aware of the distinctions among our senses. We then can begin to know the difference between what we experience directly and what we imagine to be true. Here is an exercise that can be done with a partner.

Exercise V.
Developing Self-awareness

Sit down with someone in a place where you will not be interrupted for half an hour. When you are comfortable, look into each other's left eye. Breathe and look, nothing else. Taking turns, begin to report to each other what you are aware of. A good place to start is with your senses: "This is what I hear/touch/smell." Next, share with each other what you are aware of: "I am aware of my breathing/my thought/your hair/my fantasies." Next, share with each other things you imagine to be true: "I imagine you are angry/bored/tired." Be as open as you can be to all that you are feeling. This is a moment to learn to expand your consciousness, to be aware of everything that is going on, true and imagined. Expanding your awareness can feel silly or irrational at times, but with practice you will be able to develop your intuitive capacity into a very useful tool.

Item 2. *Develop a Relationship With Your Spirituality*

When you develop a relationship with your spirituality, you find a connection to an energy and a power that is both part of, and greater than, yourself. Some people talk about a relationship with God or Jesus. Others simply speak of it as a relationship with an inner voice or a higher power. In either case, what is essential is that you have a relationship with a part of yourself that is separate from ego and personality. When we talk about relationship, we mean a dynamic connection with someone, or something, that changes, grows, and lives.

We cannot speak for everyone about how it feels to be connected to one's own spirituality, because the experience for everyone is unique. The experience of someone studying Zen practice would be different from that of the person studying the Torah or the life of Jesus. However one experiences it, in our moments of deepest connection, struggle ceases and we can relax and surrender to a force that is greater than ourselves.

Developing a relationship with one's spirituality can be difficult for ACOAs for a number of reasons. For many of us raised with the church, the teachings of our childhood religions have played an important role. Even if we do not subscribe to the teachings of our church now, they continue to influence how we think about life. For some, our childhood religion has taught us that as much as God is loving, he will punish us for our sins. We remember that trespassing against God was a daily temptation, and that being good takes vigilance and hard work. Many of us spent our childhood waiting for God to discover how really bad we were. Jake tells us of the terror the church instilled in him.

> **Jake:** As a four-year-old, I would see the devil. What was most terrifying is that he suddenly peeked out from behind the couch in the living room, and he always smiled. He smiled as though he was up to something, and wanted me to join him. I remember him hiding behind the altar rail and taking peeks at me during Sunday sermons.

Since Jake and his family were suffering from his father's alcoholic outbursts at the time, it is possible that Jake's visions of the devil were an objectification of the family pain, a vision of the bad in his life. In Jake's case, the church did not give him a sense of security, but instead gave him the vocabulary and images to see the wrongness he felt. Dora tells us she left the church for another reason.

> **Dora:** I could not tolerate anymore viewing myself as a sinner. I also had a hard time believing in a God who would let me and my brother suffer so much. My father went to church every Sunday after being drunk and beating us up on Saturday night. I remember him in church, praying and pious, and I wondered what people would think if they knew the truth. I couldn't understand a community that treated a man like this with respect. I felt the church had let me down.

Spiritual development happens when a child feels safe with his parents and projects that feeling onto God or another force. As a child's world expands to include friends, and then colleagues, his experience of God grows bigger as well. Many ACOAs did not have the original experience of surrendering to and trusting their alcoholic or abusive parents, and it is then hard for them to find faith and spirituality in a world that seems malevolent and unfair. Perhaps if our childhood had been happier, we would have been able to focus on God as a loving, rather than punitive, presence. Often it seemed that survival depended on mental acuity and rationality, and to make the leap of faith and accept God seemed too scary and involved too much faith.

As we grow, we learn that God is an internal experience and dwells within us. For women, this can often be difficult to accept, because God as a "he" is different and separate from them. Many Western religions continue to teach them that God is an authority outside of themselves, and they struggle against surrendering to him. As women begin to think of God as female, or as Goddess, the experience of the divine can become integrated within them. They can think less in terms of surrender and more in terms of opening up to their highest potential.

ACOAs have trouble connecting with their own spirituality because there is so much noise in our minds we can't find the quiet within the storm. Our minds protect us from facing the pain in our hearts through fantasy, denial, and avoidance. This hardly creates an encouraging environment to connect with one's spirit. The voice of the spirit speaks quietly, and we must allow ourselves to hear it. It is necessary to empty our hearts of past pain before we can let our spirits enter. We must be able to find the eye of the storm where there is quiet, where the spirit resides. To do this, we must confront the storm. The good news is that it's not necessary to get rid of all the pain before we can experience the joy of spirit. Rather, each time we open ourselves a bit more, we create room for spirit. So although our process may feel like crossing a vast desert, there are oases of green to be found along the way.

When we can overcome these obstacles and develop a relationship with our spirituality, we stop fighting against our destinies. We are aware of what we can and cannot change, and we know the difference. Our lives are a combination of creating what we want for ourselves and accepting what is.

Karen: Developing a relationship with my sprituality has been an ongoing process, but being diagnosed as having cancer has accelerated that process. I saw that there were certain things about my cancer that I could control, and things I could not. I could not change the diagnosis, and ultimately, I could not change whether I would live or die because of it. I was, however, able to choose how I would respond to the cancer, and I've used it to improve the quality of my life. One of the most important ways I've done that is to deepen my personal relationship to spirit. For me, this meant accepting the cancer as part of my destiny, and not pushing it away. I've had to open my life to whatever happens, including death, and the sense of trust I've developed has given me the strength to deal with whatever comes. I've had to rely on my resources and ask for help when those resources are not enough. I have developed a connection with something inside myself that will help and sustain me. I am here now for my life, accepting it and knowing that I do not face it alone.

In our extended workshops, we do a breathing exercise called Holonomic Integration, created by Stan and Christina Grof, pioneers in the investigation of altered states of consciousness. It is an exercise that allows people to discover their own inspiration, and not one that is prescribed for them. Each participant lies on his back, relaxes, and breathes. A partner sits next to the "breather" offering nonintrusive attention. The exercise is accompanied by powerful and emotionally provocative music. The depth and frequency of breathing are increased, and eventually everyone finds himself following the music into a state of consciousness that is individually meaningful.

The range of experience during this exercise is broad. Some people reexperience painful past events and cry and rage at them. Some reexperience their birth and relive the release and trauma. Some people experience what appear to be events from previous lives, while others have strong experiences of God and their connection to universal love. Others are blissful, and while they can't articulate their experience, you can see it in their radiant faces.

This exercise provides people with a transpersonal experience. It is an awareness that they are connected to more than their bodies and emotions—they are connected to a spiritual realm as well. Having this experience often changes the context of people's lives. It enlarges the arena within which they exist, and spirit becomes an active force rather than a distant idea. Whatever pain a person might be experiencing is eased by the knowledge that one's self is not static and limited. With this comes a sense of optimism and hope, because one realizes the endless bounds of each person's potential.

Molly, a thirty-nine-year-old participant in one of our workshops, had been depressed and withdrawn the entire time we were together. During the breathing exercise, she had an experience that altered the way she looked at the world.

> **Molly:** I began by breathing deeply, and was carried away by the music, and then I felt as though I was being filled with light and rising up to a place filled with angels. The angels were singing, too, and I joined them. Then I saw that the angels were people I knew, and that the other people in the workshop were singing with me. I think I recognized then the basic angelic nature in all of us that has been hidden by our pain and inhibitions. When I saw that, I saw the angelic nature in myself as well, and I felt as though a great weight had been lifted from me.

It requires a commitment to want to develop a relationship with your spirituality, and a necessary first step. Sometimes the path that takes you there is long, and passes through the dark side of your soul, and it may not be the way for everyone. But simply making the choice to connect with your spiritual self starts the ball rolling, because commitment alone is a powerful thing. It is a big step to choose to open yourself up to the pain, and have enough trust that you can survive what you feel, no matter how horrible it is.

Our parents may have developed their relationship to spirit by going to church, and for some of us, that may still work. Others may find that the church has lost its power, that they need to change churches or create their own. All over the country people gather in groups that are not "church," but in which they celebrate their love together. In workshops, AA meetings, support groups, women's groups, men's groups, singing groups—anywhere it is safe to tell the truth and where there is mutual respect among the members—spirit and love reside. In the sharing and support that occur in these groups, people feel safe to explore their relationship to spirit. Most of these groups do not require that the members accept a certain dogma. Rather, they require that the members be themselves, be supportive, and thrive in a community atmosphere.

Item 3. *Life Is a Process, Not a Product*

> When we say life is a "process," not a "product," we are pointing out that life happens in increments. We take two steps forward and one step back, and we learn by degrees. We learn by making mistakes, because only through our mistakes can we tell when we are off base. ACOAs have unrealistic standards much of the time, and expect instant achievement, and they forget that learning comes from trial and error, not just trial and success.

Life is not about being perfect all the time. It is an ongoing process of learning, growing, and changing. Goals are important, but the act of trying to reach them and learning along the way is equally important. When we view life this way, we can honor the daily events in our lives, and see all that happens to us—the pain as well as the pleasure—as valuable experiences that make us who we are. With this view, we have less of a tendency to view our experiences as either good or bad, but accept what happens as an opportunity to learn and grow.

As we learn to honor the process of our lives, we stop trying to do what is "right" and "appropriate" and "expected" all the time. We align ourselves with our spirit by listening to our inner voice instead. As we are learning to recognize our inner voice, we make mistakes along the way. Never are we more challenged to remember that life is a process, and that learning is achieved through trial and error, than when we are learning to trust ourselves.

Learning that life is a process requires faith. We have to give up our notion that we know where we should be and what we should have achieved, and accept where we are instead. We surrender to the fact that God, the universe, our higher power, is in charge of our lives. Our faith allows us to trust that life has a perfection all its own.

Many people who grew up in unhealthy homes did not have the support that allowed them to learn from their mistakes and ask for help when necessary. Lonnie, thirty-six, the mother of two and an avid piano player, is one such person. While she had patience to know that she still had a lot to learn and a long way to go on the piano, she was not so understanding of herself in other areas of her life.

> **Lonnie:** One year I was appointed head of the committee for the Christmas Fair at my children's school. It was an important fund-raising event, and I had lots of ideas about what crafts and games would sell well. I thought I could do it, but then I realized I was in a big mess and I felt like a jerk. I don't know how to organize, I can't delegate authority (and end up doing it all by myself), and I have no idea how to negotiate disagreements. There was a group that splintered off and were doing what they wanted, and that made me feel stupid. My family was fed up at how frantic I was getting over this, but I was terrified of being a failure.

What is striking about Lonnie is the amount of anger she directs at herself for not knowing something she was never taught. With support, Lonnie was finally able to go to the other members of the committee and admit that she was in over her head. In order to do that, though, Lonnie had to accept the fact that life is for learning, not necessarily for knowing, and that she could value this experience for all that it was teaching her. This was a very different view of life than she usually had, the one that said she was supposed to be perfect and competent all the time. As Lonnie developed a relationship with her faith, she was better able to accept herself and her weaknesses. She recognized that she was developing exactly as she should, and that it was the wounded little girl inside her, not the grown woman, that strove for perfection and blamed herself for the family pain. She could then value her experience as an opportunity to see herself and grow, and not as an opportunity to dwell on her failings and beat herself up.

When we view our lives as a process, and not a product, the satisfaction and inner peace can be great.

> **Karen:** I went through a two-week period where I was reviewing in my mind all the terrible things I'd ever done to people. Particularly, I remembered an incident where I had been the landlady to two young women, and I had broken my word to them. I didn't remember their names or where they were, so I couldn't get in touch with them and tell them how sorry I was. I kept going over and over what had happened, and how badly I'd acted, and I felt awful about myself.
>
> Then something switched in me, and I realized that after the incident with the two women, I had never again broken my word to anyone in the same way. The event had taught me the importance of integrity and honor, and in realizing that, it had been an important learning experience, instead of something to regret and hate myself for.

In order to start living life as a process, we must stop beating ourselves up for everything we do wrong. We must recognize our intentions and strive for our goals, but at some point we must move out of the way and "let go and let God." "Let go and let God" is a phrase frequently used in AA that means letting one's connection with one's spirit be the guide. It is a suggestion to stop struggling, stop worrying, stop trying to be perfect, and let the process of life happen. To "let God" means to trust ourselves and the path we are on, to believe that life is unfolding as it should, and it includes even those things we consider mistakes.

> **Karen:** Twice in one year, many years ago, I was led by an inner voice, which I mistook to be the voice of truth, to financially support two men who claimed their great metaphysical knowledge could solve all the problems that plagued the world. I laugh now at my innocence, but at the time I really believed, and was prompted by my desire to be involved with those people. I see now that I learned some important lessons from the experience, that it made me more savvy and better able to discern who is trustworthy and who is not. Before I could honor what I learned, though, I spent years cringing at my naïveté and gullibility in believing these people.

As in Karen's example, many ACOAs tend to focus on their failures and weaknesses. An important part of our recovery is to focus on our successes and strengths. In the course of our lives, we accomplish much, but often disregard our accomplishments as trivial, simply because we don't know how to feel good about ourselves and are uncomfortable with the feelings of success and satisfaction. When we begin to acknowledge our successes, we learn to rely on ourselves and trust our actions.

Exercise VI.
Goal Setting: Note Your Successes

Every morning make a list of the goals you want to accomplish for the day. Be sure to include even the small, obvious things, such as getting dressed or feeding the cat. As you accomplish each goal, cross it off your list. Every time you cross something off, you'll be noting an accomplishment. Take pleasure in it! When you look at your list, you'll see that you are a person who can keep your word, someone who carries out what she says she'll do, instead of someone who can't do anything. This may seem to be an insignificant exercise, but your mind begins to notice that you are someone of accomplishment. Increased self-esteem will eventually take hold.

Item 4. *"I Am Not to Blame, nor This Time Are You"*

Many ACOAs are so entrenched in believing that "life is all up to me" that they are stuck in thinking that everything is their fault. Conversely, others believe that they are responsible for nothing and everyone else is to blame. Most of us are unable to see that there are some things in life that we are responsible for, and some things that we are not. Resentment and guilt are at opposite ends of the same spectrum, and when we are unaware of one feeling, we often overexpress the other.

As we struggle to stop blaming—either ourselves or others—we often accept the notion that says we are responsible for our lives, but distort it to mean we are to blame for all the mess in our lives. We then find ourselves in the same situation we were in as children, that is, directing all the anger and blame at ourselves and then feeling guilty for all the mistakes we've made. In our black and white view of the world, we think that if we can't point a finger at someone else, we'll have to point it at ourselves. Of course some of the misery and suffering in our lives is of our own creation, but much of what happens to us is out of our control. We must begin to see that taking responsibility is not the same as being at fault.

Ken Wilbur, a leading theorist of transpersonal psychology, writes in an untitled manuscript about the notion that we are responsible for creating our own reality:

> It mistakes the correct notion "Godhead creates all" for the narcissistic notion that "since I am one with God I create all." Wrong. That position makes two profound mistakes . . . namely: one, that God is an intervening parent for the universe, instead of its impartial reality or suchness; and two, that your ego is one with that parental God, and therefore can intervene and order the universe around.

These ideas, Ken Wilbur says, are the narcissistic, magical thinking of a four-year-old. It is also a painful way to think, because we then burden ourselves with blame for everything that has gone wrong. When Terry and Gale's baby died, for instance, well-meaning friends offered explanations and reasons, thinking it would make it easier for all to bear the loss. Being told that they had "chosen" the death of their child felt cruel, but this was merely some people's desire to understand the divine plan. Why the baby died was not such an important question. What was important for Terry and Gale was to accept the experience, which meant facing their grief. It meant recognizing the fact that life is a mystery that we often can't control.

As we let go of our need to assign blame and reason for all that has happened, we are able to be with what is. We accept our feelings, our regrets for what was, and our yearnings for how it might have been, and our priority becomes to know ourselves and our experiences, rather than trying to figure out who is to blame. We accept our feelings of rage at those who have hurt us, but we don't get dragged down by it. We experience the anger, know that is is part of the path toward healing, and when we are ready to let go of it, we do. As we begin to forgive, compassion replaces blame.

Darlene, a thirty-three-year-old hairdresser, had been enraged at her father for years, and was in therapy to work on this. Her anger toward her father was so strong that even his name provoked an outburst against him. Although not an alcoholic, her father was angry, critical, and verbally abusive, and Darlene had feared him all her life.

> **Darlene:** I grew up not knowing much about my father at all. One day after my mother died, I was going through some old family papers, and I discovered something about my father I'd never known. It seems that he'd had a dream when he was younger, to escape the mill town his family had been in forever, to save money and go to the university and make something of himself. But my mother had gotten pregnant with me, and my father was forced into a marriage he didn't want. With the marriage went all his dreams.
>
> For the first time, I saw that his marriage to my mother had been an act of love toward me, and that my father, despite it all, had supported me and encouraged me to do well and to live out his dream. When I was able to understand the extent of his sacrifice, I was able to forgive him. The feelings of resentment and fear I had toward him didn't simply disappear, but they receded into the background, and were replaced by an understanding on my part that he had done the best he could.

After this realization, Darlene was able to feel compassion instead of hatred toward her father. She no longer saw her father's anger and belligerence as his fault, but rather a condition of his circumstances. Through this, Darlene was finally able to accept this man as the loving father she'd wanted all her life.

Many ACOAs, when they are able to forgive their

parents, find that in the place of anger and disappointment there emerges a relationship of caring and pleasure. The facts of childhood are not changed, merely forgiven.

> **Karen:** I spent my life being angry at my father, for not saving me from my alcoholic mother, and also for loving my sister more. By the time I was forty-three, I wasn't actually angry anymore, but I seldom saw my father, and when I did, it wasn't fun. One night I woke up out of a dream with an understanding of what had gone on in my family with a clarity I'd never had before, and I understood that my father had chosen my sister because I rejected him when he returned from war. It wasn't that he decided which daughter to love more, it was that I was too angry at him to welcome him home. He had been through a war, but so had I with my mother, and somehow, we were never able to connect. I saw that there was no one to blame, and from that moment, I felt forgiveness for everyone in the family, and began to enjoy a relationship with my father.

For the women in the above examples, there were no real steps to forgiveness; rather it was just a state that they both accepted. Forgiving is not something we simply decide to do or say. It happens over time as part of the process of healing ourselves.

We must break away from the position of automatically blaming. To do this, we must become aware that blame and resentment often mask guilt and powerlessness. When we can accept these feelings within ourselves, we are able to let go of the concept of "fault" and move on. We do this by looking to see what is under our resentment, because often it covers guilt. For instance, do you resent your mother because she didn't stand up to your father's abuse, and because you feel guilty for not having protected her? Is the resentment you feel toward your sister for her endless variety of woes fueled by your guilt in not being able to make things better for her?

As Carl and Stephanie Simonton, specialists in nonmedical approaches to living with and recovering from cancer, discuss in their book *Getting Well Again*, people often allow resentments to pile up for years. They maintain a catalogue of hurt and humiliation which they constantly reenact in their minds, and each time they remember the incident, they restress their bodies. This, the Simontons believe, can cause illness.

Unresolved resentment often becomes generalized, so that a woman's resentment toward her father can affect her feelings about all men, or a man's resentment toward his parents for never keeping a promise can lead him to believe that no one is trustworthy. In the same way, the resentment about what happened in our childhood can affect the way we see our lives today and make it hard for us to believe that things can change.

We can resolve our resentment and blame in two steps. First, we can reexperience the underlying emotion. In some instances, this will be anger, and you may not be able to express that anger directly at the person who has caused it. For someone to hear your anger is not as important as your feeling and experiencing it. Second, it may be important to confront some people directly. Often, though, this person is no longer living or is still drinking, which makes a direct confrontation impossible or unproductive. In this case, talking to a photograph of him, visiting his grave, writing him a letter you may never mail, screaming things you never intend for him to hear, may more than suffice if you put your heart in to it.

Exercise VII.
Doing the Work of Letting Go of Painful Relationships

Although "letting go" appears to be a passive step in overcoming wounds, the ability to do so comes through experiencing and dealing with powerful feelings that ultimately lead the way to the place where the heart "lets go." Here is a simple way to do this on your own. Sit with a pillow in front of you. Relax and take a few deep breaths. Start to imagine that the pillow is your parent sitting in front of you, giving you focused attention. Breathing deeply, begin to speak, addressing your parent directly, and allow your feelings to rise. If you are angry, experiment with hitting the pillow, allowing your body to help you in expressing and releasing your rage. Hold the pillow against your face and shout into it. Keep it simple and honest. You don't need to justify yourself.

If what you feel is grief, hold yourself and rock, letting the sadness have its own movement. Don't worry about making sense. It is your wounded child who is feeling and healing here. You can trust your body and your feelings to provide just the experience you need. The goal is not to get rid of anything, but rather to expand your capacity to be alive with feeling.

Sometimes we run the risk of getting even more attached to our resentment when we reenact the pain in an attempt to resolve it. Having a therapist at this stage can be crucial. As we reexperience the anger we feel toward our parents, we feel our harsh self-accusatory stance soften. As we accept that life is a process and not a product, we forgive ourselves for our mistakes and our imperfections. At some point, we can even begin to see this world from our parents' point of view. They did not deliberately try to hurt us, but we see that somehow their dreams were destroyed and they lost control of their lives. Addicted to alcohol, or out of control with their abuse and rage, they were locked into a pattern of behavior stronger than themselves. When we accept that in many cases they did their best, we begin to forgive.

Only when we allow ourselves to accept the mystery of life can we open up to the spirit within each of us. In becoming one with our spirit, we let go of the need to be in control and can accept whatever life brings us. We can then accept a paradox in our lives—that we are responsible, but also humbled by the events we can't control. Learning to know the difference is the crucial thing. As we do, we forgive ourselves for not being perfect and accept that we are on the path of learning. We see that life is a process and that we are its students.

CHAPTER 10

Toward Emotional Sobriety: Forming Intimate Relationships

As you may recall from Chapter 5, the key to switching from pain avoidance to pleasure-seeking is the rekindling of the physical feelings of pleasure and excitement that come so easily to most adolescents as they emerge through puberty.

Adult sexuality is clearly different. By adulthood, men and woman have experienced emotional wounds, and although we look for excitement and fireworks in our sexual lives, we realize that there needs to be a commonality in the area of values, interests, and experiences with the people we date and marry. In essence, sexual interest is the gate we pass through toward the higher pursuit of adult intimacy.

In this chapter, we will look at how sexuality and physical pleasure are directly interrelated with the capacity to be intimate. By drawing on our instincts for pleasure-seeking that emerge in adolescence, we can learn to provide for ourselves and our loved ones the qualities of sexual excitement, focused attention, and respect that lead to intimacy and delight in each other over the long haul.

The key element in making the switch to healthy pleasure-seeking is attaining a self-awareness of your sexual needs and sexual history. This enables ACOAs to separate the needs of the wounded child from the needs of the adult identity which takes delight in equal, intimate relationships. Unfortunately many ACOAs have been unaware of the importance of exploring their sexuality. Most therapists don't talk much about sexual relationships with their clients, figuring that if they work out other problems—past hurts, power dynamics, etc.—the sexual arena of their lives will automatically improve. In addition, Janet Woititz in her book *Adult Children of Alcoholics*[1] argues that ACOAs have no more problems than other people in the area of sexuality. Our experiences and those of our clients contradict this belief. We feel that it is vital for ACOAs to examine their sexuality for three main reasons:

1. It is a primary area of pleasure. All the ways in which we try to be pain-avoidant show up in the realm of sexuality. Learning to tolerate the sheer pleasure of our sexuality opens us up to pleasure in every area of our lives.

2. It provides ACOAs with a new and healthy definition of sexuality beyond the sex act itself. When we talk about someone who has a healthy sexuality, we're talking about a person's aliveness—how much he is willing to meet life head-on without closing down and shielding himself from the intensity of life.

3. It is the key to unlocking many areas of sexual and emotional dysfunction found among ACOAs. As infants ACOAs are awake, aware, and alive. But through the series of shamings that ACOAs experience as children, they close down emotionally, learning such ideas as "sex is bad" and "touching yourself is evil." They get scared and feel that survival depends on being in control. Letting go into sexual pleasure frightens ACOAs because of the lack of control it represents. Soon, instead of being open sexually, ACOAs become inorgasmic, ejaculate prematurely, or get lost in fantasies, choosing partners who are inferior or abusive like our parents, or wanting someone to take care of them. This was the case with Robin.

Robin: When I was a little boy, my parents, who were cut off from their own feelings, were unable to allow me to have my own. If I cried or felt scared, they would tell me to grow up and act like a big boy. If I was angry, they'd tell me I was tired and send me to my room. To please them and get the attention I longed for, I learned to keep all my feelings inside. I smiled when I didn't feel happy, and acted grown up, but the little boy inside me did not go away.

As I grew up, I began to see that the little boy inside me was running the show. He wanted the warmth he'd never received, and my sexual urges only increased the search for love and attention. I see now that what I really wanted was a warm mommy for a lover, and not a woman with needs and desires of her own.

When I met my wife, I was full of expectations for our future. She was a therapist, warm and sensitive, and I was sure I had finally found someone to take care of me. She also had a wounded child within her, and had come from an alcoholic and abusive family in which her feelings were constantly denied and ridiculed.

She was looking for many of the same things I was, and was attracted to my warmth, and we got married. I think that each of us was secretly seeking a parent. Beneath her facade of the powerful professional woman was a hurt little girl, and behind my manly exterior was that wounded little boy. When it became obvious what we both wanted, we freaked out. My wife didn't want to take care of me—she got paid for doing that all day—and I didn't want to be her daddy. When a conflict arose, my wife was sure she wouldn't get taken care of, and she'd demand that I act like a man. So again I was trapped, just as I had always been, having to pretend I was feeling something I wasn't, in order to be loved.

Robin wrote this as he was about to begin therapy. He had a good understanding of the dynamics of his relationship, but he couldn't seem to break the pattern of struggle. The love

Robin and His wife felt for each other was there, but the wounded children inside them were clamoring for their own attention.

People who grow up in alcoholic or abusive families know that being close to someone can be a very painful experience. The wounded child deep inside is both self-protective and scared of being hurt, but also longs deeply for the love and nurturing that they were never given. ACOAs, unless they were lucky enough to have a grandparent or some loving adult in their lives, do not know what it means to be nurtured, supported, and loved. They saw that the parent who drank or was out of control, that the person who was supposed to love them the most, was abusive and critical, and there was no way to escape injury. As a result, ACOAs are distrustful of those closest to them, a distrust that is at the core of their being.

As adults we now pay the price for this in our own intimate relationships. When our relationships are peaceful, many of us think something is wrong, that there is no passion left. We create passion by creating crises: dramatic leave-taking followed by equally dramatic returns, violent fights followed by tender reconciliations. We often are unable to recognize, or even appreciate, when someone is loving us in a consistent, healthy manner. We are afraid to let go, to acknowledge our passion and sexual feelings, because we don't know where those feelings will take us, and as we learned growing up, the unknown is a dangerous place. So we enter our sexual relationships only partway; half of us is there, the other half is still in the realm of our self-protective coping persona.

The problem boils down to our failure to focus on the pleasure that can be derived from a relationship, a failure that grew out of our earliest relationships with our families. Instead, we organize our lives—and our intimate relation-ships—from a position of pain avoidance. The more conscious you are about how you do this, the greater hope there is that you can make a switch toward a pleasure-seeking focus in your life. Let's look at some pain-avoidant reasons we get into relationships. While each of these reasons for being in an intimate relationship can be a fine motivator, in the long run they form a shaky foundation for intimacy that crumbles under the pressures of everyday life.

• *Security*. When we were children, we looked to our parents to provide us with the necessities of living and basics of security—food, clothing, shelter, affection—whether they did or did not do so effectively. Now as adults we look to our intimate relationships to provide us with that security, and often look for the parenting we never had. Unfortunately it is too late for that, and such expectations make impossible demands on a relationship. Adult sexual relationships are between equal adults, not parent and child. Security exists within yourself when you feel potent as an individual in the diverse spheres of your life—professional, sexual, spiritual.

• *Fear of abandonment*. Many of us were emotionally "abandoned" in childhood, and as adults we are terrified of being alone. Because we do not believe that we can survive on our own, or that we can properly take care of ourselves, we enter into relationships erroneously believing that anything is better than being alone. We feel that our need to be taken care of is imperative, and we end up staying in a relationship not out of choice, but out of what we see as a life-and-death necessity. In our clinical experience, we have seen again and again that the romantic notion of "I can't live without you" is an acting out of a desperate dependency that has little relevance to a healthy, adult relationship. At times, we are aware of the extent of our dependency, and realize that the person we are with is not the right one for us, but the alternative of being alone is too scary. It is natural, then, to resent and be critical of someone on whom you are dependent, causing further conflict in the relationship.

• *Passion and drama*. Because many of us are addicted to excitement and the rush of adrenaline it produces, we find ourselves drawn to the people who bring passion and drama to our lives. Instead of choosing people who are stable and dependable, we hook up with people who keep us guessing, keep us on our toes, and guarantee us an endless ride on the roller coaster of excitement. We confuse excitement and upheaval with love, and we are reassured by the familiar ups and downs of the relationship. The chaos protects us from what we are really feeling, thus serving the pain-avoidant function.

In this kind of relationship, sexual feelings are driven by a desperation to hold on, rather than by the pleasure that can be derived from another's presence. Your fear that your partner may not really love you reinforces the image of yourself that you have had all along: that you are unworthy of love. As Groucho Marx put it, "I wouldn't want to belong to any club that would have me as a member."

As ACOAs we similarly feel that anyone who could love us (since we are fundamentally unlovable) must be a fool. And when someone attempts to love us just for who we are, we back away from his or her intimacy and hide our fear behind the excuse of boredom. When we choose a partner who keeps us perpetually wondering and worrying, someone who fills our lives with passion and drama, we are too busy trying to make ourselves wanted to feel the underlying self-hatred and sadness.

• *Merging*. At some weddings, the bride and groom perform a ritual of merging. The man and woman each take a candle, and with their candles they light a third and blow out their own, thereby becoming one. The ritual is a symbolic reenactment of the moment of release when the ego surrenders to the experience of oneness—fusion. The misconception here is that this is a static state that couples aim to attain. Rather, it is a fleeting moment that leaves the individuals to lead their own separate lives until the next time. Born out of a fear of confronting and accepting our basic aloneness, even our vernacular reinforces this idea that two people become one, when we talk about "our better half" or our "soulmate."

Ironically, in our practice, we often see that couples who are emotionally involved to this extent have difficulty generating sexual excitement for each other regularly, because they see themselves as one. Healthy sexual excitement requires separation and an awareness of the differences between people.

Being in a state of fusion actually reduces the ability to experience sexual pleasure, for the excitement is to be found in the coming together of two separate beings. In the same way, if you hold someone's hand for a long time, you lose the acute sensation of touching. The thrill comes from contact at the boundaries, and merging ends up depriving us of the healthy excitement of our very individual sexuality.

• *Loyalty.* Perhaps this is the toughest pain-avoidant reason to be in a relationship, because we place such value on loyalty. To be able to hang in there, to stick it out when things get tough, is commendable, and not only provides a certain amount of satisfaction but prolongs the life of the relationship as well.

Even as children, with the fear of abandonment looming close by, we were loyal to relationships and to people we knew weren't right for us. Because we are afraid of the pain involved in separation, we have developed a tolerance for the intolerable, and truly believe that we wouldn't find anything better anyway. In our pain-avoidant stance, we continue to allow ourselves to be mistreated, and are loyal to the end to the person who mistreats us. We do not demand that our relationships be good and satisfying, and by avoiding the possible pain of loss, we also avoid the possibility of finding a fulfilling and loving relationship.

Finding Pleasure in Another's Company

It is a great mystery why some relationships and marriages are successful, while others fail quickly, and no one really knows the exact components that make each unique partnership thrive. We believe, though, that in healthy relationships there is a fundamental understanding that the right reason to be in any intimate relationship—sexual, platonic, familial—*is to enjoy the pleasure of another's company*. The pleasure to be found in another's company is profound, and does not require a lot of fireworks or romantic ideals. It is peaceful, and fills you with a sense of well-being and gratitude for the other's presence in your life.

Even if this understanding of pleasure exists between partners, we must realize that healthy intimate relationships are not fun and happy all the time. Fighting, for instance, is generally not fun, but serves a very real purpose of sorting out and airing conflict. A fight, however, does not require loud voices, verbal attacks, or violence.

When conflict arises, healthy people do not withdraw. Nor does the healthy person resort to offensive tactics such as blaming and manipulation, for that is also a form of withdrawal. Rather, when faced with conflict, the healthy person acts within his own boundaries, and states his desires and needs in a simple, nonaccusatory way.

Having Sex and Talking About Sex Constitute "Quality Time"

It should go without saying that a healthy sexual attitude is an essential component in an intimate relationship, yet most people find it difficult to talk about sex. Just about anyone who seeks psychotherapeutic help will tell you that he or she doesn't really have a problem in the area of sexuality. Further exploration, however, reveals fear and anxiety that are rarely verbalized. A person's coping mechanism disguises this anxiety, and it takes time and careful self-examination to uncover the true feelings. When you discover that talking about your sexual concerns with your partner helps keep pleasure alive in the relationship, you will have discovered a strong incentive to open up and talk, despite the anxiety that may ensue.

But why does it become increasingly difficult at times to sustain a high level of physical pleasure and emotional satisfaction in an intimate relationship? When we begin to explore this question, we must resist blaming the relationship itself. Too many couples avoid the real problems they are facing by treating their relationship as a separate entity, an organism with a life of its own. A relationship is made up of the two people involved, and cannot have a mind and feelings of its own. When people talk about "working on the relationship," what they really mean is the need to work on themselves. Hopefully the focus is on developing a capacity for healthy pleasure. But as we have seen time and time again, pain-avoidant people are afraid of pleasure just as they are afraid of pain, because they are essentially afraid of feeling in whatever form it takes. Pain-avoidant people have no choice but to avoid life in all its forms.

Let's see how this lack of focus on real pleasure manifests itself in the beginnings of an intimate relationship. We previously mentioned the tendency to merge as a pain-avoidant reason to get into a relationship, such as in Paul's case.

> **Paul:** I used to place great focus and intent on my sexual excitement. The problem with this was that I would get myself so excited by another person that my mind would turn to mush, and I'd lose my ability to see the other person realistically, rather than as the fulfillment of my fantasies. What would happen is that I'd mentally erase all the data about this woman that did not support my fantasy. I attributed to her qualities that enhanced my excitement for her but did not actually exist. I didn't always feel good around her, but I kept telling myself otherwise. Inevitably the relationship ended disastrously.

Paul, like most pain-avoidant people, put the cart before the horse. He got involved with his fantasies of romance and "happily ever after" rather than attending to the realities of the situation, the other person, and how he really felt deep inside. It is a critical task of psychotherapy to help the individual develop a relationship with another that is a harmonious, fulfilling, and pleasurable interaction between the fantasies of the mind and the real-life experience of body feelings.

When we pursue a life of Emotional Sobriety, there is a key principle to remember: Healthy people fall more and more profoundly in love when they share the pleasure of sex with each other. This can begin with a look, a hug, or a kiss, all of which result in a delightful body feeling that leaves us grateful and wanting more. Therefore, you had better be very clear that the person you are having sex with, whether it is kissing or intercourse, is someone you want to fall in love with. This is, in many ways, a pitch for bringing back the old ideas of courtship into a relationship. A healthy relationship with your sexuality is one in which sexual feelings precede love, commitment, and fidelity. First you feel excitement about another person. From that comes courtship and eventually some sort of consummation along the sexual continuum, followed by love, commitment, and fidelity. This course of building a relationship occurs when you truly enjoy the pleasure of each other's company, not just the pleasure of your fantasies.

If this pleasure in another's company is the basis of a healthy relationship, then we see that there are three problem areas to focus on, several skills to develop, and a few things to remember, in order to put Emotional Sobriety into your sexual life and keep the pleasure flowing in your relationship over the long haul.

Problem Areas to Focus On

Have a Sense of Your Capacity for Excitement

Some ACOAs, scared of any feeling at all, contain their excitement to the point where they are unable to feel much of anything. But for most of us, the addiction to adrenaline is so established that we *love* to be excited, and when we are, we express it all over the place. If we have feelings, we state them loudly and often to whoever will listen, believing that our feelings have a force and strength that we could not bear if we did not discharge them. We are sensitized to feelings, and in us, they are so acute that sitting quietly with whatever is going on inside feels impossible.

This is certainly true with sexual feelings. When we feel aroused, the sexual feeling fills us to overflowing, and we believe that if we don't act on it, we will burst. So instead of our sexuality being an aspect of our capacity for pleasure and feeling good, it bullies us into having sex prematurely, or with people who are inappropriate for us, or at times when our loyalty and love may really belong to someone else.

This rush to express our excitement stems from our belief that we cannot bear the anxiety, and for some, the pain of containing it—on either the feeling or the sexual level—and has us behaving like bulls in a china shop. We self-disclose inappropriately, scaring people away with the intensity of our sharing, before we know whether or not they really want to know our feelings. We also frighten potential partners when we dive pell-mell into fantasies about the future before we have gotten to know each other in the present.

Sharing feelings is an important aspect of intimacy, but being able to do it appropriately and out of a feeling of choice rather than compulsion is vital. The ability to contain excitement, is part of the ability to tolerate being with oneself and to have choice in how one wishes to live life. Learning to contain excitement is learning to be in charge of oneself instead of at the mercy of adrenaline. As we are learning to contain our excitement, there will be times when we simply cannot sit with the feelings. We can learn that masturbation is a legitimate outlet for sexual arousal. Writing in a journal, punching pillows or screaming in our car is a way to express and release feelings without burdening anyone else. These options allow us to choose when we will self disclose and when we will not. Our excitement then becomes ours to share or not as we choose, and we no longer feel bullied by the feelings that we have.

For those who have learned to contain their excitement to such an extent that they cannot feel it at all, the problem becomes not how to hold excitement back, but how to bring it forward. Going numb is a survival technique learned by children who felt that their aliveness was under attack, and the problem they face in recovery is learning how to rediscover the excitement they have spent a life time repressing.

Excitement—both sexual and emotional, lives in the body, and it is to the body that we must return to reclaim our aliveness. People who don't feel, don't inhabit their bodies. Instead they use addictions—to substances, to adrenaline, to work, to spacing out, to fantasizing and planning—in order to block their awareness of physical sensations. If you are someone who is unaware of excitement, we recommend spending some time each day tuning into your body and learning to be aware of your sensations and feelings.

Exercise VIII.
Discovering the Life of Your Body

Sitting or lying quietly, breathing naturally, and quieting your mind, begin to notice what is happening inside your body, inside your torso. At first just let your attention be on your insides—get used to focusing in this way. When your thoughts begin to wander, bring your awareness back to your insides, noticing what it feels like in your body as you breathe in and out. And now begin to scan your body: starting with your head, noticing what it *feels* like inside, feel your face, and down your neck, being aware of any tension that you feel, any sensations that are there. Continuing downward, notice what is happening in your chest, around your heart, in your solar plexus, your belly, and so on. Just notice. When you discover that there is a sensation, a tension or feeling, stop and be with it. Don't try to figure it out, just breathe and let it be. Get into the middle of it, if you can—embrace it as an experience, and see what happens. Tolerate it.

It is very freeing to realize that we don't have to *do* anything about feelings, we can just *have* them. And they are not in our minds, they are in our bodies. If you do this exercise regularly, you will begin to discover that sometimes when you stay with a feeling, you are able to name it—"I feel sad" or

"That's anger." You may even cry or want to yell and scream. Allow the feelings in your body to lead you, and if tears come, let them. If at any time you realize that you are analyzing your experience, just come back to the feelings in your body. When you pay attention to your excitement in this way, some of what you feel may be sexual. Allow that, too, recognizing that it is part of your aliveness and nothing to be ashamed of.

Support Others' Excitement About You and About Life

When you experience a mutual attraction for someone, it is delightful and easy to support and enjoy that person's excitement. Sometimes, however, the feelings of excitement that another has for you involve anger, disappointment, or hurt—or sexual desire that you do not want to reciprocate—and it becomes more difficult to support the person's excitement. Even unbridled enthusiasm may be frightening in its intensity. When you do not share your partner's excitement, or when it makes you uncomfortable, learning to still be there for him increases the level of freedom in the relationship, and thus the level of love.

Because ACOAs are pain-avoidant, whenever our partners make us uncomfortable with their feelings, we attempt to manipulate them so that they will change that feeling, or at least keep quiet about it. The often unarticulated rules that we establish in our relationships set limits on our partners. The fear is that the unknown will rock the boat. The problem is that in outlawing each other's excitement, we also rule out what is most lively, most sexy, and most oriented toward pleasure.

In order to support our partners' excitement, we must deal with our own fear and with the belief that it is our responsibility to do something about our partners' feelings. ACOAs, who feel obligations in all aspects of their lives, also often feel that if their partner is sexually aroused, they have to do something about it. It is the pain of this belief that often causes the ACOA to withdraw, to start a fight, or to blame his partner for experiencing sexual feeling that he does not share.

Once you understand, however, that your only obligation is to be honest about your own truth, then you can let go of the burden that your partner's arousal places on you, and simply enjoy his excitement. You may then choose to hold your partner while he masturbates, to listen to him as he fantasizes, or to simply love him for desiring you. When you are able to support his excitement, then you do not require that he denies it as a prerequisite for being in a relationship with you.

Similarly, when you realize that your partner's feelings require nothing more of you than that you attend to them, you are able to allow a freedom in the relationship that says that who both people are is okay. In Karen and Terry's relationship, she is much more excitable than he is, but because of his family's tendency to label him as the troublemaker, he is very vulnerable to that excitation. In the beginning of their partnership, when Karen became excited (often expressing this excitement as anger), for example, Terry would withdraw or criticize her. The rule that was being established was that Karen's anger or disapproval was not okay. For a while Karen kept her anger in check, but in denying her excitement, she began to treat Terry with kid gloves, resulting in the loss of some honesty, closeness, and fun in their relationship.

One day Karen confessed to him that she felt she spent too much time tending his ego, and that she didn't like it. Terry saw that by not supporting Karen's excitement, he was censoring her honesty, an aspect of her personality that he valued. In order for Terry to be able to support her excitement, however, Karen had to learn to contain hers. Expression of her anger and disapproval were too strong for the injured part of Terry to tolerate. For months, whenever Karen's excitement was too much for him, Terry would simply say, "Ouch." He didn't criticize, he simply let her know how he felt. Since there was no criticism to defend herself against, Karen was able to open herself to hearing and seeing the effect her words had on Terry, and slowly she began to learn how to contain her excitement enough so that she could express it in a way that Terry could hear.

While there are still occasions when Karen gets so angry

or upset that the censor is overruled, because of the work they have done on this together, Terry is more able to tolerate it. They both know that when either of them is excited, it means something is brewing, there is something to learn. They are able to face the excitement, open to the pleasure it brings, instead of denying it out of fear of the pain.

Bob and Ann's relationship is an example of how feelings of intimacy and closeness are enhanced when a couple is able to support each other's sexual excitement. Ann, thirty-seven, was a social worker, who, like most therapists, had undergone some therapy herself. Her therapy had been supportive but had encouraged her coping mechanisms, rather than help her face her deep hurts. During an exercise in one of our workshops she suddenly remembered an incident that had occurred when she was fourteen. Her father had questioned her about her virginity and she remembered feeling humiliated and frightened by the look in his eyes, a look that was both seductive and hateful. The memory of this incident awakened Ann to her feeling of being sexually abused, although she was sure her father never touched her.

In the wake of these feelings, Ann began to become aware of the reason she had little sexual feeling for Bob. Her father had shamed and frightened her so badly that she came to believe that sex was forbidden and that her interest in it was a bad and dangerous thing. Bob's excitement for her reawakened the fear that she felt with her father, and she was unable to support, much less respond to, his sexual interest in her.

In follow-up couples therapy, when pushed to say what might be sexually arousing for her, Ann revealed a secret. She said she felt ashamed of her sexual passions, because they were laced with fantasies about being ravished and swept away. She kept this a secret from her husband, believing that he would not respond positively to her, but would hate her as her father had. As therapy helped her understand her feelings of shame and excitement, she began to share her secrets with her husband, and he was filled with a curiosity about her. He then felt free to discuss his own fears and secrets, and they began to reveal their secrets more routinely. This support for each other's excitement became part of their daily lives and that replaced the dread of each other's judgments.

Being Responsible for Your Own Wounds

When you are wounded, if you have not made significant progress in your recovery, then chances are you will choose to become involved with someone else who is also wounded. Most of us choose mates who have the same qualities as our parents, hoping that this time we will be able to work through the relationship and resolve the pain. Until we have recovered, though, we lack the skills to do anything differently, and so the same dynamic that created our childhood misery entraps us again. Also when we choose someone who is wounded, we are picking someone who is full of injury and need. Then we ask that this child grow up and act like our mommy or daddy—a task that he or she clearly cannot do. In most ACOA relationships, there are two injured children trying to act grown-up, both trying to get the parenting that they never received.

Instead of feeling the disappointment of failing again to get what you needed as a child, it is easy to blame your partner for not giving it to you. But as we have said before, it is not the task of your sexual partner to act as your parent. Still, when you feel pain, it is tempting to believe that if your partner would change, you would feel better. Blaming your partner for your unhappiness, however, is a dead end. If you get locked into looking outside yourself for the source of your pain, you will never be able to face it, and it will never release its grip on you.

Your past is not your partner's fault, and he or she can't fix it. You do have a right, though, to ask that your partner be as clear and honest as he or she can be. You do not need anyone to add to your anxiety by giving you mixed messages, or blaming you for a past that was not your fault.

Skills to Develop

Learn to Mind Your Own Process and Admit Your Projections

Denying much of our own inner process, ACOAs project in others what we cannot admit about ourselves. This is particularly significant in intimate relationships where our partners become a mirror for unacknowledged and unacceptable parts of ourselves. If you want to know what you don't like about yourself, notice what you criticize in your partner.

Carol and Marion, both in their thirties, and together for five years, came to our couples workshop because they had lost all feelings of love and affection under the constant barrage of Carol's criticisms of Marion. Marion loved Carol deeply, but was unhappy in the relationship. She was feeling abused by Carol's anger at Marion's "wimpiness," her lack of aggression and drive. As we encouraged Carol to experience her vulnerability instead of her anger, she became aware of a deep fear that she would not be able to take care of herself, and she began to see that the qualities she criticized in Marion were the very qualities that she most feared in herself. As she was able to own her fear, her need to lash out at Marion diminished. Once Marion no longer had to protect herself from the criticism, and instead felt supported by her lover, she was able to be more assertive.

Focusing on your partner, even if it is not projection, is almost always a mechanism to avoid your own pain. In Karen and Rick's relationship, for example, Karen had Rick all figured out but when she talked about them as a couple, it was Rick's behavior that she focused on. Her observations about him were astute, but her inability to mind her own process was destroying their relationship.

Rick: Karen was always telling me what was going on inside my head, and this left me no real room for my own feelings and perceptions. I just couldn't hear myself think with Karen around. But Karen was usually so quick and good with her readings of me that I didn't feel I could compete, and I ended up withdrawing from her.

Karen: In therapy I began to see that when I told Rick what his problems were, I was fostering in him what I dislike the most—dependency. When I started focusing on my own process, I saw that I was really afraid to be with a man, because I was so scared that if I loved him, he would leave me. By criticizing Rick, I would draw my attention away from my fear of abandonment and feel less afraid because of it. But once I'd acknowledged this, I couldn't cover up my fear anymore. Rick was a man and he wasn't leaving me. It was my criticism of him that was making him withdraw.

As tempting as it is to try, the fact is we cannot change things by focusing on someone else. When we are continually telling our partners how we think they ought to be, we are simply creating resistance in them. The only way we can effect change is to recognize our projections and take responsibility for our own thoughts, feelings, and behavior. If most of your conversations with your partner start with "you," you are probably not minding your own process, and you need to start paying attention to your own fears and needs. Only when you acknowledge what they are can things change. Focusing on your partner is simply a distraction from being aware of yourself.

Learn to Give and Receive Appropriately

The inability to trust those closest to us, and the fear that those we need the most are also those that cause us the most pain, create a wariness in us that makes achieving intimacy difficult. Giving and receiving love means giving out good energy from the heart one minute, and in the next, opening your heart to take it in. These are two separate skills, and for those who grew up in alcoholic or unhealthy homes, often one or both of these skills are not developed.

For ACOAs, caretaking, a form of giving, is often more well developed than the ability to receive love. It allows us to feel in control and give out what we want the most. In a sense, it is a way to live vicariously. Caretaking, however, is not love. The trouble for many ACOAs is a belief that you can't have one without the other. We assume that we can't receive love unless we take care of another and give up a part of ourselves. We secretly believe that if someone loved us, he or she would do the same.

Often ACOAs get wrapped up in resentment about how much they do for their partners, or about the fact that their partners don't take care of them in the same way. Feeling angry about being trapped in a caretaking role is a denial that you are in that role because you chose it, and that you chose it to protect yourself from the risk of wanting to receive, or because you feel unworthy to be given to, or because it feels comfortable and safe in its familiarity.

The way to extricate yourself is not to get mad at your partner, but to start examining the fear you experience when you are in the receptive role. If you are mad at your partner for not giving to you, it may be that your wounded child is expecting a kind of parenting which it is too late to ever receive. This is not to say that healthy adults don't get angry at each other when the give-and-take in their relationship gets out of balance, for certainly they do. Sometimes it requires careful negotiation to get things on track again. Often when relationships aren't working, it is because neither partner has the skill to negotiate, and expectations are unvoiced and probably unreasonable as well.

The clients who have the most trouble committing themselves in relationships are those who believe that being in love means giving everything all the time. Too much was demanded of us as children, and we often still feel the burden of those expectations. We think that being intimate means holding nothing back for ourselves, and we are unable to say "no." The sad thing about this is that we are also unable to say "yes." For example, we find it difficult to seek our own sexual pleasure, and so we withdraw our investment from the sex act. When we don't experience sexual union and satisfaction with a partner, it is difficult to open our hearts. Although we think that it is selfish to ask for our own satisfaction, we resent our lack of it and blame our partners. The "unselfishness" that we take pride in has a backlash of bitterness and disappointment. Still, many of us would prefer to experience disappointment and resentment rather than have our partners feel it toward us, so we tend to give in when we don't want to rather than take a stand for what we want.

Learn to Communicate

In their childhoods, ACOAs did not learn that it is safe to say what they think and feel. As a result, they either are unable to express anything they feel or are operating under such a compulsion not to be silenced that feelings just spill out without regard to their affect on others. As you work on your recovery, there may be many things that you need to express to your partner. Old hurts, fears, and secrets erode the love in a relationship, and it is necessary to be truthful with one another. Here are some guidelines for learning effective communication with your partner:

• *Go slowly.* Often our first reaction is an impulsive one, and is not what we really want to communicate. By recognizing that we are prone to jumping quickly to conclusions, we can let the first impulse pass over us and wait until we are sure of what we want to say.

• *Pay attention to timing.* Is this a time when your partner will be able to pay attention to what you are saying and hear you? Does he want to hear it now? *When* we choose to say things can be as important as how.

• *Pay attention to balance.* Make sure that you express all your feelings, not just the angry and disappointed ones.

When we constantly express our anger, we forget to remind our partners that we value our relationship and their love. If all a partner hears about is anger and disappointment, he will soon be discouraged about his ability to love and be loved.

• *Value the importance of how and what your partner is hearing, not just how and what you are saying.* Successful communication is both transmission and reception. Sometimes we get so involved in the momentum of expressing ourselves that words just tumble out without any concern for how they are being received. It is important to express ourselves in a way that allows our partners to listen and take time to digest what they have heard before responding.

• *Learn to edit and discriminate in what you say.* If our feelings were repressed and denied as children, we might overcompensate and go overboard with them now. Certainly many of us have felt that therapy has given us license to say whatever we feel, but there may be times when some of what you feel is better left unsaid. Learn to discriminate between those things that are important for your partner to hear and those things that can be hurtful and better not voiced.

Learn to Be Honest in the Sexual Act

Most of us are scared of sex. We are afraid of opening up, afraid of the energy involved, and afraid that we may not be good at it. Movies and advertisements show us what it means to be sexy, how we should respond, and what we should feel. Our anxiety about not meeting our own expectations cuts us off from our true response, and we get so involved in an act that we forget that sex is supposed to feel good and be fun.

If we have been sexually abused as children, or have had sexual experiences that felt painful and frightening, then each time we have sex, those feelings will be reawakened, and we will find it very difficult to lose ourselves in pleasure. Unfortunately when that happens we tend to ignore the painful feelings and try to bully our way through, hoping that somehow the sex will be wonderful enough to carry us past our fear. This doesn't usually work for long. Sex becomes too uncomfortable, and we begin to avoid it, thus denying a part of ourselves which is most alive.

Sexual intimacy brings to the surface all of our unmet childhood needs, our childhood sexual conflicts, hurts, and traumas, which have been hidden behind the coping persona. The triangle of mother, father, and self is very much a factor when intimacy is at stake. The more intense the intimacy, the more this will arise. Wendy and Ken, both children of alcoholics, are examples of how one couple faced their childhood wounds and grew closer together.

Wendy, a social service administrator, was the daughter of an alcoholic father and an emotionally unstable mother. Wendy's father had been seductive toward her when she was a child, and her mother's rage was often provoked by this. Still, Wendy was loyal to both her parents and worked hard to maintain the appearance of a happy home. She appeared to all to be a bubbly, upbeat young woman. Ken's father had abandoned his wife and family, leaving Ken at an important stage in his life and wounding him deeply. Rather than acknowledge his hurt over his father's desertion, Ken was only aware of feelings of contempt toward his father.

Wendy and Ken began therapy because they believed they were suffering from sexual dysfunction. Ken wanted to make love much more often than Wendy did, and expected daily lovemaking as an assurance of love. As a result, Wendy felt guilty much of the time, and Ken felt resentful. The problem, however, while manifesting itself in Wendy and Ken's sexual relationship, in this case really had more to do with unresolved childhood issues. Through daily lovemaking and orgasm, Ken was trying to comfort the abandoned, wounded child within himself. Wendy had spent her life denying her feelings in order to take care of her family, but as an adult she no longer wanted to sacrifice herself to anyone else's needs.

To help Ken and Wendy see that their individual sexual problems were rooted in their childhoods was not an easy task. Wendy's case was easier because her need to break out of the caretaker mode in order to be sexual was obvious to her. She could see that although she did not want to respond to Ken sexually, she had so much shame and guilt that she had put her own sexual needs second to his. Wendy gradually came to resent this, and she enjoyed sex with Ken less, had fewer orgasms, and poured her passion into her family and career. Ken's situation was harder to deal with because he had had no male role models growing up, and thus looked to women to make him feel like a man through sex. It was important for Ken to acknowledge the deep hurt caused by his father's desertion so that he could stop turning to Wendy to make his hurt go away and feeling like a resentful little boy when she refused. Getting him to focus on the fact that his problem was with his father, not with Wendy, was difficult.

As you can see from this story, sorting out childhood injuries from the conflicts of a current intimate relationship can be quite complicated. Wendy and Ken suffered from the split between their wounded child's needs and their adult sexuality. They could only heal this by separating from their emotional entanglements with their parents, and by being honest about their sexual feelings.

Most of us do not know how to speak openly about our sexual feelings and needs. We grew up with the message that sex was shameful and not to be discussed, and it is difficult to reverse that learning just because we are now sexually active. If sex has become a battleground or an issue that is painful and confusing for you, here is a suggestion:

Exercise IX.
Talk About Sex as You Do It

The point of this exercise is to slow down the sex act to such an extent that you are able to be aware of your feelings at every moment, with plenty of time to share those feelings with your partner. You will be telling your partner when you feel good, as well as when you feel uncomfortable. Never let a feeling go by without asking your partner to stop so that you can explore what it is that you feel. In order for you and your partner to be allies in this, it is important that you not blame each other for anything, but simply report how you feel. It is also important that you agree that you will go no further than feels comfortable to both of you. Thus, there is no expectation that either of you has to have an orgasm or be satisfied. This is a time to be close, and to discover the feelings that both of you have, as well as to learn what gives each of you pleasure. Remember, personal pleasure is a worthy goal when it is in the spirit of harmlessness.

Hopefully this exercise will release blockages so that sex will get to be more fun, but it may not happen immediately, and it is important to build trust between you, taking all the time that you need. If your commitment is to true intimacy, then you know that neither of you needs to sacrifice yourself for the other, and that for sex to really work between you, both of you must follow what you want. If one of you becomes really turned on and the other isn't, part of the sharing will be about the pain and frustration of wanting something you cannot have—or the obligation you feel to respond even though you aren't drawn to it. There may be times when one of you has to cry about an incident just remembered, and the other will be there to hold and comfort. This exercise is not about having intercourse, but about clearing the blocks to having pleasure in sex and getting to know one another.

Things to Remember on
The Road to Recovery

There are a few things to remember which will ease the task of developing Emotional Sobriety. Nobody is perfect, life and relationships are for having fun, and if you keep your eye on the bigger picture, you can ease off on the demands you make of your partner.

Understand That Sometimes I'm Not Okay, You're Not Okay, and That's Okay

It's a hard fact to swallow, but the truth is, when people are close to each other in intimate relationships, they often hurt each other. They may not mean to, but it will happen sometimes. The wounded child in each of us still clings strongly to the notion that love means never hurting someone, and if we are hurt by the one we love, we view it as a deliberate act instead of simply carelessness or lack of sensitivity.

If you have been with someone for years, you may have a bag full of resentments, and in order to release them, you must see that there are times when you have hurt your partner, too. You need to let bygones be bygones, and enjoy your relationship, instead of focusing on past hurts and wrongs. You will be more likely to be able to forgive yourself as well if you have compassion and respect for your friends and lovers, and accept that they are doing the best they can, given their strengths and weaknesses.

At the same time, we do not believe that love means never having to say you are sorry. In fact, we think that relationships thrive on apologies. If you injure your partner and are able to express true remorse for having hurt him, then your partner feels heard and acknowledged, and has an easier time letting go of his anger or hurt.

Remember to Have Fun

In order for your relationship to work, both of you have to be committed to recovery. But as you go through this process, remember to have fun. It is important that you and your partner enjoy your time together. We are often so serious, and so determined to "work" on the relationship, that things can get pretty grim. We forget that fun is for fun, and the purpose of a relationship is the pleasure to be derived from the contact between two people. Having fun does not necessarily mean having a manic kind of high. It can be simple, quiet, and nonactive, a time to enjoy the presence of the other. In spending time pursuing simple pleasures, we can find the time to connect with and rediscover the excitement that fueled the attraction in the beginning.

Discover Your Own Unique Path

At some point in recovery, after grappling with our emotional issues, we may become aware that our life has a purpose and that our destiny is more than simply the effects of our childhood. At this point we are ready to contend with our aloneness and open ourselves to following the direction that beckons to each of us, that resonates so deeply within us that it captures our imagination, our vitality, our life force. For each individual this is unique—it may be that one person's true path is to be a writer, another's to work with children, and still another's to open deeply to the spiritual side of life.

At this point we become willing to face our journey ourselves and no longer try to make our lives work through a relationship. It can be frightening to let go of the struggle we have with a partner. We have taken refuge for so long in its familiarity, but this is a step of letting go of all that we have clung to and embracing the unknown instead. This step, however, does not *deny* the issues between you and your partner. It includes a thorough understanding of them, and cannot be taken prematurely. It is not a way to escape the difficulties, but a way to move beyond them

When we realize the complete picture—that we are greater than the sum total of life's effects on us—then we begin to ask some of the larger questions: Who am I in my aloneness? Who is the self that stands alone? What is the purpose of my life? Who am I at my essence? What is the nature of my inner self? As you begin to ask these questions about yourself, you recognize that your partner's life may or may not be about asking these same questions. You no longer cling to each other for meaning, but instead support each other in your quest for the meaning inside.

After nine years of marriage, Rosie and Hans were about to give up. Rosie's criticisms of Hans's lack of manliness eroded his self-confidence, and Hans's withdrawal left Rosie feeling abandoned and afraid. During a confrontation in which they admitted how miserable they both were in the marriage, they made a commitment to "mind their own process," focus on their own inner work, and stop criticizing and commenting on each other's progress. They chose Jungian therapy, which focused mainly on their dreams, and found a new place of sharing as each began to peel away the levels of fears and beliefs that obscured their inner beings.

> **Rosie:** I still see Hans as someone who has a little boy in him, but it is no longer the whole story about him. That is just one aspect—an aspect that he grapples with—but he is so much more than that. I have come to respect his journey and the riches that he is uncovering as he explores his inner life, and to see that although our journeys are not the same—my issues arc definitely different from his—they are certainly parallel. Hans does have to deal with a childhood which involved a lot of pain, and he is doing that. But opening to his inner life involves much more than simply coming to terms with his alcoholic parents. If his life is to be an expression of who he truly is, then he must separate from me and connect with his own particular journey—and he is doing that. I am plumbing the same sort of depths in myself—learning to accept who I truly am and to value it. I have great respect for Hans now. As I face my destiny, how I am doing depends much less on Hans, and I find that I can allow him the time and space to do his journey his way. I am so thankful that we decided not to split up. At this point he is truly my best friend.

Hans: What was most frightening to me as we took this step was that there was no guarantee that as we each became willing to walk our own path, we would stay together. I was very attached to Rosie, and there was a part of me that would have preferred to be with her rather than with my true self. I had to let go of my dependence on her, and there was no guarantee that I'd find anything to replace her. I just had to let go into the void. It turned out that what I found in the void was the beginnings of myself. But I didn't know that when I let go.

At this point I can't imagine us going back to the place where we blame each other for our dissatisfaction. We still get angry at each other, and we still do get entangled, but we are very quick now to recognize just what is happening and to stop. This feels to me like the last step—learning how to be in a relationship and still have separate journeys. Rosie, for example, has certain parts of her that she will never be able to share with another person. The point is not for her to blame me for that, or to search for someone she might be able to share with, but to embrace those parts of herself alone. I am aware of the magnitude of the task, and I have tremendous respect and love for her. I support her on her journey, and she supports me on mine.

A few lines written by Ginny and Roger Jordan, friends of ours, and therapists in Boulder, Colorado, express the depth that can be found in a relationship when both partners are willing to do the work of embracing their own inner selves.

Marriage is a vessel. It is substantial and real.
It is also elusive and invisible.
We approach it filled with expectation, hope and promise.
Yet we come to it empty, not knowing what mystery it contains.

The vessel of marriage is a paradox.
It contains both the mundane and the sacred.
It holds the urge for union
And it holds the need for autonomy.
Within the vessel of marriage we feel our wounds
And within the same vessel we feel our wholeness.
The vessel of marriage is ancient.
It reaches back to the beginning of the human race.
Carry it carefully.
And also carry it lightly, for joy's sake.
Allow spontaneity to keep your vessel alive.
Allow your imagination and creativity to change its
     shape or
     color, for it contains a universe of possibilities.
When others drink from the vessel which is your
     marriage,
     they take in the wisdom of your experience.
This is true service.
Respect its boundaries as well.
They are there to protect the love which is yours and
     yours alone.
Like water, marriage reflects.
Look deeply and you will see your own soul.
When you know your own soul something greater can
     be born.
Be as a midwife to the spirit which lies dormant in your
     union.

There Are Times to Say Good-bye

As we recover and find our Emotional Sobriety, what we
may have to recognize about our relationship is that it will
never work. We may have chosen each other out of pain
avoidance rather than to pursue pleasure, and when we
become healthy, we are no longer a match. Some things we

can change, some things we cannot, and we must learn to recognize the difference.

If you feel abused by your partner, it is important not to tolerate it. Speak up for yourself, leave the house, seek help. As children we were not responsible for the abuse that went on, but as adults we are responsible for protecting ourselves. Protection means not letting people take advantage of you. As you become clearer about your boundaries, about what you are and are not, about what you want and don't want, your partner's behavior may begin to change in response. If it does not change, then you must understand that you have reached the limits of what you can do, and know when is the time to leave. Just because you are familiar with abuse and constant acquiescence does not mean that is what's best for you. You can learn to recover from "Don't mind me" to insist that you be treated with kindness and respect and that your desires and concerns be honored in the relationship.

CHAPTER 11

Recovery as a Path

The things we learn through our suffering can ultimately teach us how much there really is to enjoy in life. All of us have something in our lives that is difficult to deal with—a relationship, an illness, our career. For adult children of alcoholic and abusive families, it is always difficult to deal with our parents and our past. Our parents have made us who we are today, the good part of us as well as the bad, and our past has taught us some important lessons. These are not things we can simply ignore. It is very easy, and even reasonable at times, for us to go through life feeling sorry for ourselves because of all the bad experiences we've lived through. Certainly much of what we did experience was awful, but there is nothing we can do about what is in the past—what's done is done. The only thing we can change now is how we choose to view what happened. We can allow the tragedy of our childhood to take control of us, or we can find a way to accept what was and move on toward a life of pleasure and fulfillment. This acceptance is, in part, our recovery.

You cannot cheat on arriving at this acceptance, and you can't pretend to accept something when really you don't and have no intention to. You can't grow flowers on top of a cesspool and expect to hide what's underneath forever. You have to start where you are now, with your pain, sorrow, and resentment about the past. Once you face the truth of your past and the reality of your pain, then you can let it go, and get on with your life without dragging your alcoholic or abusive parents around with you. But it takes time.

Beth is a woman who showed Karen that an attitude of acceptance about life is not only possible but leads to personal satisfaction and meaning. By accepting her past, Beth grew into a compassionate and understanding person who exuded an aura of inner peace. There was still regret when she thought about her past, but it no longer preoccupied her.

> **Karen:** Several years ago, I took a workshop in which we were asked to go back into our past and name all the tragedies and betrayals that had occurred. My partner was Beth. As she talked about her past, I was appalled at all the awful things that had befallen her. Many people close to her had died, and she herself had a brain tumor with a prognosis that was unclear. Her first husband had been abusive, and now she was in love again, and feared that she was sterile because of the treatment she received for the tumor. My life seemed like a fairy tale in comparison to Beth's. Hers was the saddest story I had ever heard.
>
> When we got to the part of the workshop where we were to talk about the benefits of our tragedies, Beth had no problem at all. She had a deep curiosity about the human condition, and accepted her life because it had provided her with almost all the experiences one person could have. Not only was she accepting of what had happened, but she was grateful as well. I could see that life had taught her compassion and respect and had given her a depth and a calmness I did not have.
>
> My mouth fell open as I listened to her. I still thought that what had befallen me was a great tragedy, and I couldn't think of anything positive about my

relationship with my mother. I wanted to be where Beth was, but I couldn't be. The turning point came for me after I had done some healing around having grown up with an alcoholic mother, and I realized that everything that had happened to me, all the therapy, training, and workshops I had done, had come together to allow me to do the work I'm now involved with. Though I'm not quite ready to go to my mother's grave and say "Thank you," I realize that without the childhood I had, I wouldn't be doing this work and finding it so fulfilling. I found a way to turn my childhood pain into something useful for myself and others. Having an alcoholic mother forced me to learn things about myself.

Both Karen and Terry have worked hard for some measure of satisfaction and inner peace in making the switch from the avoidance of pain to the pursuit of pleasure. In the process, we've learned a great deal about ourselves. We feel that we now have a knowledge and wisdom about the human condition that our pain has taught us, and we see that the most difficult times of our lives were also the most intense times of learning. The year Karen separated from the man who would eventually become her husband was agonizing, but through it she learned to take care of herself. Terry's divorce and job losses were a shock to his self-esteem, but pushed him to move beyond his arrogant and cavalier approach to life and to other people.

Over and over, we hear people say that a divorce, a death, or a crisis at work forced them to confront some frightened part of themselves. Through this confrontation, they developed parts of themselves they never knew they had. In the end, they felt that the experience allowed them to grow in new and satisfying ways.

Moving at Your Own Pace

It is important to let yourself be where you are now and not try to force the changes. If you are not ready to accept the pain in your life, then you must honor that. Each of us must look at ourselves in the mirror and be honest—something that is very hard for ACOAs because many of us are perfectionists and want to get everything right. When we hear about the importance of accepting the past, we try to do it now. We try to rush recovery and skip steps, particularly the painful ones about our childhood. Beth's remarkable acceptance of her life came only after years of crying and feeling cheated. Acceptance is not found within yourself until you do your work, and part of this is feeling the pain. Acceptance is a place to get to at your own speed. We are so vulnerable to thinking we are doing something wrong or that we should be feeling something else that we often harm ourselves by moving at a pace we don't feel comfortable with.

Karen: I was working with my friend Robert Gass on some personal problems, and I told him I thought that I should be crying, and because I wasn't, I was doing therapy wrong. "You know, Karen," he said, "different vegetables have different growing times. If you plant a radish, it is a radish in thirty days, broccoli takes forty-five, lettuce twenty-three. You can't say that broccoli is wrong because it takes longer to mature, and that lettuce is right because it grows faster. We each have our own path to follow, and you're doing just right for a cabbage." Although I found the analogy hilarious, I also understood what he said, and it allowed me to accept my own path and my own speed of growth.

When we move at our own pace, we also need help, because we can't do it all alone. We need the help of a therapist, a teacher, or a group of trusted friends with whom we feel safe enough to examine ourselves. When we get stuck, we realize that being stuck is part of the process of breaking free.

We now can suggest eleven specific steps for you to take on your path to recovery.

Step 1. *Learn the facts about what it means to grow up in an alcoholic or abusive family.* People who grow up in unhealthy families are suffering, and only recently have they known the name of their disease. When we discover the facts about growing up in an unhealthy family, we begin to understand and accept what is wrong. By learning the effects our alcoholic and abusive parents had on us, we begin to feel less crazy, and to know that there is a name for, and a predictability to, what we feel. The label "adult child" allows us to ask for help and admit that we are having trouble in our lives. When you label yourself, it is a relief to discover that you are not alone, that there are other people who act and feel as you do. When you learn the facts, you begin to know what you are up against, and you start to know where to begin. You give yourself hope to live a better life.

Step 2. *Break through the denial.* Even after we have identified our parents as alcoholic or abusive, we still have a strong tendency to say things weren't so bad. For so long, we have numbed ourselves to what happened, or accepted our experiences as normal, that we have forgotten much of what went on, and it may take years to remember. Buried in our denial is the shame we feel for our family and our deep fear of being hurt. It is a slow process to finally admit what hurts, since pain avoidance has been our mechanism of survival for so long.

Step 3. *Share the stories.* When we tell others what happened, we take off our masks and let some light into the recesses of our shame and fear. When we share our stories, we see that we are not alone. As we hear others speak, we begin to remember more and more and we feel secure in a community of people like ourselves. We begin to recognize in other people's stories things that happened to us. When others cope with their shame, we learn to cope with ours, and our sense of isolation is diminished.

Sometimes we hear people in our workshops complain about adult children meetings they attend, saying that many people simply go over their stories again and again. While we do acknowledge that there is a danger of getting stuck in a rut just telling our stories, we think that the people who complain may be reacting to the pain they hear. It is difficult to hear about abuse that others have suffered. As we listen, we are reminded of our pain, which we would prefer to forget.

Step 4. *Feel the feelings*. This is perhaps the most important step toward recovery. Too often ACOAs gloss over their experiences by saying things such as, "You know, it was the usual drunken scene." Inside that "usual drunken scene" is a scared child whose world is exploding in front of her face. By avoiding the particulars and the details, we continue the denial on another level. We cannot recover from the hurt if we do not feel it.

Often, though, tears cover anger and anger covers tears. Sometimes when we feel most hopeless, we behave most controlling. When we feel guilty, we may blame everyone around us. This was the behavior we saw as we grew up, because alcoholics are never able to freely express what they feel, but cover their true emotions with more acceptable, less threatening ones. When we say it's important to feel your feelings, cry your tears, and express your rage, some people in our workshops say they cry all the time or get angry often. To them it seems as though they are doing the work and finding no relief. Tears that flow endlessly are surely a cover to mask deeper and more intense experiences. In the same way, anger can be protective, and often just covers feelings of vulnerability, as in Barbara's case.

> **Barbara:** Behind my facade of the paper lion, I'm really just a mouse with a slingshot. If people get beyond my first line of defense, I have nothing left to protect myself with.

People rarely crossed or contradicted Barbara because she seemed so powerful and tough. Her cover of fierceness fooled almost everyone.

In therapy, we can appear to be doing the emotional work without really doing it. Maybe we want to please the therapist (we are people-pleasers) and have a few good "feelings" that simply fool the therapist and ourselves into thinking we are doing what we are expected to do. Recovering real feelings is scary stuff, and in therapy, ACOAs have to move slowly, testing the safety and trust around them. The deeper the emotion, the more vulnerable the ACOA feels.

> **Terry:** Perhaps because I was an aspiring therapist myself, I had difficulty in therapy. Every time I would ask for help, half of me was opening up, while the other half was simply looking for more technique to live my life more masterfully. I'd learn whatever it was my current mentor had to offer me, without ever really admitting I was injured. I see now why it was that I had to fall so far, and so hard, before I could feel my true feelings.

ACOAs not only fool others but also themselves, as in Terry's case. To take off the masks takes time and help.

Step 5. *Become aware of the decisions you made when you were a child.* Think back to the lessons you learned and your responses to them. Often self-destructive decisions were made when the pain was too great or too confusing to tolerate. Women who, as little girls, "learned" from watching their abusive fathers that "love hurts" need to remember that they were only children when they reached that conclusion. Reconnecting with that child allows the woman to see that her conclusions were natural, given the situation then, but now they may not necessarily be true. When we are aware of the childhood decisions we made about life, we can, as adults, reevaluate the decisions and see that life can be different, and possibly better, than we ever thought it could be.

Step 6. *Collect a data base.* People who grew up in

unhealthy homes did not know what was normal and what was bizarre. Now we need help knowing what is appropriate and what is not. Some of us don't know how to nurture, while others need to learn how to be a friend. Some don't know how to act around their boss, or they don't know how to behave at a party. Learn by watching other people, and see how they succeed in relationships and in their careers. Make sure you pick as models people you admire and trust.

Step 7. *Allow dependency, consciously and appropriately*. ACOAs have never been allowed to be dependent on anyone who was stable and dependable. This often becomes a problem when they try to form a romantic partnership, because either they are overdependent or they adopt an attitude of "I don't need you." In the safety of the therapeutic setting, ACOAs can depend on someone and have the experience they lacked as children. By facing dependency needs directly and depending on someone, they also learn independence, over time, as the therapist acts as teacher as well as therapist.

Step 8. *Monitor your behavior*. Once ACOAs begin to understand the dynamics of having grown up in dysfunctional families, they can catch themselves when they act on impulse or assume that things are as they were in childhood. We can begin to use our will when we catch ourselves responding in old ways that are pain-avoidant. When our partners get angry, we begin to see that they are merely expressing themselves, not re-creating our parents' abusive behavior toward us. Instead of responding with tears and the urge to run away, we can stay and try to understand the dynamics and reality of a situation.

Step 9. *Develop a relationship with your own spirituality*. We recommend that you pursue a search for meaning in your life. Meditation can be valuable in this search, because a quiet mind is the setting for the wise and loving voice inside you that we call the higher self. Meditation can take many forms and is derived from many traditions, but the unifying idea is that the mind must be quieted enough to receive the true self, which is usually buried underneath the chatter of the ego. When we meditate, we gradually achieve a state of "emptiness," and we can receive feelings directly from our hearts.

Step 10. *Uncover your self.* Your self is who you are, the real you underneath the ideas you have of who you are and how you ought to be. The self is below the level of your mind, and even of your personality. It is the authentic you. Your purpose in life is to be yourself and express who you really are—your joys, enthusiasm, creativity, and desires—but many of us have forgotten this in our dedication to being good, generous, and responsible.

How do you get in touch with your inner self when you are living a life that is not really your own, but fits someone else's expectations? Stop denying the truth within you, and start listening for the message from the voice deep within. At one point in her life, Karen heard, and finally listened to, her inner voice.

> **Karen:** My mother lived in a distant town, and her death was very slow and drawn-out. I spent a month with her as she got progressively worse until she was hardly awake during the days at all. My husband needed me home with him and our three young children, and so I went to the hospital for what I thought would be the last time. My mother was so out of it, she didn't understand I was saying good-bye.
>
> At the airport, I felt very uncomfortable, and as I got on the plane, I heard a voice inside me that said, "You don't want to get on this plane." I had never heard a voice inside me before and I was shocked and frightened by it. I ignored it, though, and went to my seat, telling myself not to worry. As the plane taxied, the voice continued, and I became convinced that the plane would crash. It was too late to turn back and I was trembling in my seat.
>
> As we got to the end of the runway, a torrential downpour started and the sky was filled with lightning. The pilot's voice came over the loudspeaker and announced that we couldn't move and we'd just have to wait. I made my way to the stewardess, guided by

my "voice," and told her about my concerns. The pilot offered to take me back to the gate.

As soon as I was out of the airport, I made my way to the hospital, thinking my mother had surely died. When I entered the intensive-care unit, she was sitting up in bed, watching as I came in. "Mom," I said, "did you know I had to turn a plane around to get to you? I thought you wanted me." "I did," she said. The nurse then told me that my mother had been asking for me all afternoon.

That afternoon I spent with my mother was lovely and she was alert. We used that opportunity to say good-bye. We needed that extra time before either of us was ready to let go of the other, and if I hadn't listened to my inner voice and gotten off the plane, we would not have had it.

Often the heart speaks in whispers which are drowned out by the roar of our minds. "Don't," says the mind, "you'll get hurt. Don't trust, stand back, say "no," retreat, withdraw." So how do we know when our inner voice is speaking, and not just the voice of our personality? It is a hard task, and we learn by acting out different parts of ourselves and seeing what happens. We learn that when we listen to the voice that tells us we will fail, we are listening to the voice that tells us not to try, to avoid disappointment, and we miss out on some of life's greatest challenges. We begin to notice that certain messages from our inner selves have a tone and feeling to them, sometimes pushing, sometimes not, and we begin to recognize which ones are caused by fear. We discover that when we listen to the quietest voice within us, the one that whispers behind the clamor, things often turn out for the best. Often our hearts tell us something that is so contradictory to what we have learned from our experience and our past that we find it hard to listen.

Guilt, a fear of pleasure, and a sense that you don't deserve good things block your access to your self. It takes courage to listen to yourself, but when you do, the message from the true self comes through strong and it is wonderful. The jolt of listening to our hearts fills us with energy and excitement. Our desires and preferences are our compass to move toward aliveness, for when we ignore what we want and fill our lives with "shoulds," we bury ourselves. Dedicating our lives to being good so we can win approval extinguishes the self. When the self is dead, why live? Only by fulfilling who you really are can you connect with the joys of living. You have a right to be who you are, and if your self is buried, you need to dig until you can join again with that voice that belongs to the true inner self.

Step 11. *Get help.* Often in our workshops, people ask advice on what we think the most effective help is, and here are some suggestions.

• Workshops in which the ACOA is given information about growing up with alcoholism. These workshops have exercises designed to allow the participant to reconnect with childhood pain, examine current behaviors, and try out new ones for the future.

• Group therapy where one can try out new behavior, receive feedback from others, and feel supported. As we've mentioned before, a group situation helps break the sense of isolation the ACOA feels by having others tell similar stories and lend encouragement.

• Community meetings of Adult Children of Alcoholics and abusive parents are valuable as well, especially in con-junction with therapy and groups or workshops led by trained professionals. The "Anonymous" traditions (AA, OA, DA, NA, SLA, Al-Anon, etc.) are truly wonderful resources and we recommend them to you highly. The steps to recovery are compassionate and clear, and they work. Like most helping organizations, though, they are only as helpful as the individ-uals involved. Different meetings have different tones, and a bad meeting one week might be followed by a good one the next. We encourage you to give the meetings in your area a chance to be helpful, and keep trying if you don't like the first few you attend.

• Individual therapy where one can further explore and integrate issues brought up in a workshop. The therapist must be familiar with ACOA issues. The kind of therapist you want may depend on your personality. If you tend to hide your doubt and confusion behind arrogance and confidence, you may want a therapist who will push you hard. If you are someone who collapses into self-doubt, you may need someone who is gentle and accepting.

Some therapists focus on helping their clients develop new ways of behaving, believing that if a person can change how he acts, his life will change as well. If ACOAs simply learn new behaviors, however, without facing the pain within themselves, the pain is simply pushed further away, and will still find a way to make its presence known. We believe that the best therapy combines an exploration of the past with a new plan for the future.

Learning to Forgive

On our path to recovery is the important step of forgiveness, not because we believe that forgiveness is an ethical or moral must, but because when we carry resentment in our bodies, it hurts us. Chances are that if you haven't forgiven your parents, you haven't forgiven yourself either. Until you can forgive yourself for the past, you can't move into the future. Forgiving and letting go of the past allow us to see our future with fresh and innocent eyes.

Nancy taught of the great value of forgiveness.

Nancy: It's always been hard for me to trust men because I assumed they were all like my father. As I learn to forgive my father for the pain he caused me, I begin to see that some of the impulses my boyfriend has toward me are actually very generous and loving. I couldn't see that for a long time, because I thought he was just like my dad, and I was always waiting for the hurt. This only made my boyfriend mad, and in many ways, I fulfilled my own prophecy.

Forgiving allows us to love ourselves as well. Hanging on to resentments makes us hard and unloving toward ourselves and toward others. When we harbor resentment toward our parents, it does not stay neatly contained as we hope, but often comes out in unexpected ways.

Sondra: When I behave like my mother, which I do more often than I would like to admit, I just hate myself. It's awful to hear her voice coming out of my mouth, and feel her feelings in my body. I wish I didn't hate her so much, because in the end I hate myself, too.

Some of us may not want to forgive our parents because we don't want to give them that satisfaction. Our parents, though, especially if they are still drinking, may not even care if we forgive them or not. We are not doing it for them, we are doing it for ourselves. Forgiving is also not something we can simply decide to do; rather it happens over time as we go through a process of healing.

What is the process that leads us to forgiveness? How is it that we are able to forgive?

1. *Like the steps in the path to recovery, it is important to feel the feelings.* Taking time to do feeling work should be considered as important a part of your day as exercise and eating right. If you have not opened yourself up to do the emotional recovery work, then you are not ready to forgive. There is an emphasis in some "New Age" thinking on "letting go" and embracing the "light," not harboring the "dark," emotions. This can be dangerous, because it asks us to deny a whole aspect of our being.

We can be filled with pain and anger as well as filled with guilt for having these feelings, but when we take the time to know what we feel, we can move back through our anger and fear and find Emotional Healing. As you reach this point, you find forgiveness, but there are no shortcuts to this process. At times you'll feel ready to forgive, and at times you'll find yourself as full of resentment and anger as before. Remember that this is a "two steps forward, one step back" process.

Thus, it is important not to rush to forgiveness, for if it is premature, it can only be a continuation of denial. We tend to want to have our feelings about the past over and done with, for once and for all. Tired of rehashing what was, we sometimes think that we are letting go when we are really just pushing our pain further away, continuing the avoidance that we learned in childhood.

> **Karen:** When my mother was dying, I wanted very much to heal the hurt between us, so I told her that although I'd been angry at her for many years, I now forgave her. This, in fact, wasn't true. It was simply a continuation of the pattern of me taking care of her all the time. But at the same time, I was also taking care of myself, because I didn't want to live with the guilt of having never resolved my relationship with my mother.

At the time of Karen's mother's death, there was still too much unexplored territory in Karen's life for her to truly forgive, and the "forgiveness" she spoke of grew slowly out of clearing away her rage and hurt. For Karen, completing the work of forgiveness has been an ongoing process that has involved years of deep digging into the past and the pain. But it has finally led her into a place of compassion for her mother and an acceptance that she really did try to be a good parent. Karen has found peace in this.

> **Terry:** Forgiving my father seems to come in waves. I go along on my merry way for a time before I'm forced by some pain or anger to look inside myself. As I take the time to address the feelings inside, I inevitably run into the same old blocks of feeling that trip me up again and again. In most cases, I'm still denying that my father really hurt me, that the things he did had a profound influence on my development. Each time I

go through this cycle, I find myself forgiving him a little more. I don't forgive his actions—many of them were cruel. It's him I find myself forgiving.

2. Another step toward forgiveness is *creating distance and disconnecting*. Psychologist John Bradshaw believes that "healthy families disintegrate in orderly fashion." We have seen that unhealthy families don't. ACOAs find themselves enmeshed with their parents and siblings well into adulthood. Growing up is, in part, about separating and establishing one's own life, but unhealthy families often don't encourage this. The irony here is that while the family members don't feel good about the closeness, they do not know how to pry themselves away. In order to forgive your parents, you must separate from them, because it is impossible to feel the pain of the past if you are still trapped and still living with the same dynamics in the present.

Terry: I was first aware of how I was overly involved with my mother when I heroically tried to intervene in her financial difficulties with my stepfather. Clearly it was none of my business, and even my mother, who had put me up to it, was angry. My dilemma was how to extricate myself in a constructive way. When I stopped calling, my siblings told me how much I was hurting her. When I saw her, I was aloof and reserved. It was as though our entire family system was designed to keep us mixed up with each other. Finally I learned to hold my ground, to keep things in proportion, and let time do the real work of loosening those emotional ties.

3. Another step in the process of forgiveness is *creating boundaries you can live with*. Once you are ready to visit your parents again, you need to establish boundaries that you can feel comfortable with. Choosing the timing and length of a visit may help (a whole weekend may be too much at first), and mixing up the visit with other activities can break up the time. You need to avoid the drinking times by taking a walk or going

to bed. At first you may feel guilty about disappearing, but part of your recovery involves making your needs important.

4. *Learn to act instead of react, to break old patterns of behavior when you are with your parents.* When you act, you are the author of your own life, and you make choices about the way you would like things to happen, the goals you would like to achieve, the people you would like to be with. When you live life in the reactive mode, you are pushed from crisis to crisis, and the adrenaline rush makes you think this is a fun way to live. You then depend on external forces to guide your life.

> **Josh:** At some point, I realized that when I was at home, I always let my father set the tone. Somehow I lost my personality when I was there, and forgot that in my life I was really a different kind of person. Why did I leave that personality and those skills behind? Eventually I learned to be more active in setting the tone, and if my father was critical of me, I told him to stop and walked away. I began to establish a pattern when we were all together, of noticing the good things in life, and commenting on the good parts of each of us.

5. *Create a history of success.* Our childhood was filled with failure: discussions that ended in argument, holiday gatherings that ended in violence, promises that were never fulfilled. Now in our adult lives, we must create success with our families. Set yourself up so that once your boundaries are established, your interactions with your family are successful. For instance, call home in the morning when things are okay, and not at night when there is drinking. End a visit early if it means leaving on a successful note rather than dragging it out until things fall apart. Notice when your interactions are successful and build on that.

6. *Accept the members of your family for who they are, and give up your unrealistic expectations for them.* Most of us, even as adults, still carry around an ideal image of who our

parents should be. We often hold on to the idea that our mother or father will take us away from the bad, but in reality, few parents can ever live up to this fantasy. What we need to realize is that our fantasy is a child's fantasy. As adults we must rescue ourselves when we are in trouble. Persisting in holding on to those expectations for our parents keeps us locked in a pattern of hope and disappointment that runs our lives. As long as we expect heroics from them, we will be let down. We must learn to accept them for who they are, even if that means admitting the bad.

7. Finally, in order to forgive others, *you must be able to forgive yourself.* First you must believe that you did the very best you could all along. Our tendency is to be extremely self-critical and hard on ourselves and believe that we didn't do what was right. In truth, there were very limited options open to us and we did only what we could.

As you forgive yourself, you will be able to stop blaming yourself and others. As you begin to accept responsibility for your actions, you stop pointing the finger at everyone else, and begin to see that in unhealthy families, everyone gets stuck in patterns of behavior he or she can't get out of. You were not just a victim of parental abuse, you were part of a poorly functioning family. Start accepting that you have learned from your mistakes. You only make the same mistake as many times as you need to get it right, and learning is a trial-and-error endeavor.

Addressing the Unforgivable

We have spent a lot of time talking about forgiveness, but we must also admit that sometimes people are simply not forgivable. A woman in one of our workshops told us the story of how her alcoholic and schizophrenic mother had beaten three of her siblings so badly they died. For years, this woman attended Catholic school, and learned to turn the other cheek as she was taught, pretending nothing had happened.

When we spoke of forgiveness to her in our workshop, she erupted, wailing that she could never forgive her mother, that the things she had done were not forgivable, and that she had been denying her true self by pretending they were. For her, admitting that the things her mother had done were not forgivable was an important part of her recovery. "I need to remember how crazy my mother was," she said, "and I can't be nice about it any longer."

In the "My Turn" section of *Newsweek* a man named Joseph Queenan wrote that he could not forgive his father for all the pain he had caused. He described his father as a "textbook alcoholic," terrorizing his wife and children, unable to hold a job, lazy, and often a liar. He had humiliated his family over and over again.

> I hated my father for the first twenty years of my life. I don't hate him anymore—today I understand some of the roots of his behavior. . . . I understand, but I won't forgive. And so a word about the etiquette of contrition. To all those who want to wipe clean the slate and launch brand-new relationships with those they may have harmed during their binges, stupors and rages, I would urge caution. If you're trying to pull your life together at a very late date—terrific. If you're genuinely sorry for whatever you've done and whomever you've harmed, tell them so. If feeling good about yourself is the only way to stay away from the bottle, feel free to feel good about yourself. Just don't think that a belated apology makes everything even-steven. And don't go sticking your hand out waiting for someone to shake it. Keep it to yourself.[1]

What is important is to honor what you feel. Some of us may be at a place where forgiveness is right. Others may not be ready, and may never be ready to forgive their parents for the pain they caused. Too often we have tried to believe what we knew wasn't true, to say things we knew were lies, and to hope for things we knew would never happen, and perhaps now there may be pressure on us to forgive as well. Because of this, we are tempted to skip some of the steps and to get to forgiveness prematurely. If you are hurt, you must feel the hurt, perhaps for a year, maybe for ten.

Only by experiencing what is real for us at the moment can we change. Ignoring the pain does not work, it only prolongs the problem. Perhaps your siblings have forgiven your parents, and you wish you could work at their speed, but you must follow your own unique path and listen to your feelings. As much as you might wish that you could forgive, if you're not ready, you're just not ready—and that's okay.

Parenting

Of all the distress that we see, perhaps the most poignant is the pain of ACOAs who are unable to avoid hurting their children in the same ways they were hurt. For this reason, we talk about parenting here, too, because if we do not follow the path to recovery, the endless cycle of abuse and unhappiness will never be broken.

It is possible to break the cycle of suffering we experienced. Terry is a new father and has not yet had to face many of the challenges his son's assertion of self are sure to bring. Karen has three nearly grown children, and has been through most of the cycle. In our experience of working with ACOAs, we do see that untreated ACOAs repeat the mistakes their parents made. They do so either through unconscious imitation, or, in an attempt to act as unlike their parents as possible, they overcompensate and create opposite problems. In either case, they are not acting out of free choice. We also see that ACOAs who clear up some of the pain associated with their childhoods can in fact change, and when they do, the way they raise their children changes as well. We are fortunate to be of a generation to whom help and therapy are very available. We are therefore also the generation that can stop the suffering. Even if your children are grown, it is not too late. Support, love, and acceptance heal many wounds.

As parents many of us have sworn over and over not to do to our children what was done to us, but despite all our efforts and best intentions, we still find ourselves acting and sounding like our parents. Some ACOAs are so afraid of this happening that they decide not to have children at all. They simply don't trust themselves not to be like their parents. We do not have positive family role models, and often our actions are activated by feelings that lie below our level of awareness.

Amy was an unwanted child, and had felt it her entire life, not only from her parents but from her brothers as well. If it hadn't been for her grandmother, it's hard to believe Amy would have survived emotionally at all. As an adult her deep need for the closeness she didn't receive as a child almost destroyed her relationship with her own daughter.

> **Amy:** I was so determined not to be like my parents were with me that I tried to make my daughter Susan into my best friend and confidante. That was fine when she was little, but when she started to want her own space, I started feeling neglected and hurt. I was determined to stay involved by becoming more of a mother when she was ready for less. I had our relationship all backward, but I couldn't help myself because I was hurt inside. After a lot of work on myself, it's still hard for me to let my daughter grow at her own pace, but she is beginning to believe me when I say my parents weren't so great. I have cried buckets of tears for the wounded child inside of me, and I am finally beginning to find some peace within myself.

Amy needed to learn to separate her own needs from those she perceived to be her daughter's. She could not do this as long as she was living her life in reaction to the way her parents had treated her as a child.

Like Amy, parents who are uncomfortable and unresolved about some of their own issues project those feelings onto their children. Parents who feel guilty about their own lack of honesty will see a lack of integrity in their children. Parents who feel bad about their quick tempers will have a hard time tolerating their children's anger, and parents who are afraid to confront life head-on may urge their children to sneak and lie.

> **Megan:** My father has hurt his whole life because of his own father's stinginess with money. But my father is just as tight, and he doesn't realize that when he withholds money from his children, we think he doesn't love us. It's hard not to feel that he doesn't want to see you very much when he makes you pay your own fare from college to go home for Thanksgiving. It's almost as if my father had no choice but to act that way.

What can we do about our blindness? How can we interrupt the cycle of pain that is being passed from generation to generation? How do we give our children the love and support we never got? We must recognize the inadequacies we have as parents, and the stressful parts of parenting that are hard to accept. Knowing that parenting styles are influenced by childhood experience, we can be alert to the tendency of the wounded child within us to influence the way we interact with our children. We must become aware of our fear that we aren't doing something right, an uncertainty as to the best way to act in a given situation, a feeling that we are "winging" the whole thing. For some parents, the amount of neediness inside is so great that there is little left to give a child. They want to be taken care of instead of being the caretaker. Being able to admit this is a big step toward protecting your children from your unconscious rage over your childhood.

Having grown up in alcoholic or abusive homes, we have the tendency, even if we are not addicts in the normal sense, to be "alcoholic" in our behavior. Being calm, consistent, and coherent are not necessarily things we are good at.

Karen: I remember when my children were little, hearing myself scream at them. It occurred to me that although I was completely sober, I sounded like I was in an alcoholic rage. It was then that I realized how much my own childhood was affecting the way I parented, and I knew I needed help.

As parents, with our ACOA tendency to see things in black and white, we tend to blow things out of proportion. We may hit the roof if we find out that our children have experimented with drinking or drugs, thinking that one sip or one puff will lead them to addiction. We forget that experimentation is a part of adolescence. We are such perfectionists, we find it hard to tolerate our children's mistakes, and don't give them the leeway necessary to learn by doing.

The chaos of our childhood has injured us, and many of us may have developed a fearful startle reflex, as if we had survived a war. Thus, it may be difficult for us to withstand the noise and commotion children make. We wish we could be calm and sit back, but we are rattled to the bone. When things get out of control, so do we.

Because control is such an important issue for us, many of us have problems when our children begin to assert themselves, and have their own opinions and way. For ACOAs, their own children's adolescence can be an intolerable time, and they may get locked into fighting instead of supporting.

Because of our own unresolved pain, we are often sad, and our children pick up on this.

Karen: I remember my youngest child, Max, said to me when he was three, "Mommy, how come you never smile?" It was a shock for me to realize then that he was learning about life from me, and because I was so sad, I couldn't do anything about the expression on my face. I wanted so much to provide my children with the happiness that I never had that I made a big deal out of events like Christmas. I tried to hide my sadness then, but my children could always see it.

Often we try to give our children all the things we never had and end up paying so much attention to their feelings that we never punish them, never let them feel bad. In doing this, we are actually making our children anxious, because in our overprotectiveness, we send them the message that they cannot tolerate painful feelings or handle life without our protection. As a result, they grow up scared and lacking sufficient autonomy.

Recovery Is Our Greatest Gift to Our Children

To be good parents, we must solve our own problems, because if we don't, we will tend to hurt our children in the same ways that we were hurt. In particular, if we don't face the wounded child within us, the unexpressed pain of that wounded child will affect our daily functioning. Until we listen to that wounded child, our parenting decisions come right out of our pain-avoidant coping mechanisms, and we end up inflicting more pain than ever. In working with ACOAs, we've seen so many people repeat their own childhood in the way they bring up their children, it often seems as though there is no choice. We've seen the man who complained that his father loved his brother better turn around and favor one of his children over the other. We've listened to the woman complain about how her mother left her so often, and then witnessed her leaving her own kids. We've worked with parents who cruelly tease their children, as they were teased by their parents.

In order to break these patterns that are passed from generation to generation, each of has to become fully conscious of what our childhood was like, and how we felt about it. By bringing light to our past, we can stop following the path blindly and find our own direction. And as you strive toward becoming a better parent, remember that there is no such thing as the *perfect* parent. Don't be too hard on yourself when you make a mistake. A baby that doesn't sleep through the night, a child that won't nap, a child that cries a lot, can stress any parent, and it is important to recognize that much of it has to do with a child's nature, and isn't your fault.

Our parents were too caught up in their problems, too busy drinking, to teach us certain things—how to deal with money, how to be a friend—and when we raise our children, we may not know how to teach them these things either. This is where a trusted group of friends can be an important support in child rearing. We can learn by watching them and seeing how they treat these issues in their family.

A client of Karen's was very upset that her daughters would not obey her on an issue she thought was important. She felt like a failure as a mother because they wouldn't listen to her, and she was sure this meant that they'd have problems later on in life. What her daughters refused to do was wash their feet before they got into bed. Karen told her, "I don't wash my feet before I go to bed, and neither do my children. In fact, I don't know anyone who does." This was startling information to the mother, as she'd never stopped to consider that maybe her daughters didn't wash their feet because they thought it was silly and strange. When she finally accepted that she was being obsessive, and that her intense desire for foot washing was something she had learned from her obsessive mother, she stopped badgering her children.

Sometimes when we have a baby, particularly a first baby, we are so anxious to do a good job that we forget how important our relationship with our spouse is. The child ends up taking all our energy, and as one parent comes in the door, the other hands him the baby like a hot potato and leaves. Granted having a child is stressful, but we must learn to save time for our relationship with our spouse and the enjoyment of each other's company.

Most important, we need to go easy, forgive our mistakes, and realize and work on the limitations our background has given us. We do the best we can at loving our children, and when we make a mistake, we'll have another chance to get it right. Participants in our workshops ask us for the magic formula for being a good parent, but of course, there is no such thing. Recovery is an ongoing process, and if you dedicate yourself to it, it will work.

Karen: When my first husband and I separated, we decided that the two youngest children would live with me, and Alex, the oldest, would stay with his father. Even though the decision to divorce was mutual, Alex came to believe that I had left him, and he was furious with me. During the seven years I lived apart from Alex, he was so full of his own and his father's anger that the times we spent together were tumultuous and difficult. When Alex came to visit, he physically abused his brother and sister and disrupted the household.

I was in great pain about my relationship with Alex and went to many professionals for help, and what I saw was that I needed to get my act together. I could not heal Alex until I could heal myself. When Alex was fourteen, I insisted that we needed to spend more time together, alone. We began to talk about all the things that had happened over the years, and little by little he expressed his hurt, and the tide of our relationship began to turn. Soon we were ready to live together again.

When Alex was eighteen, he said to me: "For years I was angry at you because I was thinking that I wasn't getting enough love or attention from you. And then one day I noticed that you were listening, that you did care, and you did love me. I stopped being mad then." Alex and I were on the wrong track for so long, there were times I thought it was hopeless. I believed I would die a sad old lady, and my deepest regret would be over my relationship with my first child. Instead, it is a relationship that brings me great pleasure.

Most often, though not always, unhappy situations can be changed. You just have to know what moves to make. Sometimes it means more love and more structure, or less attention and fewer rules. As our children develop, our roles as parents do as well, until we are ready to let go of our position as protector and problem solver and let our children lead their own lives. It's hard for us to know when to let go, because our role models were not good. Parents who were involved in alcohol and their own problems either let go of us too early or attempted to control our every movement, perhaps even until this day. We have to somehow search for an appropriate middle ground.

There are as many different parenting styles as there are parents. Some of us may care a great deal about table manners, while others value academic achievement most highly. Some parents let their children watch television all night while others forbid it. Some parents are indulgent to the point of spoiling their children, while others are not. You can't make yourself be a different kind of person with different values than you have. In order to find the parenting style that is yours, you must honor yourself first.

Taking Stock of Our Good Points

As we work on our recovery, it is essential to remember that there are positive elements to being an ACOA.

• *We have been through a war and have learned about winning our battles.* The fact that we have gotten this far attests to our strength. As we move toward our recovery, we can rely on this strength and confidence to see us through. There may be times when we feel it is all too much, and we will collapse, but we haven't collapsed yet and can rely on the fact that we are survivors.

• *We are great in a crisis.* We have already discussed the down side of being good in a crisis—we get hooked on a crisis mentally and rely on the adrenaline to make us feel alive. But the positive side of this is that when something goes wrong, we are able to act. We respond immediately and know just what is needed when.

• *We are very loyal friends.* Sometimes we hang on when things aren't good for us, but we don't give up when the going gets rough. We are always willing to work things through, and thus are able to have the pleasure a long-term relationship can bring.

• *We are good at taking care of others.* With our great sensitivity, we can tell what other people need. We know what it is we wish other people would do for *us,* and we are able to provide it for *them.* It is no accident that ACOAs gravitate toward the caretaking professions—we are good at it!

• *We are sensitive people.* We became highly sensitive during our childhood, and sometimes it was as if we had antennae all over our bodies. We could tell when someone had too much to drink, when someone was about to get angry. The down side of this is that it can become too much for us, and we become flooded with feelings and information that don't belong to us. The positive aspect is that this allows many of us to be psychic. Our sensitivity allows us to tune into people at a deep level, and this makes us good friends and listeners.

• *We have an acute awareness of when something is right and when it is wrong.* It's as though we have a tiny Geiger counter inside us that lets us know when something is even the smallest bit askew. In groups, this kind of sensitivity is valuable because it allows the ACOA to sense conflict or untruths that most people are not aware of.

• *We can be effective agents for social change.* Because we have so often been the scapegoat, we know when things are unfair, and we fight back. The scapegoat, fueled by his anger over how unjust his childhood was, can compensate for it by addressing his energies to the greater injustices and inequities in the world. He feels acutely what it means to be unloved, an outcast, unheard, and can empathize with those on the fringes of society. Working for social change often provides an outlet for, and a positive expression of, childhood anger.

• *We have been forced to know ourselves.* If our pain had not been so real and intense, many of us would never have taken the time to get to know ourselves. We would still be leading unexamined lives, much like our parents. We have opened up new worlds for ourselves.

• *We have learned to question, and have a choice about how we respond to what happens to us from now on.* As children in unhealthy homes we had no choice, and we were forced to act in specific patterns of behavior that were designed to control us and stabilize the family. As children we learned to numb ourselves to the pain, but as adults on a path of recovery we are becoming aware of our feelings. We can be in charge of our own destiny and can make the choice to move toward pleasure.

Finally Embracing Life

We remember a story from the news a few years ago about a woman whose life was filled with mishap and sorrow. Instead of giving in to the tragedies that plagued her life, she grew increasingly stronger, more courageous, and was filled with an inner peace. She is an example of how one can learn from, and survive, misfortunes in life.

The woman was in New York City, walking down the street, when a crane toppled over and trapped her underneath. It hovered over her in a precarious position for hours, and as workers tried to free her, people wondered whether the crane might fall and kill her. The woman knew the circumstances and spent the hours preparing to die. Several volunteers put themselves at risk to be with her as the rescue attempt went on, and the woman talked to them about dying and gave them messages to deliver to her children in the event of her death. Finally the crane was removed and she was saved.

A year later, television did a follow-up story on her, and it turns out that the crane incident was not the first bad thing to happen to her, nor was it the last. There had been many disasters in her life—her legs had been badly injured in this accident, the man she loved had been killed in a holdup—but her attitude toward these tragedies was amazing. Instead of bitterness and fear, she was full of acceptance and peace. At the time of the interview, it seemed she had finally found peace, absorbing the shocks into the inner calm that characterized her life.

We might all wish that the things that happened to us never occurred, but the fact is, they did, and our experiences have tempered us and made us stronger, wiser, and more compassionate in a deeper way. Like the woman who was caught under the crane, we have begun to face and accept our pain because we have learned that the only way to live is to open up to life, and pursue the pleasure it has for us.

Recovery means coming out of your cocoon and truly embracing life. As we have seen, embracing life means embracing all of it, the pain and the pleasure. We no longer need to deny our hurt because we have learned to tolerate it. Pleasure is not so frightening anymore either, because we have discovered that we can let go of control and still have the bad things and the good things that happen to us become opportunities to grow and learn. When we are willing to let go of our picture of how life should be and admit that it "may not be so," we allow ourselves to be surprised by what life has to offer.

In recovery, we no longer think of our lives in tragic terms, because we treasure the wisdom and strength we have found in ourselves. We have deepened our sense of compassion and understanding, knowing the difference between being swallowed up by someone else's feelings and caring for them from within the boundaries of our separate selves.

We have learned to love, no longer afraid that if we allow ourselves to get close, we will get hurt. We understand that love and dependency are not the same, and we are able to be whole and separate, capable of taking care of someone, as well as allowing ourselves to be cared for. We are able to tolerate it when we have a fight with a loved one, knowing that anger and love do not rule each other out.

Our depression, fear, and anxiety lifts and we are able to

have fun and delight in things. Life no longer seems to be so serious all the time, and we can play and be silly. Our addiction to adrenaline and excitement no longer rules us, so that we can now enjoy the silence and the calmness within, no longer afraid of the pain we might find there. We can find Emotional Healing.

We have learned to disentangle ourselves from the past, so that while we are conscious of what happened, we no longer dwell on it and let it rule us. Healing the pain has allowed us to put it to rest, and move on, so that at some point, we no longer identify ourselves as ACOAs. We are ready to live our lives in the present and for the future, no longer trapped by things that happened so many years ago.

We are ready to pursue pleasure, aware that if we are willing to face the pain, we will also open up to the delight that life offers. As we learn to bear the pain of the past, there is room in our hearts to feel good. Through recovery, we learn to embrace life, and we no longer expect that life will be a bowl of cherries all the time. The Buddha says that "life is suffering," and we accept that sometimes this is true. We don't run away when things get hard, and as we let go of our pain-avoidant mechanisms, we begin to have more pleasure.

A friend once said that he thought that humans, like flowers, were meant to open themselves up. Like flowers opening toward the sun, we all can tilt our faces to the heavens to receive the energy of love. When we take in love, we breathe it out again, and create an environment where it is safe to experience pain and also know pleasure.

Notes

Introduction
1. Herb Gravitz and Julie Bowden, *Guide to Recovery* (Holms Beach, Fla.: Learning Publications Inc., 1985).

2. Pat Perrin and Wim Coleman, "Addictions and Consciousness," *New Realities* Sept./Oct. 1987.

3. Janice Keller Phelps, M.D., and Alan E. Nourse, M.D., *The Hidden Addictions and How to Get Free* (Boston: Little, Brown & Co., 1986).

Chapter 1
1. Janet Woititz, *Adult Children of Alcoholics* (Pompano Beach, Fla.: Health Communications, 1983).

Chapter 2
1. Stanley Keleman, *Emotional Anatomy* (Berkeley, Calif.: Center Press, 1985).

Chapter 4
1. Sharon Wegscheider, *Another Chance: Hope & Health*

for Alcoholic Families (Palo Alto, Calif.: Science and Behavior, 1980).

2. Claudia Black, *It Will Never Happen to Me* (Denver, Col.: M.A.C., 1981).

Chapter 9
1. O. Carl Simonton and Stephanie Matthews Simonton, *Getting Well Again* (Los Angeles, Calif.: James L. Creighton, J.P. Tarcher, 1978).

Chapter 10
1. Janet Woititz, *Adult Children of Alcoholics* (Pompano Beach, Fla.: Health Communications, 1983).

Chapter 11
1. Joseph Queenan, "My Turn," *Newsweek*, Aug. 31, 1987.

INDEX